DEC 10 2009

Praise for *The Official Ubuntu Book*

Linux Journal Readers' Choice Awards 2008 Favorite Linux Book, Honorable Mention. (linuxjournal.com)

". . . this is an item of choice for any serious Ubuntu collection or software designer's library."

—Jim Cox, Midwest Book Review

". . . this one (Ubuntu Linux book) is at the head of the pack for getting started with your penguin experience. . . ."

—Tom Duff

"Benjamin Mako Hill et al. have produced an excellent book that speaks to everyone who uses or is considering using Ubuntu."

—James Pyles, reviewer, "The Linux Tutorial"

"Well written in an easy-to-follow format. Full of information for folks new to Linux or just new to Ubuntu. Even nontechnical users would find this a very helpful resource."

—Ben Gerber, Arsgeek.com

"I'd recommend picking it up if you are running Ubuntu."

—Tony Lawrence, owner of aplawrence.com

D0924076

The Official Ubuntu Book

Fourth Edition

DALY CITY PUBLIC LIBRARY
DALY CITY, CALIFORNIA
DISCARDED

The Official Ubuntu Book

Fourth Edition

Benjamin Mako Hill

Matthew Helmke

Corey Burger

With Ivan Krstić, Jonathan Jesse,
Richard A. Johnson, and Jono Bacon

PRENTICE
HALL

Upper Saddle River, NJ • Boston • Indianapolis • San Francisco
New York • Toronto • Montreal • London • Munich • Paris • Madrid
Capetown • Sydney • Tokyo • Singapore • Mexico City

S

005.43
LINUX
(UBUNTU)
2009

Many of the designations used by manufacturers and sellers to distinguish their products are claimed as trademarks. Where those designations appear in this book, and the publisher was aware of a trademark claim, the designations have been printed with initial capital letters or in all capitals.

The authors and publisher have taken care in the preparation of this book, but make no expressed or implied warranty of any kind and assume no responsibility for errors or omissions. No liability is assumed for incidental or consequential damages in connection with or arising out of the use of the information or programs contained herein.

The publisher offers excellent discounts on this book when ordered in quantity for bulk purchases or special sales, which may include electronic versions and/or custom covers and content particular to your business, training goals, marketing focus, and branding interests. For more information, please contact:

> U.S. Corporate and Government Sales
> (800) 382-3419
> corpsales@pearsontechgroup.com

For sales outside the United States please contact:

> International Sales
> international@pearson.com

Visit us on the Web: informit.com/ph

Library of Congress Cataloging-in-Publication Data

Hill, Benjamin Mako, 1980–
   The official Ubuntu book / Benjamin Mako Hill, Matthew Helmke, Corey Burger. — 4th ed.
      p. cm.
   Includes index.
   ISBN 0-13-702120-8 (pbk. : alk. paper)
   1. Ubuntu (Electronic resource) 2. Operating systems (Computers) I. Helmke, Matthew.
   II. Burger, Corey. III. Title.
   QA76.76.O63O34348 2009
   005.4'32—dc22   2009020517

Copyright © 2009 Canonical, Ltd.

This book is published under the Creative Commons Attribution-ShareAlike 3.0 license, http://creativecommons.org/licenses/ by-sa/3.0/.

Printed in the United States of America. This publication is protected by copyright, and permission must be obtained from the publisher prior to any prohibited reproduction, storage in a retrieval system, or transmission in any form or by any means, electronic, mechanical, photocopying, recording, or likewise unless permitted under the Creative Commons Attribution-ShareAlike license 3.0. For information regarding permissions, write to:

> Pearson Education, Inc.
> Rights and Contracts Department
> 501 Boylston Street, Suite 900
> Boston, MA 02116
> Fax: (617) 671-3447

ISBN-13: 978-0-13-702120-8
ISBN-10:   0-13-702120-8
Text printed in the United States on recycled paper at Courier in Stoughton, Massachusetts.
First printing, June 2009

This book is dedicated to the Ubuntu community. Without your tireless hard work and commitment, none of this would be possible.

Contents at a Glance

Contents

Foreword to the First Edition

IT'S A SMALL CELEBRATION for me to write this foreword—almost exactly two years after the first meeting of a small group of free software professionals that turned into the Ubuntu project. A celebration because two years ago none of us would have predicted that our dream would spawn several million CDs, three or four million enthusiastic users, hundreds of commitments of support from companies large and small, a minor prime time television reference, and now *The Official Ubuntu Book*.

The dream that brought us together can be simply expressed:

> To build a world-class operating system for ordinary desktop computer users, that is genuinely free and freely available, that is immediately useful, and that represents the very best that the free software world can achieve today.

In setting out to build a platform for "ordinary desktop computer users," I had no idea that I would have the privilege of meeting and working with so many *extra*ordinary desktop computer users. Some of those extraordinary individuals are the authors of this book, people who both understand the importance of the free software movement and have the talent to have been real contributors to its success. Others make up the backbone of the Ubuntu community—the small but dedicated army of a few hundred people that works to produce a new release of Ubuntu every six months. They are at the heart of a network that reaches out through the global free software community—through the world of Debian, an extraordinary project in its own right and without which Ubuntu could not exist, and on out to the thousands of projects, large and small, that produce the code and documentation that we pull together and call *Ubuntu*.

While this huge extended community can often appear to be fractured and divided along infinitesimal ideological lines, we are all broadly in agreement about four key ideas, and it is those ideas that are central to the Ubuntu promise:

- That our software should not come with a license fee. That we should be able to share our software, modify it, and then share our modifications, too.

- That this free software should be the best version available, including regular security updates, and not a tease for a better, commercial product.

- That full-scale, high-quality commercial support from local and global companies should be available for this free platform.

- That this software should be usable in as many languages as possible and usable by as many people as possible regardless of disability.

The 17 of us who met in London two years ago come from a very wide variety of countries and backgrounds, but we all agreed that the goal of producing a platform that could live up to that promise was a worthy one, one that we would devote ourselves to wholeheartedly.

For several months we worked quietly. We wanted to come to the world not only with a manifesto but also with a clear demonstration of work done toward our goals, something that people could test and comment on. We had no name (though industry insiders called us the "Super-Secret Debian Startup"), and, as a result, we hosted most of our work at www.no-name-yet.com. We were looking for a name that could express the beauty of the free software community development process—collaboration, interdependence, sharing, standing gently on the shoulders of giants, and reaching for lofty goals. The only word that comes close to that, of which I'm aware, is the African word *ubuntu*. It is found in many forms in many different African languages. And so we adopted it as the name of our project.

We knew that our first release would have blemishes—warts—and gave it the codename "The Warty Warthog." We called ourselves "the warthogs" and coordinated our work on the #warthogs IRC channel. Today, for better or worse, that's turned into a tradition of codenames such as "Breezy

Badger" and "Dapper Drake." As lighthearted as they sound, these code-names come to embody the spirit of our community as it works toward a particular release. This next one—Dapper—is exactly that: a man emerging from youth, professional, bold, confident, and energetic. This is our first release that is designed to meet the needs of large organizations as much as developers and engineers. In the same way, the Ubuntu community has moved from being something of a rebellion against the "Linux establishment" to a strong and professionally organized group.

What Makes Ubuntu So Popular?

First, this is the time for free software to come to the forefront, and Ubuntu is very much the beneficiary of the vast amount of work that has gone into building up a huge body of work in the GNU/Linux world. That work has been underway for nearly 30 years, in one form or another, but Ubuntu is one way in which it is suddenly becoming "visible" to the non-specialist computer user. We are in the middle of a great overturning of the industry status quo. The last time that happened, in the mid-1990s, was when the world suddenly found itself connected to itself—by the Internet. Every major company, especially those in the field of technology, had to examine itself and ask the question, "How do we adapt to an Internet world?" Today, every major technology company has to ask itself the question, "How do we adapt to a free software world?"

I would speculate and say that Ubuntu represents an idea whose time has come. We did not invent the free software movement—that honor goes to Richard Stallman and many others who had a vision far more profound at a time when it was hard to see how it could ever become reality. But Ubuntu has perhaps the honor of bringing that vision to a very wide audience in a form that we can all appreciate. I hope that the real visionaries—those who have led the way—will appreciate the decisions and the choices we make in bringing you this project. Some will take exception—I know Linus prefers KDE to GNOME, for example, so he's likely to be more of a fan of Kubuntu than Ubuntu. But in general, the ideas that others have had, the principles of the free software movement, are well expressed in Ubuntu.

Second, Ubuntu is a project on which you can have a real impact. It has the benefit of deep and reliable financial backing and a corporate team to give it muscle, but it is in every regard an open project, with participation at the highest levels by true volunteers. We work in a fishbowl—our meetings take place online, in a public forum. That can be tricky. Building an operating system is a fast-paced business full of compromise and tough decisions in the face of little information. There are disagreements and dirty laundry, and mistakes are made. (I should know; some of them are mine. You should hear the one about the Warty Warthog desktop artwork.) The transparency of our environment, however, means that we can count on having robust conversations about our options—all of them, even the ones the core team would never have dreamed up. It also means that mistakes are identified, discussed, and ultimately addressed faster than they would be if we lived and worked behind closed doors. You get a better platform as a result.

We work hard as a community to recognize the contributions of all sorts of individuals—advocates, artists, Web forum moderators, channel operators, community event organizers, writers, translators, people who file and triage bugs . . . whatever your particular interest or talent, we will find a way to integrate your contribution.

Perhaps most important is the way our approach to community differentiates Ubuntu from other free software projects with similar vision. We try to do all of this in a way that recognizes that disagreements are important but prevents those disagreements from creating deep divides in our community. Our code of conduct may not be perfect, but it reminds each of us to remember the meaning of the word *ubuntu*—that each of us has our best impact *through* the relationships we maintain with one another. Finding common ground and maintaining healthy communication are more important for us as a community in the long run than a particular technical decision or the specific choice of words with which to translate "File" into Spanish. Our community governance structures—our Technical Board and Community Council—exist to ensure that debates don't become personal and that decisions can be taken after all sides have been heard.

If you are a software professional or curious about Linux, this book and this platform are an excellent choice. You will learn about the world of Ubuntu and, indirectly, Debian and GNU/Linux. These are great foundations for working with the tools that I believe will come to define the "standard," the everyday computing base upon which we build our homes and offices.

I once heard a proprietary software vendor say, "Linux is more expensive because skilled Linux professionals are more costly." This is true. It means, of course, that Linux skills are more valuable! It won't be true forever because the world of Linux is expanding so rapidly that sooner or later we will have to accept a position in the mainstream, and that takes off some of the "geek points" associated with being part of the "future of technology." But right now, without a doubt, being ahead of the curve on Linux and on Ubuntu is the right place to be. If you're this far into this foreword, you are clearly going to make it. ;-)

It's difficult for me to speculate on what the future might hold for the Ubuntu project. I know that I along with many others are loving the opportunity to be at the center of such an exciting initiative and are committed to seeing where it leads us over the coming years. I believe that it will become a pervasive part of our everyday computing environment, so I would like to help make sure that we don't make too many mistakes along the way! Please, come and join us in the fishbowl to help ensure we do a very, very good job.

—Mark Shuttleworth
Ubuntu Founder
April 2006

Preface

AS WE WRITE THIS, it is several years since we penned the first edition of *The Official Ubuntu Book* and a year since the third. The last year has seen Ubuntu continue its explosive growth. Updating this book drives this fact home in striking ways. For example, the number of users and posts in the Ubuntu Forums has nearly doubled since the last edition of this book a year ago. Again. The number of officially supported flavors of Ubuntu have been added to. Again. Once again, we feel blessed that *The Official Ubuntu Book* has been able to benefit from, and perhaps in a small way even *contribute* to, that success. Ultimately, that success paved the way for the second, third, and now the fourth edition of the book that you're reading now.

In the process, this book, like Ubuntu, is beginning to mature. Like Ubuntu, we have now put together our piece a few times and are beginning to get more comfortable. Our job as authors, like that of the Ubuntu developers, now involves more updating and polishing than it used to. Distributed under a free license, a once-risky book on a once-risky operating system is, just a few short years later, as close to a sure thing as an author, publisher, and if we have done our job well, a reader, could hope for.

And yet with success comes responsibility to our readers and to our users with high expectations. Ubuntu's success is built in part of maturity and excellence, and it cannot sacrifice these qualities if it will succeed. We cannot either. Our job as writers is complicated because we need to accurately reflect and represent both while catering to an increasing and increasingly diverse group of users.

As we've noted in the prefaces to previous editions of this book, being *Official* has carried with it a set of rights and responsibilities. Our book's title means that we must attempt to reflect and represent the whole

Ubuntu community. While we, as authors, are expected to put ourselves into the book, it is understood that it can never be to the detriment of the values, principles, technologies, or structures of the Ubuntu community.

Doing this has been complicated as Ubuntu has grown. In each edition, we have added a new chapter, because the Ubuntu community has grown to include new projects. In each revision of this book, we have needed to add to the list of related projects, tools, and community initiatives. As the Ubuntu community grows, it is impossible to give a complete accounting of what Ubuntu has to offer. Creating a summary requires some hard decisions. At the end of the day, we are constrained by page count and our own limited schedules.

Meanwhile, as with earlier editions, we needed to write this book about a new release of Ubuntu while that version was under active development and was being redesigned, rethought, and rebuilt. Every day, Ubuntu grows in different, unpredictable ways, and this growth has increased exponentially with the size of the community and the diversity of the userbase. Our book's development process had to both match and track this process as our content was crafted, rewritten, adjusted, and allowed to mature itself.

As in the previous edition, the contributors to this book go well beyond those listed on the book's cover. As in the first three editions, the recipes included in Chapter 6 have been elicited from and designed in consultation with the community. But while the community contributions are sometimes less visible in other chapters, they are no less present. Invisible to most readers, dozens of members of the community left their mark on different parts of the text of this book. Although this degree of participation led to a writing process that was as hectic, and at times frustrating, as the process that builds Ubuntu, we hope we can remind readers of the level of quality that this process inspires in our book's subject. In the places where we achieve this, we have earned our book's title. With that goal in mind, we look forward to future versions of Ubuntu and editions of this book wrought through the same community-driven process.

Acknowledgments

SPECIAL THANKS TO Mark Shuttleworth, Andrew Rodaway, and Jane Silber for all their efforts to get this book out into the world for both new and veteran Ubuntu users. Thanks also to Victor Ferns, director of Canonical, Ltd., for his attention to the project. Many people at Canonical, including Kat Kinnie, Julian Hubbard, Ivanka Majic, Cezzaine Haigh, and James Troup, provided immeasurable assistance in the production of this book.

We reached into the Ubuntu community for a top group of reviewers, each of whom greatly contributed to the strength of the manuscript, including Alan Pope, Jorge O. Castro, Jonathan Riddell, and Oliver Grawet. Our thanks extend back to this group of reviewers for help with the previous editions: Kyle Rankin, Dennis Kaarsemaker, Matthew East, Quim Gil, Dinko Korunic, Abhay Kumar, Jaldhar Vyas, and Richard Weideman.

We received a truly global response from the Ubuntu community when the call was put out on The Fridge for solutions to common problems. Valuable recipes were collected from Alabama, Australia, California, England, Germany, Illinois, India, Jamaica, Massachusetts, Mauritius, Minnesota, the Netherlands, Paris, Prague, Quebec, and Sweden. Hearty thanks go to the following avid Ubuntu users for sharing their knowledge: Tim Aretz, David Bain, David Bolin, Alan Barnard, David Clayton, Manu Cornet, Scott Dier, Kevin Goldstein, Oskar Jönefors, Keith Kyzivat, Jason LaPrade, Freddy Martinez, Avinash Meetoo, Julien Rottenberg, Stephen Sandlin, Matěj Šmíd, David Symons, Paul van Genderen, and Andrew Zajac. James Stanger also pitched in with a very useful section on how to print from Ubuntu.

And finally, we appreciate the efforts of the Prentice Hall team, including Debra Williams Cauley, Carol Lallier, Kim Arney, Linda Begley, Richard Evans, Kim Boedigheimer, Mark Taub, John Fuller, and Elizabeth Ryan.

About the Authors

Benjamin Mako Hill is a Seattle native working out of Boston, Massachusetts, USA. Mako is a long-time free software developer and advocate. He was part of the founding Ubuntu team, one of the first employees of Canonical, Ltd., and coauthor of *The Official Ubuntu Server Book*. In addition to some technical work, his charge at Canonical was to help grow the Ubuntu development and user community during the project's first year. Mako is currently a fellow at the MIT Center for Future Civic Media, and a researcher and Ph.D. Candidate at the MIT Sloan School of Management. Mako has continued his involvement with Ubuntu as a member of the Community Council governance board, through development work, and through projects such as this book.

Matthew Helmke has been an Ubuntu user since April 2005 and an Ubuntu Member since August 2006. He serves on the Ubuntu Forum Council, providing leadership and oversight of the Ubuntu Forums, as well as on the Ubuntu regional membership approval board for Europe, the Middle East, and Africa. He has written articles about Ubuntu for *Linux+* and *Linux Identity* magazines, along with books and articles on this and other topics. He recently closed his consulting business in Morocco and began a Master's degree program at the University of Arizona in Tucson, Arizona, USA.

Corey Burger lives in Victoria, British Columbia, Canada, and is a long-term user and contributor to Ubuntu. A member of the Ubuntu Canada and the Community Council, he has been involved with Ubuntu since its first release. Corey is currently a geography student and has most recently worked for a Canadian Linux company. He also contributes to Open-StreetMap and works to promote Ubuntu on Vancouver Island. Corey speaks regularly about Ubuntu, OpenStreetMap, and open source to a wide variety of audiences.

Ivan Krstić is a software architect and researcher currently on leave from Harvard University. Until recently, he worked as the director of Security Architecture at the One Laptop per Child project, a nonprofit organization that aimed to provide $100 laptop computers for children in the developing world. In 2008, *eWEEK* magazine editors declared him one of the top three most influential people in modern computer security, and the editors of *CIO Insight and Baseline* magazine named him one of the top 100 most influential people in all of IT.

Jonathan Jesse is a full-time Microsoft Windows consultant specializing in IT lifecycle management products. Beginning with the Hoary Hedgehog release, he joined the Ubuntu Documentation Team by proofreading and submitting patches to the mailing list, then worked on the Kubuntu documents. Currently, Jonathan is involved in working on bugs for the Kubuntu Team, the Ubuntu Wiki, and the Laptop Testing Team. Ubuntu and Kubuntu have given Jonathan a way to give back to the community without having to be a developer, and he encourages everyone to come help him out.

Richard A. Johnson is a contributor to Kubuntu and Edubuntu from Chicago, Illinois, USA, and a long-term member of the Ubuntu community. In 1994, while serving in the U.S. Navy, he purchased a computer at the base PX. Upon starting it up later that day, Richard noticed the immediate issues with the modem as well as the sound card. The next day at work, he searched the Internet on "How to fix Microsoft Windows." One of the first results was the Slackware Linux distribution, at which time he downloaded to numerous floppy disks to install later at home. Now Richard hacks on the Kubuntu, Edubuntu, and Debian GNU/Linux operating systems, as well as the award-winning K Desktop Environment (KDE). He enjoys spending a vast majority of his free time hacking on, and spreading, freedom.

Jono Bacon (www.jonobacon.org) is the community leader for Ubuntu. Previously, he was a consultant for the United Kingdom's government-funded OpenAdvantage (www.openadvantage.org) center in England, where he worked with businesses, educational and charitable organizations, and individuals to help them move to open source software and open standards. He is the cocreator of the popular LugRadio podcast (www. lugradio.org).

Introduction

WELCOME to *The Official Ubuntu Book, Fourth Edition*!

In recent years, the Ubuntu operating system has taken the open source and IT world by storm. From out of nowhere, the Little Operating System That Could has blossomed into a full-featured desktop and server offering that has won over the hearts of users everywhere. Aside from the strong technical platform and impressive commitment to quality, Ubuntu also enjoys success because of its sprawling community of enthusiastic users who have helped to support, document, and test every millimeter of the Ubuntu landscape.

In your hands you are holding the official, authorized guide to this impressive operating system. Each of the authors selected to work on this book has demonstrated a high level of technical competence, an unbridled commitment to Ubuntu, and the ability to share this knowledge in a simple and clear manner. These authors gathered together to create a book that offers a solid grounding to Ubuntu and explains how the many facets and features of Ubuntu work.

About This Book

At the start of every book, on every bookshelf, in every shop, is a paragraph that sums up the intentions and aims for the book. We have one very simple, down-to-earth aim: to make the Ubuntu experience even more pleasant for users. The Ubuntu developers and community have gone to great lengths to produce an easy-to-use, functional, and flexible operating system for doing, browsing, and creating all kinds of interesting things. This book augments that effort. With such an integrated and flexible operating system, this guide acts as a tour de force for the many things you can do with Ubuntu.

The Scope of the Book

With so much to cover, we had our work cut out to write a book that could cover the system in sufficient detail. However, if we were to write in depth about every possible feature in Ubuntu, you would need to buy a new bookcase to store the sheer amount of content.

Part of the challenge in creating *The Official Ubuntu Book* was selecting the topics and content that can be covered within a reasonably sized book. We have identified the most essential content and written only about it. These chosen topics not only include installation, use of the desktop, applications, multimedia, system administration, and software management, but also include a discussion of the community, online resources, and the philosophy behind Ubuntu and open source software. As a bonus, we decided to squeeze in a chapter full of useful troubleshooting recipes that you can use when you need to troubleshoot problems, and we expanded our discussion of projects related to Ubuntu that will be of interest to you. We believe this book provides an ideal one-stop shop for getting started with Ubuntu.

The Menu

Here is a short introduction to each chapter and what it covers.

- Chapter 1—Introducing Ubuntu: This spirited introduction describes the Ubuntu project, its distribution, its development processes, and some of the history that made it all possible.

- Chapter 2—Installing Ubuntu: We walk through the installation process one step at a time to clearly describe how anyone interested may begin using Ubuntu on their own computer.

- Chapter 3—Using Ubuntu on the Desktop: This is an informative and enjoyable introductory tour of the Ubuntu desktop, the applications included, and ways to configure and customize your desktop.

- Chapter 4—Advanced Usage and Managing Ubuntu: We explore some of the advanced ways to use Ubuntu, including managing the system. These features are not vital if you want to use the computer only as a simple tool, but once you learn how to install and manage software, use hardware devices and printers, interact with remote computers, use the terminal, and run some Windows programs under

Ubuntu, you will find your overall experience even more rewarding and enjoyable.

- Chapter 5—The Ubuntu Server: This introduction to Ubuntu Server installation and administration includes coverage of command-line package management, basic security topics, and advanced installer features like logical volume management and RAID.

- Chapter 6—Support and Typical Problems: Packed to the seams with lots of small, independent recipes, this chapter teaches you how to solve problems or meet unique requirements in your setup.

- Chapter 7—The Ubuntu Community: The Ubuntu community is larger and more active than many people realize. We discuss many of its facets, including what people like you do to build, promote, distribute, support, document, translate, and advocate Ubuntu—and we tell you how you can join in the fun.

- Chapter 8—Using Kubuntu: The most popular spin-off project from Ubuntu is Kubuntu. This chapter provides a solid introduction and primer for getting started.

- Chapter 9—Using Edubuntu: We offer in-depth coverage of the Edubuntu project and community, an Ubuntu derivative designed for educators and the schools in which they work.

- Chapter 10—Ubuntu-Related Projects: There are a number of Linux distributions based on Ubuntu that you will find interesting and possibly useful. We discuss some of these as well as projects that are integral to the creation of Ubuntu, such as Launchpad and Bazaar.

- Chapter 11—Introducing the Ubuntu Forums: For hundreds of thousands of people, the Ubuntu Forums have provided the first glimpse of and interaction with the greater Ubuntu community. Especially for new users, this has become the most important venue for support. We explore the forums and the people, history, and processes that have built them.

- Appendix A—Welcome to the Command Line: You can begin to take advantage of the power and efficiency of the command line with the clear, easy-to-use examples in our brief introduction.

- Appendix B—Ubuntu Equivalents to Windows Programs.

The Ubuntu team offers several installation options for Ubuntu users, including CDs for desktop, alternate install, and server install. These three CD images are conveniently combined onto one DVD included in the back of this book, allowing you to install Ubuntu for different configurations from just one disk. There is also an option to test the DVD for defects as well as a memory test option to check your computer.

The first boot option on the DVD, Start or Install Ubuntu, will cover most users' needs. For more comprehensive information, check the Help feature by selecting F1 on the boot menu. You can also refer to Chapter 2, which covers the Ubuntu installation process in detail.

You can find the DVD image, the individual CD images (for those who don't have a DVD drive), and Kubuntu and Edubuntu images on www.ubuntu.com/download.

CHAPTER 1

Introducing Ubuntu

- **A Wild Ride**
- **Free Software, Open Source, and GNU/Linux**
- **A Brief History of Ubuntu**
- **What Is Ubuntu?**
- **Ubuntu Promises and Goals**
- **Canonical and the Ubuntu Foundation**
- **Ubuntu Subprojects, Derivatives, and Spin-offs**
- **Summary**

THIS CHAPTER INTRODUCES THE Ubuntu project, its distribution, its development processes, and some of the history that made it all possible. If you are looking to jump right in and get started with Ubuntu, turn right away to Chapter 2, Installing Ubuntu. If you are interested in first learning about where Ubuntu comes from and where it is going, this chapter provides a good introduction.

A Wild Ride

In April 2004 Mark Shuttleworth brought together a dozen developers from the Debian, GNOME, and GNU Arch projects to brainstorm. Shuttleworth asked the developers if a better type of operating system (OS) was possible. Their answer was "Yes." He asked them what it would look like. He asked them to describe the community that would build such an OS. That group worked with Shuttleworth to come up with answers to these questions, and then they decided to try to make the answers a reality. The group named itself the Warthogs and gave itself a six-month deadline to build a proof-of-concept OS. The developers nicknamed their first release the Warty Warthog with the reasonable assumption that their first product would have its warts. Then they got down to business.

It's difficult, particularly for those of us who were privileged to be among those early Warthogs, to imagine that the brainstorming meeting behind the Ubuntu project took place just five years ago. Far from being warty, the Warty Warthog surpassed our most optimistic expectations and *everyone's* predictions. Within six months, Ubuntu was in the Number 1 spot on several popularity rankings of GNU/Linux distributions. Ubuntu has demonstrated the most explosive growth of any GNU/Linux distribution in recent memory and had one of the most impressive first years of any free or open source software project in history.

It is staggering to think that after less than six years, *millions* of individuals are using Ubuntu. As many thousands of these users give back to the Ubuntu community by developing documentation, translation, and code, Ubuntu improves every day. As many thousands of these users contribute to a thriving advocacy and support community—both online and in their local communities—Ubuntu's growth remains unchecked. Ubuntu subprojects, a list of efforts that contains the now-mature Kubuntu, Edubuntu, and Xubuntu projects, are extending the reach and goals of the Ubuntu project into new realms.

Meanwhile, millions of pressed Ubuntu CDs have been shipped at no cost to universities, Internet cafés, computer shops, and community centers around the world. You can find Ubuntu's familiar human-colored background and title bars almost anywhere people use computers. I have personally seen strangers running Ubuntu on trains in Spain, in libraries in Boston, in museums in Croatia, in high schools in Mexico, and in many more places too numerous to list here.

Over the years, Ubuntu has continued to mature. The public took even more notice of Ubuntu beginning with the release of Ubuntu 6.06 LTS, the first polished release with long-term support for both desktops and servers, and followed later by the next long-term support release, Ubuntu 8.04 LTS, and now 9.04, the most recent release. With these and other releases in between, Ubuntu has proven it intends to stick around for the long term. Even with this maturation, the project maintains its youthful vigor, its ambitious attitude, its commitment to its principles, and its community-driven approach. As the project ages, it is proving that it can learn from its failures as well as its successes and that it can maintain growth without compromising stability. We've come a long way—and we're still only getting started.

Free Software, Open Source, and GNU/Linux

While thousands of individuals have contributed in some form to Ubuntu, the project has succeeded only through the contributions of many thousands more who have indirectly laid the technical, social, and economic groundwork for Ubuntu's success. While introductions to free software, open source, and GNU/Linux can be found in many other places, no introduction of Ubuntu is complete without a brief discussion of these concepts and the people and history behind them. It is around these concepts and within these communities that Ubuntu was motivated and born. Ultimately, it is through these ideas that it is sustained.

Free Software and GNU

In a series of events that have almost become legend through constant repetition, Richard M. Stallman created the concept of free software in 1983.

Stallman grew up with computers in the 1960s and 1970s, when computer users purchased very large and extremely expensive mainframe computers, which were then shared among large numbers of programmers. Software was, for the most part, seen as an add-on to the hardware, and every user had the ability and the right to modify or rewrite the software on his or her computer and to freely share this software. As computers became cheaper and more numerous in the late 1970s, producers of software began to see value in the software itself. Producers of computers began to argue that their software could be copyrighted and was a form of intellectual property much like a music recording, a film, or a book's text. They began to distribute their software under licenses and in forms that restricted its users' abilities to use, redistribute, or modify the code. By the early 1980s, restrictive software licenses had become the norm.

Stallman, then a programmer at MIT's Artificial Intelligence Laboratory, became increasingly concerned with what he saw as a dangerous loss of the freedoms that software users and developers had previously enjoyed. He was concerned with computer users' ability to be good neighbors and members of what he thought was an ethical and efficient computer-user community. To fight against this negative tide, Stallman articulated a vision for a community that developed liberated code—in his words, "free software." He defined free software as software that had the following four characteristics—labeled as freedoms 0 through 3 instead of 1 through 4 as a computer programmer's joke:

▪ The freedom to run the program for any purpose (freedom 0)

▪ The freedom to study how the program works and adapt it to your needs (freedom 1)

▪ The freedom to redistribute copies so you can help your neighbor (freedom 2)

▪ The freedom to improve the program and release your improvements to the public so that the whole community benefits (freedom 3)

Access to source code—the human-readable and modifiable blueprints of any piece of software that can be distinguished from the computer-readable version of the code that most software is distributed as—is a prerequisite to freedoms 1 and 3. In addition to releasing this definition of free software, Stallman created a project with the goal of creating a completely free OS to replace the then-popular UNIX. In 1984, Stallman announced this project and called it GNU—another joke in the form of a recursive acronym for "GNU's Not UNIX."

Linux

By the early 1990s, Stallman and a collection of other programmers working on GNU had developed a near-complete OS that could be freely shared. They were, however, missing a final essential piece in the form of a kernel— a complex system command processor that lies at the center of any OS. In 1991, Linus Torvalds wrote an early version of just such a kernel, released it under a free license, and called it Linux. Linus's kernel was paired with the GNU project's development tools and OS and with the graphical windowing system called X. With this pairing, a completely free OS was born—free both in terms of price and in Stallman's terms of freedom.

All systems referred to as Linux today are, in fact, built on the work of this collaboration. Technically, the term *Linux* refers only to the kernel. Many programmers and contributors to GNU, including Stallman, argue emphatically that the full OS should be referred to as GNU/Linux in order to give credit not only to Linux but also to the GNU project and to highlight GNU's goals of spreading software freedom—goals not necessarily shared by Linus Torvalds. Many others find this name cumbersome and prefer calling the system simply Linux. Yet others, such as those working on the Ubuntu project, attempt to avoid the controversy altogether by referring to GNU/Linux only by using their own project's name.

Open Source

Disagreements over labeling did not end with discussions about the naming of the combination of GNU and Linux. In fact, as the list of contributors to GNU and Linux grew, a vibrant world of new free software projects sprouted up, facilitated in part by growing access to the Internet. As this community grew and diversified, a number of people began to notice an unintentional side effect of Stallman's free software. Because free software was built in an open way, *anyone* could contribute to software by looking through the code, finding bugs, and fixing them. Because software ended up being examined by larger numbers of programmers, free software was higher in quality, performed better, and offered more features than similar software developed through proprietary development mechanisms. It turned out that in many situations, the development model behind free software led to software that was *inherently better* than proprietary alternatives.

As the computer and information technology industry began to move into the dot-com boom, one group of free software developers and leaders, spearheaded by two free software developers and advocates—Eric S. Raymond and Bruce Perens—saw the important business proposition offered by a model that could harness volunteer labor or interbusiness collaboration and create intrinsically better software. However, they worried that the term *free software* was problematic for at least two reasons. First, it was highly ambiguous—the English word *free* means both gratis, or at no cost (e.g., free as in free beer), and liberated in the sense of freedom (e.g., free as in free speech). Second, there was a feeling, articulated most famously by Raymond, that all this talk of freedom was scaring off the very business executives and decision makers whom the free software movement needed to impress in order to succeed.

To tackle both of these problems, this group coined a new phrase—open source—and created a new organization called the Open Source Initiative. The group set at its core a definition of open source software that overlapped completely and exclusively with both Stallman's four-part definition of free software and with other community definitions that were also based on Stallman's.

One useful way to understand the split between the free software and open source movements is to think of it as the opposite of a schism. In religious schisms, churches separate and do not work or worship together because of relatively small differences in belief, interpretation, or motivation. For example, most contemporary forms of Protestant Christianity agree on *almost* everything but have separated over some small but irreconcilable differences. However, in the case of the free software and open source movements, the two groups have fundamental disagreements about their motivation and beliefs. One group is focused on freedom, while the other is focused on pragmatics. Free software is most accurately described as a social movement, while open source is a development methodology. However, the two groups have no trouble working on projects hand in hand.

In terms of the motivations and goals, open source and free software diverge greatly. Yet in terms of the software, the projects, and the licenses they use, they are completely synonymous. While people who identify with either group see the two movements as being at odds, the Ubuntu project sees no conflict between the two ideologies. People in the Ubuntu project identify with either group and often with both. In this book, we may switch back and forth between the terms as different projects, and many people in the Ubuntu community identify more strongly with one term or the other. For the purposes of this book, though, either term should be read as implying the other unless it is stated otherwise.

A Brief History of Ubuntu

There was a time when writing a history of Ubuntu may have seemed premature. However, the last several years have been busy ones for Ubuntu. With its explosive growth, it is difficult even for those involved most closely with the project to track and record some of the high points. Importantly, there are some key figures whose own history must be given to fully understand Ubuntu. This brief summary tries to quickly give you the high points of Ubuntu's history to date and the necessary background knowledge to understand where Ubuntu comes from.

Mark Shuttleworth

No history of Ubuntu can call itself complete without a history of Mark Shuttleworth. Shuttleworth is, undeniably, the most visible and important person in Ubuntu. More important from the point of view of history, Shuttleworth is also the originator and initiator of the project—he made the snowball that would eventually roll on and grow to become the Ubuntu project.

Shuttleworth was born in 1973 in Welkom, Free State in South Africa. He attended Diocesan College and obtained a business science degree in finance and information systems at the University of Cape Town. During this period, he was an avid computer hobbyist and became involved with the free and open source software community. He was at least marginally involved in both the Apache project and the Debian project and was the first person to upload the Apache Web server, perhaps the single most important piece of server software on GNU/Linux platforms, into the Debian project's archives.

Seeing an opportunity in the early days of the Web, Shuttleworth founded a certificate authority and Internet security company called Thawte in his garage. Over the course of several years, he built Thawte into the second largest certificate authority on the Internet, trailing only the security behemoth VeriSign. Throughout this period, Thawte's products and services were built and served almost entirely from free and open source software. In December 1999, Shuttleworth sold Thawte to VeriSign for an undisclosed amount that reached into the hundreds of millions in U.S. dollars.

With his fortune made at a young age, Shuttleworth might have enjoyed a life of leisure—and probably considered it. Instead, he decided to pursue his lifelong dream of space travel. After paying approximately US $20 million to the Russian space program and devoting nearly a year to preparation, including learning Russian and spending seven months training in Star City, Russia, Shuttleworth realized his dream as a civilian cosmonaut aboard the Russian Soyuz TM-34 mission. On this mission, Shuttleworth spent two days on the Soyuz rocket and eight days on the International Space Station, where he participated in experiments related to AIDS and genome research. In early May 2002, Shuttleworth returned to Earth.

In addition to space exploration and a slightly less impressive jaunt to Antarctica, Shuttleworth has played an active role as both a philanthropist and a venture capitalist. In 2001, Shuttleworth founded The Shuttleworth Foundation (TSF)—a nonprofit organization based in South Africa. The foundation was chartered to fund, develop, and drive social innovation in the field of education. Of course, the means by which TSF attempts to achieve these goals frequently involves free software. Through these projects, the organization has been one of the most visible proponents of free and open source software in South Africa and even the world. In the venture capital area, Shuttleworth worked to foster research, development, and entrepreneurship in South Africa with strategic injections of cash into start-ups through a new venture capital firm called HBD, an acronym standing for "Here Be Dragons." During this period, Shuttleworth was busy brainstorming his next big project—the project that would eventually become Ubuntu.

The Warthogs

There has been no lack of projects attempting to wrap GNU, Linux, and other pieces of free and open source software into a neat, workable, and user-friendly package. Mark Shuttleworth, like many other people, believed that the philosophical and pragmatic benefits offered by free software put it on a course for widespread success. While each had its strengths, none of the offerings were particularly impressive as a whole. Something was missing from each of them. Shuttleworth saw this as an opportunity. If someone could build *the* great free software distribution that helped push GNU/Linux into the mainstream, he would come to occupy a position of strategic importance.

Shuttleworth, like many other technically inclined people, was a huge fan of the Debian project (discussed in depth later in this chapter). However, many things about Debian did not fit with Shuttleworth's vision of an ideal OS. For a period of time, Shuttleworth considered the possibility of running for Debian project leader as a means of reforming the Debian project from within. With time, though, it became clear that the best way to bring GNU/Linux to the mainstream would not be from within the Debian project—which in many situations had very good reasons for being the way it was. Instead, Shuttleworth would create a new project that worked in symbiosis with Debian to build a new, better GNU/Linux system.

To kick off this project, Shuttleworth invited a dozen or so free and open source software developers he knew and respected to his flat in London in April 2004. It was in this meeting (alluded to in the first paragraphs of this introduction) that the groundwork for the Ubuntu project was laid. By that point, many of those involved were excited about the possibility of the project. During this meeting, the members of the team—which would in time grow into the core Ubuntu team—brainstormed a large list of the things that *they* would want to see in their ideal OS. The list is now a familiar list of features to most Ubuntu users. Many of these traits are covered in more depth later in this chapter. The group wanted

- Predictable and frequent release cycles
- A strong focus on localization and accessibility
- A strong focus on ease of use and user-friendliness on the desktop

- A strong focus on Python as the single programming language through which the entire system could be built and expanded

- A community-driven approach that worked with existing free software projects and a method by which the groups could give back as they went along—not just at the time of release

- A new set of tools designed around the process of building distributions that allowed developers to work within an ecosystem of different projects and that allowed users to give back in whatever way they could

There was consensus among the group that actions speak louder than words, so there were no public announcements or press releases. Instead, the group set a deadline for itself—six short months in the future. Shuttleworth agreed to finance the work and pay the developers full-time salaries to work on the project. After six months, they would both announce their project and reveal the first product of their work. They made a list of goals they wanted to achieve by the deadline, and the individuals present took on tasks. Collectively, they called themselves the Warthogs.

What Does *Ubuntu* Mean?

At this point, the Warthogs had a great team, a set of goals, and a decent idea of how to achieve most of them. The team did not, on the other hand, have a name for the project. Shuttleworth argued strongly that they should call the project Ubuntu.

Ubuntu is a concept and a term from several South African languages, including Zulu and Xhosa. It refers to a South African ideology or ethic that, while difficult to express in English, might roughly be translated as "humanity toward others," or "I am because we are." Others have described ubuntu as "the belief in a universal bond of sharing that connects all humanity." The famous South African human rights champion Archbishop Desmond Tutu explained ubuntu in this way:

> A person with ubuntu is open and available to others, affirming of others, does not feel threatened that others are able and good, for he or she has a proper self-assurance that comes from knowing that he or she belongs in a greater whole and is diminished when others are humiliated or diminished, when others are tortured or oppressed.

Ubuntu played an important role as a founding principle in post-apartheid South Africa and remains a concept familiar to most South Africans today.

Shuttleworth liked the term *Ubuntu* as a name for the new project for several reasons. First, it is a South African concept. While the majority of the people who work on Ubuntu are not from South Africa, the roots of the project are, and Shuttleworth wanted to choose a name that represented this. Second, the project emphasizes the definition of individuality in terms of relationships with others and provides a profound type of community and sharing—exactly the attitudes of sharing, community, and collaboration that are at the core of free software. The term represented the side of free software that the team wanted to share with the world. Third, the idea of personal relationships built on mutual respect and connections describes the fundamental ground rules for the highly functional community that the Ubuntu team wanted to build. *Ubuntu* was a term that encapsulated where the project came from, where the project was going, and how the project planned to get there. The name was perfect. It stuck.

Creating Canonical

In order to pay developers to work on Ubuntu full-time, Shuttleworth needed a company to employ them. He wanted to pick some of the best people for the jobs from within the global free and open source communities. These communities, inconveniently for Shuttleworth, know no national and geographic boundaries. Rather than move everyone to a single locale and office, Shuttleworth made the decision to employ these developers through a virtual company. While this had obvious drawbacks in the form of high-latency and low-bandwidth connections, different time zones, and much more, it also introduced some major benefits in the particular context of the project. On one hand, the distributed nature of employees meant that the new company could hire individuals without requiring them to pack up their lives and move to a new country. More important, it meant that *everyone* in the company was dependent on IRC, mailing lists, and online communication mechanisms to do their work. This unintentionally and automatically solved the water-cooler problem that plagued many other corporately funded free software projects—namely, that developers would casually speak about their work in person and cut the community and anyone else who didn't work in the office out of the conversation completely. For the first year, the closest thing that

Canonical had to an office was Shuttleworth's flat in London. While the company has grown and now has several offices around the world, it remains distributed and a large number of the engineers work from home. The group remains highly dependent on Internet collaboration.

With time, the company was named Canonical. The name was a nod to the project's optimistic goals of becoming the canonical place for services and support for free and open source software and for Ubuntu in particular. *Canonical*, of course, refers to something that is accepted as authoritative. It is a common word in the computer programmer lexicon. It's important to note that being canonical is like being standard; it is not coercive. Unlike holding a monopoly, becoming the canonical location for something implies a similar sort of success—but *never* one that cannot be undone, and *never* one that is exclusive. Other companies will support Ubuntu and build operating systems based on it, but as long as Canonical is doing a good job, its role will remain central.

What Is Ubuntu?

The Warthogs' goal and Canonical's flagship project is Ubuntu. If you've gotten this far, you already have some idea of what that means. That said, this section tries to offer a little bit of background that is helpful in understanding exactly *what* Ubuntu is and what its goals are.

What Is a Distribution?

It's clear to most people that Ubuntu is an OS. The full story is a little more complex. Ubuntu is what is called a distribution of GNU/Linux—a *distro* for short. Understanding exactly what that means requires, once again, a little bit of history. In the early days of GNU and Linux, users needed a great deal of technical knowledge. Only geeks needed to apply. There were no Linux operating systems in the sense that we usually use the term—there was no single CD or set of disks that one could use to install. Instead, the software was dozens and even hundreds of individual programs, each built differently by a different individual, and each distributed separately. Installing each of the necessary applications would be incredibly time consuming at best. In many cases, incompatibilities and the technical trickery necessary to install software made getting a GNU/Linux system on a hard disk prohibitively difficult. A great deal of knowledge of configuration and programming was necessary just to get a system up and running. As a result, very few people who were not programmers used these early GNU/Linux systems.

Early distributions were projects that collected all of the necessary pieces of software from all of the different places and put them together in an easier-to-install form with the most basic configuration already done. These distributions aimed to make using GNU/Linux more convenient and to bring it to larger groups of users. Today, almost nobody uses GNU/Linux without using a distribution. As a result, distribution names are well known. Ubuntu is such a project. Other popular distros include Red Hat and Fedora, Novell's SUSE, Gentoo, and of course Debian.

Most distributions contain a similar collection of software. For example, they all contain most of the core pieces of GNU and a Linux kernel. Almost all contain the X Window System and a set of applications on top of it that may include a Web browser, a desktop environment, and an office suite. While distributions started out distributing only the core pieces of the OS, they have grown to include an increasingly wide array of applications as well. A modern distribution includes all of the software that "comes with an OS," that is, several CDs or DVDs containing anything that most users might want and that the distribution is legally allowed to distribute.

Ubuntu, like other contemporary distros, offers a custom installer, a framework including software and servers to install new software once the system has been installed, a standard configuration method through which many programs can be configured, a standard method through which users can report bugs in their software, and much more. Frequently, distributions also contain large repositories of software on servers accessible through the Internet. To get a sense of scale, Ubuntu includes on the order of 20,000 pieces of software on its central servers—each piece of software is customized slightly and tested to work well with all of the other software on the system. That number grows daily.

What's important to realize is that the creators of distributions do not, for the most part, write or create the applications you use. The Ubuntu team did not write Linux, and it did not write GNU—although individuals on the team have contributed to both projects. Instead, the Ubuntu team takes GNU, Linux, and many thousands of other applications and then tests and integrates them to be accessible under a single installer. Ubuntu is the glue that lets you take a single CD, install hundreds of separate pieces of software, and have them work together as a single, integrated desktop system. If you were to pick up a CD of another distribution such as Debian, Red Hat, or Novell, the software installed would be nearly identical to the software in Ubuntu. The difference would be in the way the software is installed, serviced, upgraded, and presented and the way it integrates with other pieces of software on the system.

An Ecosystem of Distributions

Many hundreds of GNU/Linux distributions are in active use today. A quick look at Distrowatch's database (distrowatch.com) demonstrates the staggering number and growth of distributions. One of the first GNU/Linux distributions was called Softlanding Linux System, or SLS. For a number of reasons, a programmer named Patrick Volkerding thought he could improve on SLS. Because SLS was free software, Volkerding had the freedom to make a derivative version of SLS and distribute it. Volkerding did just this when he took SLS's code and used it as the framework or model upon which to create his own variant called Slackware. Subsequently, Slackware became the first widely successful GNU/Linux distribution and is maintained to this day.

With time, the landscape of GNU/Linux distribution has changed. However, the important role of derivation that made Slackware possible has remained fully intact and is still shaping this landscape. Today, the hundreds of GNU/Linux distributions serve a multitude of users for a myriad of purposes: There are distributions specially designed for children, for dentists, and for speakers of many of the world's languages. There are distributions for science, for business, for servers, for PDAs, for nonprofit organizations, for musicians, and for countless other groups.

Despite this diversity, the vast majority of derivatives can be traced back to one of two parent distributions: Red Hat and Debian. While it is not necessary to understand the details of how these projects differ, it's useful to know that Red Hat and Debian offer two compelling, but frequently different, platforms. Each project has strengths and weaknesses. For almost every group making a Linux-based OS, one of these projects acts as square one (with a few notable exceptions, such as the Gentoo project).

However, while the process of deriving distributions has allowed for a proliferation of OS platforms serving a vast multiplicity of needs, the derivative process has, historically, been largely a one-way process. New distributions based on Red Hat—Mandriva and Novell's SUSE, for example—begin with Red Hat or a subset of Red Hat technology and then customize and diverge. Very few of these changes ever make it back into Red Hat and, with time, distributions tend to diverge to the point of irreconcilable incompatibility. While the software that each system includes remains largely consistent across all distributions, the way that it is packaged, presented, installed, and configured becomes increasingly differentiated. During this process, interdistribution sharing and collaboration grow in difficulty.

This growing divergence indicates a more general problem faced by distribution teams in getting changes upstream. Frequently, the users of GNU/Linux distributions find and report problems in their software. Frequently, distribution teams fix the bugs in question. While sometimes these bugs are in changes introduced by the distribution, they often exist in the upstream version of the software and the fix applies to *every* distribution. What is not uncommon, but is unfortunately *much* less frequent, is for these bug fixes to be pushed upstream so that all distributions and users get to use them. This lack of collaboration is rarely due to malice, incompetence, or any tactical or strategic decision made by developers or their employers. Instead, tracking and monitoring changes *across* distributions and in relation to upstream developers is complicated and difficult. It's a fact of life that sometimes changes fall on the floor. These failures are simply the product of distribution-building processes, policies, and tools that approach distributions as products in and of themselves—not processes within an ecosystem.

Like many other distributions, Ubuntu is a derivative of Debian. Unlike the creators of many derivatives, the Ubuntu community has made it one of its primary goals to explore the possibility of a better derivation process with Debian, with Debian and Ubuntu's common upstreams (e.g., projects such as Linux or GNU), and with Ubuntu's *own* derivatives. A more in-depth discussion of Debian can help explain how Ubuntu positions itself within the free software world.

The Debian Project and the Free Software Universe

Debian is a distribution backed by a volunteer project of over 1,000 official members and many more volunteers and contributors. It has expanded to encompass around 20,000 packages of free and open source applications and documentation. Debian's history and structure make it very good at certain things. For example, Debian has a well-deserved reputation for integrated package management and access to a large list of free software applications. However, as a voluntary and largely nonhierarchical organization, there are also several things that Debian has trouble providing. Frequent and reliable releases, corporate support and liability, and a top-down consistency on the desktop have proven to be difficult for Debian to offer.

Each new distribution exists for a reason. Creating a new distribution, even a derivative, is far from easy. In large part, Ubuntu exists to build off of the many successes of the Debian project while solving some of the problems it struggles with. The goal is to create a synthetic whole that appeals to users who had previously been unable or unwilling to use Debian.

In building off the great work of the Debian project, as well as GNU, Linux, and other projects that Debian is built on, the Ubuntu team wanted to explore a new style of derivation that focused on a tighter interproject relationship within an ecosystem of different developers. While Ubuntu tries to improve and build on Debian's success, the project is in no way trying to replace Debian. On the contrary, Ubuntu couldn't exist without the Debian project and its large volunteer and software base, as well as the high degree of quality that Debian consistently provides. This symbiotic relationship between Ubuntu and Debian is mirrored in the way that both Ubuntu and Debian depend heavily on projects such as GNU and Linux to produce great software, which they can each package and distribute. The Ubuntu project sets out explicitly to build a symbiotic relationship with both Debian and their common "upstream."

The relationship between Ubuntu and Debian has not been simple, straightforward, or painless and has involved patience and learning on both sides.

While the relationship has yet to be perfected, with time it has improved consistently, and both groups have found ways to work together that seem to offer major benefits over the traditional derive-and-forget model. It is through a complex series of technological, social, and even political processes—many of which is described in the rest of this chapter—that Ubuntu tries to create a better way to build a free software distribution.

The Ubuntu Community

By now you may have noticed a theme that permeates the Ubuntu project on several levels. The history of free software and open source is one of a profoundly effective *community*. Similarly, in building a GNU/Linux distribution, the Ubuntu community has tried to focus on an ecosystem model—an organization of organizations—in other words, a community. Even the definition of *ubuntu* is one that revolves around people interacting in a community.

It comes as no surprise then that an "internal" community plays heavily into the way that the Ubuntu distribution is created. While the Ubuntu 4.10 version (Warty Warthog) was primarily built by a small number of people, Ubuntu achieved widespread success only through contributions by a much larger group that included programmers, documentation writers, volunteer support staff, and users. While Canonical employs a core group of several dozen active contributors to Ubuntu, the distribution has, from day one, encouraged and incorporated contributions from *anyone* in the community, and rewards and recognizes contributions by all. Rather than taking center stage, paid contributors are *not* employed by the Ubuntu project—instead they are employed by Canonical, Ltd. These employees are treated simply as another set of community members. They must apply for membership in the Ubuntu community and have their contributions recognized in the same way as anyone else. All nonbusiness-related communication about the Ubuntu project occurs in public and in the community. Volunteer community members occupy a majority of the seats on the two most important governing boards of the Ubuntu project: the Technical Board, which oversees all technical matters, and the Community Council, which approves new Ubuntu members and resolves disputes. Seats on both boards are approved by the relevant community groups, developers for the Technical Board and Ubuntu members for the Community Council.

In order to harness and encourage the contributions of its community, Ubuntu strives to balance the important role that Canonical plays with the value of empowering individuals in the community. The Ubuntu project is based on a fundamental belief that great software is built, supported, and maintained only in a strong relationship with the individuals who use the software. In this way, by fostering and supporting a vibrant community, Ubuntu can achieve much more than it could through paid development alone. The people on the project believe that while the contributions of Canonical and Mark Shuttleworth have provided an important catalyst for the processes that have built Ubuntu, it is the community that brought the distribution its success to date. The project members believe that it is only through increasing reliance on the community that the project's success will continue to grow. We won't outspend the proprietary software industry. As a community, though, we are very much more than Microsoft and its allies can afford.

The nature of the Ubuntu community is described in depth in Chapter 7, which is wholly devoted to the subject. Finally, it is worth noting that, while this book is official, none of the authors are Canonical employees except Jono Bacon (and he wasn't hired as the Community Leader until the first edition of the book was already on the shelves). This book, like much of the rest of Ubuntu, is purely a product of the project's community.

Ubuntu Promises and Goals

So far, this book has been about the prehistory, history, and context of the Ubuntu project. After this chapter, the book focuses on the distribution itself. Before proceeding, it's important to understand the goals that motivated the project.

Philosophical Goals

The most important goals of the Ubuntu project are philosophical in nature. The Ubuntu project lays out its philosophy in a series of documents on its Web site. In the most central of these documents, the team summarizes the charter and the major philosophical goals and underpinnings.

> Ubuntu is a community-driven project to create an operating system and a full set of applications using free and Open Source software. At the core

of the Ubuntu Philosophy of Software Freedom are these core philosophical ideals:

1. Every computer user should have the freedom to run, copy, distribute, study, share, change, and improve their software for any purpose without paying licensing fees.
2. Every computer user should be able to use their software in the language of their choice.
3. Every computer user should be given every opportunity to use software, even if they work under a disability.

The first item should be familiar by now. It is merely a recapitulation of Stallman's free software definition quoted earlier in the section on free software history. In it, the Ubuntu project makes explicit its goals that every user of software should have the freedoms required by free software. This is important for a number of reasons. First, it offers users all of the practical benefits of software that runs better, faster, and more flexibly. More important, it gives every user the capability to transcend his or her role as a user and a consumer of software. Ubuntu wants software to be empowering and to work in the ways that users want it to work. Ubuntu wants all users to have the ability to make sure it works for them. To do this, software *must* be free, so Ubuntu makes this a requirement and a philosophical promise.

Of course, the core goals of Ubuntu do not end with the free software definition. Instead, the project articulates two new, but equally important, goals. The first of these, that all computer users should be able to use their computers in their chosen languages, is a nod to the fact that the majority of the world's population does not speak English while the vast majority of software interacts only in that language. To be useful, source code comments, programming languages, documentation, and the texts and menus in computer programs must be written in *some* language. Arguably, the world's most international language is a reasonably good choice. However, there is no language that everyone speaks, and English is not useful to the majority of the world's population that does not speak it. A computer can be a great tool for empowerment and education, but *only* if the user can understand the words in the computer's interface. As a result, Ubuntu believes that it is the project's—and community's—responsibility to ensure that *every* user can easily use Ubuntu to read and write in the language with which he or she is most comfortable.

The ability to make modifications—a requirement of free software and of Ubuntu's first philosophical point—makes this type of translation possible. This book is a case in point. While it helps explain Ubuntu only to the relatively small subset of the world that already speaks English, the choice to write this book in English was made to enable it to have the widest impact. More important, it is distributed under a license that allows for translation, modification, and redistribution. The authors of this book cannot write this book in all of the world's languages—or even more than one of them. Instead, we have attempted to eliminate unnecessary legal restrictions and other barriers that might keep the community from taking on the translation work. As a result, the complete text of the first two editions were translated in German, Japanese, Polish, and Spanish.

Finally, just as no person should be blocked from using a computer simply because he or she does not know a particular language, no user should be blocked from using a computer because of a disability. Ubuntu must be accessible to users with motor disabilities, vision disabilities, and hearing disabilities. It should provide input and output in a variety of forms to account for each of these situations and for others. A significant percentage of the world's most intelligent and creative individuals have disabilities. Ubuntu's impact should not be limited to any subset of the world when it can be fully inclusive. More important, Ubuntu should be able to harness the ability of these individuals as community members to build a better and more effective community.

Conduct Goals and Code of Conduct

If Ubuntu's philosophical commitments describe the *why* of the Ubuntu project, the Code of Conduct (CoC) describes Ubuntu's *how*. Ubuntu's CoC is, arguably, the most important document in the day-to-day operation of the Ubuntu community and sets the ground rules for work and cooperation within the project. Explicit agreement to the document is the only criterion for becoming an officially recognized Ubuntu activist—an Ubuntero—and is an essential step toward membership in the project. Signing the Ubuntu Code of Conduct and becoming an Ubuntu member is described in more depth in Chapter 7.

The CoC covers "behavior as a member of the Ubuntu Community, in any forum, mailing list, wiki, Web site, IRC channel, install-fest, public meeting, or private correspondence." The CoC goes into some degree of depth on a series of points that fall under the following headings.

- Be considerate.
- Be respectful.
- Be collaborative.
- When you disagree, consult others.
- When you are unsure, ask for help.
- Step down considerately.

Many of these headings seem like common sense or common courtesy to many, and that is by design. Nothing in the CoC is controversial or radical, and it was never designed to be.

More difficult is that nothing is easy to enforce or decide because acting considerately, respectfully, and collaboratively is often very subjective. There is room for honest disagreements and hurt feelings. These are accepted shortcomings. The CoC was not designed to be a law with explicit prohibitions on phrases, language, or actions. Instead, it aims to provide a constitution and a reminder that considerate and respectful discussion is *essential* to the health and vitality of the project. In situations where there is a serious disagreement on whether a community member has violated or is violating the code, the Community Council—a body that is discussed in depth in Chapter 7—is available to arbitrate disputes and decide what action, if any, is appropriate.

Nobody involved in the Ubuntu project, including Mark Shuttleworth and the other members of the Community Council, is above the CoC. The CoC is *never* optional and *never* waived. In fact, the Ubuntu community has also created a Leadership Code of Conduct (LCoC), which extends and expands on the CoC and describes additional requirements and expectations for those in leadership positions in the community. Of course, in no way was either code designed to eliminate conflict or disagreement. Arguments are at least as common in Ubuntu as they are in other projects and online communities. However, there is a common understanding within the project that arguments should happen in an environment of collaboration and mutual respect. This allows for *better* arguments with *better* results—and with less hurt feelings and fewer bruised egos.

While they are sometimes incorrectly used as such, the CoC and LCoC are not sticks to be wielded against an opponent in an argument. Instead, they are useful points of reference upon which we can assume consensus within the Ubuntu community. Frequently, if a group in the community feels a member is acting in a way that is out of line with the code, the group will gently remind the community member, often privately, that the CoC is in effect. In almost all situations, this is enough to avoid any further action or conflict. Very few CoC violations are ever brought before the Community Council.

Technical Goals

While a respectful community and adherence to a set of philosophical goals provide an important frame in which the Ubuntu project works, Ubuntu is, at the end of the day, a technical project. As a result, it only makes sense that in addition to philosophical goals and a project constitution, Ubuntu also has a set of technical goals.

The first technical goal of the project, and perhaps the most important one, is the coordination of regular and predictable releases. In April 2004, at the Warthogs meeting, the project set a goal for its initial proof-of-concept release six months out. In part due to the resounding success of that project, and in larger part due to the GNOME release schedule, the team has stuck to a regular and predictable six-month release cycle and has only once chosen to extend the release schedule by six weeks and only then after obtaining community consensus on the decision. The team then doubled its efforts and made the next release in a mere four and a half months, putting its release schedule back on track. Frequent releases are important because users can then use the latest and greatest free software available—something that is essential in a development environment as vibrant and rapidly changing and improving as the free software community. Predictable releases are important, especially to businesses, because it means that they can organize their business plans around Ubuntu. Through consistent releases, Ubuntu can provide a platform that businesses and derivative distributions can rely upon to grow and build.

While releasing frequently and reliably is important, the released software must then be supported. Ubuntu, like all distributions, must deal with the fact that all software has bugs. Most bugs are minor, but fixing them may introduce even worse issues. Therefore, fixing bugs after a release must be done carefully or not at all. The Ubuntu project engages in major changes, including bug fixes, between releases only when the changes can be extensively tested. However, some bugs risk the loss of users' information or pose a serious security vulnerability. These bugs are fixed immediately and made available as updates for the released distribution. The Ubuntu community works hard to find and minimize all types of bugs before releases and is largely successful in squashing the worst. However, because there is always the possibility that more of these bugs will be found, Ubuntu commits to supporting every release for 18 months after it is released. In the case of LTS (Long Term Support) releases such as Ubuntu 6.06, released in 2006, the project went well beyond even this and committed to support the release for three full years on desktop computers and for five years in a server configuration. This proved so popular with businesses, institutions, and the users of Ubuntu servers that in 2008, Ubuntu 8.04 was named as Ubuntu's second LTS release with similar three- and five-year desktop and server extended support commitments.

This bipartite approach to servers and desktops implies the third major technical commitment of the Ubuntu project: support for both servers and desktop computers in separate but equally emphasized modes. While Ubuntu continues to be more well known, and perhaps more popular, in desktop configurations, there exist teams of Ubuntu developers focused both on server and desktop users. The Ubuntu project believes that both desktops and servers are essential and provides installation methods on every CD for both types of systems. Ubuntu provides tested and supported software appropriate to the most common actions in both environments and documentation for each. This book contains information on running Ubuntu both on the desktop and on a server. The release of 6.06 LTS with long-term support successfully helped pave the way for reliable long-term server support for Ubuntu and helped grow the now-vibrant Ubuntu server community. The 8.04 release repeated this success with a more up-to-date platform.

Finally, the Ubuntu project is committed to making it as easy as possible for users to transcend their role as consumers and users of software and to take advantage of each of the freedoms central to our philosophy. As a result, Ubuntu has tried to focus its development around the use and promotion of a single programming language, Python. The project has worked to ensure that Python is widely used throughout the system. By ensuring that desktop applications, text-based or console applications, and many of the "guts" of the system are written in or extensible in Python, Ubuntu is working to ensure that users need learn only one language in order to take advantage of, automate, and tweak many parts of their computer systems.

Bug #1

Of course, Ubuntu's goals are not only to build an OS that lives up to our philosophy or technical goals and to do it on our terms—although we probably would be happy if we achieved only that. Our *ultimate goal*, the one that supersedes and influences all others, is to spread our great software, our frequent releases, and the freedoms enshrined in our philosophy to as many computer users in as many countries as possible. Ubuntu's ultimate goal is not to become the most used *GNU/Linux distribution* in the world; it is to become the most widely used *OS* in the world.

The first bug recorded for Ubuntu illustrates this fact. The bug, filed by Shuttleworth and marked as severity critical, remains open today and can be viewed online at https://launchpad.net/distros/ubuntu/+bug/1. The text of the bug reads as follows.

> Microsoft has a majority market share | Non-free software is holding back innovation in the IT industry, restricting access to IT to a small part of the world's population and limiting the ability of software developers to reach their full potential, globally. This bug is widely evident in the PC industry.
>
> Steps to repeat:
>   1. Visit a local PC store.
>
> What happens:
>   2. Observe that a majority of PCs for sale have non-free software preinstalled.
>   3. Observe very few PCs with Ubuntu and free software preinstalled.
>
> What should happen:

1. A majority of the PCs for sale should include only free software such as Ubuntu.
2. Ubuntu should be marketed in a way such that its amazing features and benefits would be apparent and known by all.
3. The system shall become more and more user friendly as time passes.

Many have described Ubuntu's success in the last five or six years as amazing. For a new GNU/Linux distribution, the level and speed of success have been unprecedented. During this period, Ubuntu has lived up to both its philosophical and technical commitments, achieved many of its goals, and built a vibrant community of users and contributors who have accomplished monumental amounts while collaborating in a culture of respect and understanding fully in line with the Ubuntu Code of Conduct. However, Bug #1 demonstrates that the Ubuntu project will be declared a complete success only when Ubuntu's standards of freedom, technical excellence, and conduct are the norm *everywhere* in the software world.

Canonical and the Ubuntu Foundation

While Ubuntu is driven by a community, several groups play an important role in its structure and organization. Foremost among these are Canonical, Ltd., a for-profit company introduced as part of the Ubuntu history description, and the Ubuntu Foundation, which is introduced later in this section.

Canonical, Ltd.

As mentioned earlier, Canonical, Ltd. is a company founded by Mark Shuttleworth with the primary goal of developing and supporting the Ubuntu distribution. Many of the core developers on Ubuntu—although no longer a majority of them—work full-time or part-time under contract for Canonical, Ltd. This funding by Canonical allows Ubuntu to make the type of support commitments that it does. Ubuntu can claim that it will release in six months because releasing, in one form or another, is something that the paid workers at Canonical can ensure. As an all-volunteer organization, Debian suffered from an inability to set and meet deadlines—volunteers become busy or have other deadlines in their paying jobs that take precedence. By offering paying jobs to a subset of developers, Canonical can set support and release deadlines and ensure that they are met.

In this way, Canonical ensures that Ubuntu's bottom-line commitments are kept. Of course, Canonical does not fund all Ubuntu work, nor could it. Canonical can release *a distribution* every six months, but that distribution will be made *much* better and more usable through contributions from the community of users. Most features, most new pieces of software, almost all translations, almost all documentation, and much more are created outside of Canonical. Instead, Canonical ensures that deadlines are met and that the essential work, regardless of whether it's fun, gets done.

Canonical, Ltd. was incorporated on the Isle of Man—a tiny island nation between Wales and Ireland that is mostly well known as a haven for international businesses. Since Canonical's staff is sprinkled across the globe and no proper office is necessary, the Isle of Man seemed like as good a place as any for the company to hang its sign.

Canonical's Service and Support

While it is surprising to many users, fewer than half of Canonical's employees work on the Ubuntu project. The rest of the employees fall into several categories: business development, support and administration, and development of other projects such as Bazaar and Launchpad, which are discussed a bit later in this chapter.

Individuals involved in business development help create strategic deals and certification programs with other companies—primarily around Ubuntu. In large part, these are things that the community is either ill suited for or uninterested in as a whole. One example of business development work is the process of working with companies to ensure that their software (usually proprietary) is built and certified to run on Ubuntu. For example, Canonical worked with IBM to ensure that its popular DB2 database would run on Ubuntu and, when this was achieved, worked to have Ubuntu certified as a platform that would run DB2. Similarly, Canonical worked with Dell to ensure that Ubuntu could be installed and supported on Dell laptops and desktops as an option for its customers. A third example is the production of this book, which, published by Pearson Education's Prentice Hall imprint, was a product of work with Canonical.

Canonical also plays an important support role in the Ubuntu project in three ways. First, Canonical supports the development of the Ubuntu project. For example, Canonical system administrators keep servers up that support development and distribution of Ubuntu. Second, Canonical helps Ubuntu users and businesses directly by offering phone and e-mail support. Additionally, Canonical has helped build a large commercial Ubuntu support operation by arranging for support contracts with larger companies and organizations. This support is over and above the free (i.e., gratis) support offered by the community—this commercial support is offered at a fee and is either part of a longer-term flat-fee support contract or is pay-per-instance. By offering commercial support for Ubuntu in a variety of ways, Canonical has made a business for itself and helps make Ubuntu a more palatable option for the businesses, large and small, that are looking for an enterprise or enterprise-class GNU/Linux product with support contracts like those offered by other commercial GNU/Linux distributions.

Finally, Ubuntu supports other support organizations. Canonical does not seek or try to enforce a monopoly on Ubuntu support; it proudly lists *hundreds* of other organizations offering support for Ubuntu on the Ubuntu Web pages. Instead, Canonical offers what is called second-tier support to these organizations. Because Canonical employs many of the core Ubuntu developers, the company is very well suited to taking action on many of the tougher problems that these support organizations may run into. With its concentrated expertise, Canonical can offer this type of backup, or secondary support, to these organizations.

Bazaar and Launchpad

In addition to support and development on Ubuntu, Canonical, Ltd. funds the development of Bazaar, a distributed version control tool, and the Launchpad project. Bazaar is a tool for developing software that is used heavily in Ubuntu and plays an important role in the technical processes through which Ubuntu is forged. However, the software, which is similar in functionality to other version control systems such as CVS, Subversion, or BitKeeper, is useful in a variety of other projects as well. More important, Bazaar acts as the workhorse behind Launchpad.

More than half of Canonical's technical employees work on the Launchpad project. Launchpad is an ambitious Web-based superstructure application that consists of several highly integrated tools. The software plays a central role in Ubuntu development but is also used for the development of other distributions—especially those based on Ubuntu. Launchpad consists of the following major pieces.

- **Rosetta:**

  A Web-based system for easily translating almost any piece of free software from English into almost any language. Rosetta is named after the Rosetta Stone, which helped linguists finally crack the code of Egyptian hieroglyphics.

- **Malone:**

  The bug-tracking system that Ubuntu uses to manage and track bugs. It both tracks bugs across different versions of Ubuntu and allows the Ubuntu community to see the status of that bug in other places, including other distributions and potentially upstream. Malone is a reference to the gangster movie musical *Bugsy Malone*.

- **Blueprint:**

  The specification writing and tracking software that Ubuntu and a small number of other projects use to track desired features and their status and to help manage and report on release processes.

- **Answers:**

  A simple support tracker built into Launchpad that provides one venue where users can make support requests and the community can help answer them in ways that are documented and connected to the other related functionality in Launchpad.

- **Soyuz:**

  The distribution management part of Launchpad that now controls the processes by which Ubuntu packages are built, tested, and migrated between different parts of the distribution. Soyuz is a reference to the type of Russian rocket that took Mark Shuttleworth to space. The word *soyuz*, in Russian, means "union."

Launchpad and its components are discussed in more depth in Chapter 10. The importance of Launchpad in the Ubuntu project cannot be overstated. In addition to handling bugs, translations, and distribution building, Launchpad also handles Web site authentication and codifies team membership in the Ubuntu project. It is the place where all work in Ubuntu is tracked and recorded. Any member of the Ubuntu community and any person who contributes to Ubuntu in almost any way will, in due course, create an account in Launchpad.

The Ubuntu Foundation

Finally, in addition to Canonical and the full Ubuntu community, the Ubuntu project is supported by the Ubuntu Foundation, which was announced by Shuttleworth with an initial funding commitment of $10 million. The foundation, like Canonical, is based on the Isle of Man. The organization is advised by the Ubuntu Community Council.

Unlike Canonical, the Foundation does not play an active role in the day-to-day life of Ubuntu. At the moment, the Foundation is little more than a pile of money that exists to endow and ensure Ubuntu's future. Because Canonical is a young company, some companies and individuals may find it difficult to trust that Canonical will be able to provide support for Ubuntu in the time frames (e.g., three to five years) that it claims it will be able to. The Ubuntu Foundation exists to allay those fears.

If something bad were to happen to Shuttleworth or to Canonical that caused either to be unable to support Ubuntu development and maintain the distribution, the Ubuntu Foundation exists to carry on many of Canonical's core activities well into the future. Through the existence of the Foundation, the Ubuntu project can make the types of long-term commitments and promises it does.

The one activity that the Foundation can and does engage in is receiving donations on behalf of the Ubuntu project. These donations, and only these donations, are then put into action on behalf of Ubuntu in accordance with the wishes of the development team and the Technical Board. For the most part, these contributions are spent on "bounties" given to community members who have achieved important feature goals for the Ubuntu project.

Ubuntu Subprojects, Derivatives, and Spin-offs

Finally, no introduction to Ubuntu is complete without an introduction to a growing list of Ubuntu subprojects and derivatives. While Ubuntu was derived from Debian, the project has, over the last four years, already developed a number of derivatives of its own.

First and foremost among these is Kubuntu—a version of Ubuntu that uses KDE instead of GNOME as the default desktop environment. Kubuntu is described in depth in its own chapter (Chapter 8) and so is not explored in any serious depth here. However, it is important to realize that the relationship between Kubuntu and Ubuntu is different from the relationship between Ubuntu and Debian. From a technical perspective, Kubuntu is *fully* within the Ubuntu distribution. Organizationally, the Kubuntu team works fully within Ubuntu as well.

A similar organization exists with the Edubuntu project, which aims to help develop Ubuntu so that a configuration of the distribution can be easily and effectively put into use in schools. That project has a dual focus on both educational and school-related software and on a Linux Terminal Server Project (LTSP) setup that allows schools to run many students' computers using one or more powerful servers and many "dumb" terminals that connect to the server and run software off it. This relatively simple technical trick translates into huge cost savings in educational settings. The Edubuntu project is treated in depth in Chapter 9.

The Xubuntu project is based on the lightweight window manager Xfce. Xubuntu is designed to be appropriate on older or less powerful computers with less memory or slower processors—or just for people who prefer a more responsive environment and a slimmer set of features. While started as an unofficial project, Xubuntu has enjoyed great popularity and has become integrated as an official part of the core distribution.

Other derivatives exist as well, such as Ubuntu Studio and Mythbuntu. A list of officially supported and recognized derivatives is available at www.ubuntu.com/products/whatisubuntu/derivatives.

In a way, it is through these derivatives that the work and goals of the Ubuntu project come together and are crystallized. It is only through the free and open source software movements' commitment to freely accessible source code that Ubuntu could be built at all. Similarly, it is only through Ubuntu's continued commitment to these ideals that derivatives can spring from Ubuntu. As a derivative with a view of distributions within an ecosystem, Ubuntu does not see the process of derivation as an insult or criticism. Far from it—Ubuntu thinks derivation is the highest form of compliment.

Outside of Ubuntu, Canonical's work is largely based around software projects such as Launchpad and Bazaar that are designed to facilitate precisely this sort of derivative process. This process, when practiced right, is one that describes an ecosystem of development in which *everyone* benefits—the derivative, Ubuntu, and Ubuntu's upstreams. Only through this derivative process does everyone get what they want.

Derivation, done correctly, allows groups to diverge where necessary while working together where possible. Ultimately, it leads to more work done, more happy users, and more overall collaboration. Through this enhanced collaboration, Ubuntu's philosophical and technical goals will be achieved. Through this profound community involvement, Bug #1 will be closed. Through this type of meaningful cooperation, internal and external to the project itself, the incredible growth of Ubuntu in its first four years will be sustained into the next four and the next forty.

Summary

This chapter introduced you to the phenomenon that is Ubuntu. It began with some free software and open source history and then moved on to the history of Ubuntu. It then covered the Ubuntu products, philosophy, and goals and the relationship between Canonical, Ltd. and the Ubuntu Foundation. It finished with some discussion of the various Ubuntu subprojects, derivatives, and spin-offs.

CHAPTER 2

Installing Ubuntu

- Choosing Your Ubuntu Version
- Getting Ubuntu
- Installing from the Desktop CD
- Installing from the Alternate Install CD
- Installing from a USB Key
- Summary

IF YOU ARE READING THIS, it is probably safe to assume that you have decided to give Ubuntu a try. You will find that Ubuntu is flexible and powerful not only as an operating system but also in how you evaluate and install it.

Trying Ubuntu is simple. The Ubuntu desktop CD is a special "live" CD. You can use this disk to run Ubuntu from the CD itself without Ubuntu removing or even interacting with your hard disk. This is ideal if you are already using another operating system like Windows or Mac OS X; you can try Ubuntu by running it from the CD, and you don't have to worry about it overwriting the data.

Choosing Your Ubuntu Version

The developers behind Ubuntu have worked to make the software as easy and flexible to install as possible. They understand that people will be installing Ubuntu on different types of computers (desktops, servers, laptops, and so on) and using different types of computers (PCs, 64-bit computers, Macs, and so on). To cater to everyone, there are two Ubuntu CDs that can be used. The DVD with this book is equivalent to the desktop CD with additional packages included.

- **Desktop:** The desktop CD is the one recommended for *desktops* and *laptops*. With this CD, you can boot Ubuntu from the CD and, if you like it, install it. Note that this is the default option on the DVD or CD.

- **Alternate install:** The alternate install CD is recommended for use in any scenario where the desktop version is unusable (e.g., not enough RAM) or inflexible (e.g., automated deployments or special partitioning requirements). With this CD, you boot into an installer and then run Ubuntu when the installation is complete.

Ubuntu 9.04 officially supports two main computer types, or architectures, and a couple of additional variations:

- **i386:** This supports all Intel or compatible processors except those that require AMD64. This includes the new Apple hardware.

- **AMD64:** If you are using a processor based on the AMD64 or EM64T architecture (e.g., Athlon64, Opteron, EM64T Xeon, or Core2), you should choose this version.

- **LPIA:** A variation of i386, LPIA stands for low-power Intel architecture and is designed for MIDs and Netbooks. The Intel Atom is a commonly used LPIA chip.

- **ARM:** ARM is low-powered chip commonly found in cell phones and similar mobile devices. ARM Inc., the makers of ARM, and Canonical have an agreement to build the entirety of the Ubuntu archive on ARM, which makes Ubuntu the first major distribution to support ARM as a standard rather than custom device–specific distribution, such as OpenWRT for routers.

You can choose between the desktop and alternate CDs depending on your requirements. For example, for your Intel Core Duo laptop you could use the i386 desktop CD, while for your Xeon server you would choose the i386 alternate CD.

TIP	**What about PowerPC?**
	Starting with the 7.04 release, Ubuntu made Power PC an unofficial architecture.

Other Ubuntu Distributions

In addition to the official Ubuntu release, some additional distributions are based on Ubuntu but are slightly different. Here are some examples:

- **Kubuntu:** Kubuntu is Ubuntu, but instead of using the GNOME desktop, Kubuntu uses the KDE desktop. See http://kubuntu.org or Chapter 8 for more information.

- **Xubuntu:** The Xubuntu distribution replaces the GNOME desktop environment with the Xfce 4 environment. Xubuntu is particularly useful for those of you who want to run Ubuntu on older hardware. See http://xubuntu.org for more or Chapter 10 for more information.

- **Netbook Remix:** This is a custom version of the standard GNOME desktop with the addition of a custom application launcher and some other Netbook-specific configurations.

Additionally, Edubuntu is a version of Ubuntu aimed at educational use and schools. It is no longer distributed on its own install CD. To install it, you should install the base or default desktop version of Ubuntu first and then use the Edubuntu CD as an add-on to install the Edubuntu environment and applications.

With a range of different distributions and options available, Ubuntu is flexible enough to be used in virtually all situations.

Is It Still Ubuntu?

Some of you may be reading about Kubuntu, Xubuntu, the Netbook Remix and wondering how different they are from the regular Ubuntu release. These distributions differ mainly in which applications and desktop interface are included. As such, they may differ quite a bit, but the underlying OS and software install system is the same.

Getting Ubuntu

Ubuntu is an entirely free OS. When you have a copy of it, you can give it to as many people as you like. This free characteristic of Ubuntu means that it is devilishly simple to get a copy. If you have a high-speed Internet connection (like DSL), head over to www.ubuntu.com/download, and select your country from the list of download sites. You can then select a desktop or alternate install CD and download it.

TIP   See the upcoming Burning a CD section for details on how to create your Ubuntu CD from the file you just downloaded.

If you are willing to wait, you can get a physical Ubuntu CD mailed to you from https://shipit.ubuntu.com. You will need an account on the Launchpad site at https://launchpad.net/ to use the ShipIt service. If you don't have one, just click on the Create a New Account link to create one. To use ShipIt, fill in the simple form and submit it. Your CDs will then be sent out.

You can also buy an authorized CD from a number of distributors, details of which can be found at www.ubuntu.com/getubuntu/purchase.

Burning a CD

When you download an Ubuntu CD, you download a special .iso file, which is the same size as a CD (around 650MB). This file is an "image" of the installation CD. When you burn the .iso file to the CD-ROM, you have a complete installation CD all ready to go.

TIP   **Which Image?**
When you are reading about .iso files, you will often see them referred to as CD images. The term *image* here does not refer to a visual image such as a photo or picture but to an exact copy of a CD.

You need to use a CD-burning application to burn your .iso file to the CD correctly. Inside the application there should be a menu option called Burn from Disk Image or something similar. The wording and details will vary according to the program that you use to burn the image. You should select the .iso file, insert a blank CD, and after a few minutes, out will pop a fresh Ubuntu installation CD.

To give you a head start, the following subsections present instructions for burning a CD in some popular tools.

In Windows with ISO Recorder   To burn your .iso file with the freely available ISO Recorder, first go to http://isorecorder.alexfeinman.com, and then download and install ISO Recorder. To burn your image, follow these steps.

1. Insert a blank CD into your CD writer.
2. Locate the .iso file you downloaded, right-click it, and select Copy Image to CD.
3. Click Next, and the recording process begins.
4. When the image has been written, click Finish to exit ISO Recorder.

In Windows with Nero Burning ROM   To burn your image using Nero Burning ROM, follow these steps.

1. Insert a blank CD into your CD writer.
2. Start Nero Burning ROM.
3. Follow the wizard prompts, and select Data CD.
4. When the wizard finishes, click Burn Image on the File menu.
5. In the Open dialog box, select the .iso file, and then click Open.
6. In the wizard, click Burn to create the Ubuntu CD. When completed, click the Done button to exit.

In Linux with GNOME   To burn your image using Linux with GNOME, follow these steps.

1. Insert a blank CD into your CD writer.
2. In the Nautilus file manager, right-click on the file you just downloaded, and choose Write to Disk. The Write to Disk dialog box opens.
3. In the dialog box, choose your CD writer and speed, and then click on Write. The Writing Files to Disk Progress dialog box opens, and Nautilus begins writing the disk.

Burning with Mac OS X   To burn your image using Mac OS X, follow these steps.

1. Load the Disk Utility application (found in your Utilities folder).
2. Insert a blank CD, and then choose Images > Burn and select the .iso file.

TIP   **Use the Right Option**
You need to ensure you use the Burn from Disk Image or similar option rather than just copy the .iso image onto the CD to be burned. If you just burn the file directly, you will have a CD containing the single .iso file. This won't work.

The Burn from Disk Image function takes the .iso file and restores all the original files from the installation CD onto the disk. This ensures you have a proper installation CD.

Installing from the Desktop CD

So let's assume you are playing with Ubuntu running from the desktop CD, and you decide you like it. You decide you like it so much, in fact, that you want to install it on your computer. Does this mean you need to get a separate CD and install it? Heck, no. Ubuntu lets you install to the hard disk by simply clicking a single icon and following the instructions—one disk to run them all.

If you don't already have the desktop CD running, pop it into your DVD/CD drive, and reboot your computer. If your computer does not boot from the CD, you should enter your computer's BIOS and change the boot order to ensure that your CD-ROM drive is tried first and the hard disk is tried next. Save your BIOS changes, and then restart again. The disk should boot now.

TIP **BIOS Problems**
If you have problems configuring your BIOS to boot from the CD, you should consult the manual. If you don't have the manual, visit the manufacturer's Web site, and see if you can download the manual.

After a few seconds, the Ubuntu logo appears and you are presented with a list of languages on top of the screen. Use the arrow keys to navigate to your language or just press Enter to choose English. After selecting a language, you'll see several options. The first option is Try Ubuntu without any change to your computer. This option allows you try out Ubuntu and install it later if you decide you want to. Alternatively, you can click the second option—Install Ubuntu—which will jump straight into the installer. Press Enter to select the first option, and Ubuntu will begin to boot. After a minute or so, the Ubuntu desktop will appear, and you can use the system right away. Under this scenario, the system is running from the CD and will not touch your hard disk. Do bear in mind that because Ubuntu is running from the CD, it will run slower than if it were installed to your hard disk.

If you decide you want to install the system permanently on your computer's hard disk, you can either reboot and click on the Install Ubuntu boot menu option or you can double-click the Install icon located on the left side of the desktop. An installer application appears that walks you through the different steps to permanently install your Ubuntu system. We will run through each of these pages in turn now.

TIP It is recommended that you back up any important files before you perform the installation. While the vast majority of Ubuntu installations can safely resize Windows partitions, installations can still result in data loss, so it is wise to be careful.

Language

The first screen you are presented with introduces you to the installation program and asks you to select your language, as shown in Figure 2-1.

Ubuntu supports a huge range of different languages. Select your language from the list, and then click Forward to continue.

Location

Now you need to tell the installer where in the world you live (Figure 2-2).

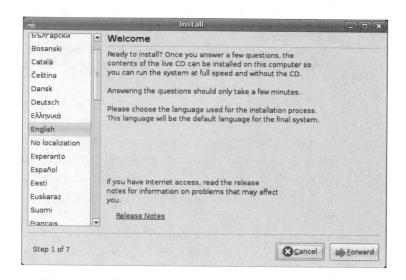

Figure 2-1 Pick your language.

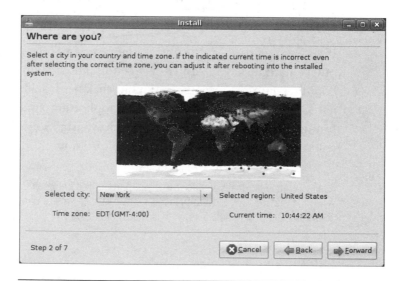

Figure 2-2 Clicking the map zooms in, allowing you to select a location more easily.

You can select your location in one of several ways. First, you can hover your mouse over the red dots in your part of the world to select the nearest location. When you are happy with the location, click it, and the map zooms in. You can then select the city nearest to you. Alternatively, use the Selected City combo box to find the city nearest to you.

When you are done, click Forward to continue.

Configuring Your Keyboard

The next screen (shown in Figure 2-3) configures your keyboard.

Choose your country from the list to select your keyboard layout. You can also use the box at the bottom of the window to test whether your keyboard layout works. Try typing some of the symbols on your keyboard (such as ", /, |) to make sure they work. If you press a symbol and a different one appears, you have selected the wrong keyboard layout.

Disk Space

The next part of the installation process prepares your hard disk for the software. This involves creating a number of *partitions* that store the Ubuntu system and your files. Hard disks are divided into partitions. Each partition reserves a specific portion of the hard disk for use by a particular OS. As an example, you may use the entire hard disk for your new Ubuntu system, or you may share the disk so that both Windows and Ubuntu are installed. This shared scenario is known as *dual-booting*. In a dual-booting situation, your hard disk typically has Windows partitions as well as Linux

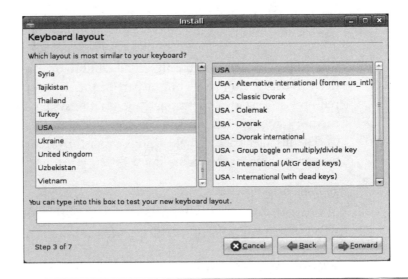

Figure 2-3 Select the correct keyboard to ensure the symbols on the keys work correctly.

partitions, and when it boots it gives you a menu so you can select whether to boot Windows or Linux.

In this part of the installer you create the partitions for your new system. This is the trickiest part of the installation and also the most dangerous. If you have existing partitions (such as a Windows installation) on the disk, it is highly recommended that you back up your important files.

TIP   Seriously, We Mean It
Really, really, really do back up any important files. If you make a mistake in this part of the installation, you could lose your files and stop your system from booting.

Deciding How You Would Like to Set Up Your Partitions Before You Create Them
If you have a clear idea of how your hard disk should be partitioned, it is easier to get everything up and running quickly.

These are the most common methods of partitioning.

- **Only Ubuntu on the disk:** If you are only installing Ubuntu on the disk and are happy to wipe the *entire disk*, your life is simple. Ubuntu can do all the work for you.
- **Dual-booting:** If you want to dual-boot your system with Windows or Mac OS X and Ubuntu, you can share the disk between your Ubuntu and Windows or Mac OS X partitions.

Regardless of whether you only install Ubuntu or you will dual-boot, you need to decide how the Ubuntu part of the disk is partitioned. Ubuntu requires at least two partitions (one for the system and one for virtual memory swap space), but you can have additional partitions if you want to. The installer tries to make things easier for you by presenting options for partitioning, as shown in Figure 2-4.

Ubuntu Only
If you are happy to erase your entire hard disk, just select the Guided—Use Entire Disk option, and click Forward. You are then asked to confirm the actions. Click Yes to continue. That's it!

Dual-Booting
Let's say you want your existing OS and Ubuntu to coexist, but you don't care about the details. Click the Guided—Resize . . . and Use Freed Space option, move the slider according to how much space you

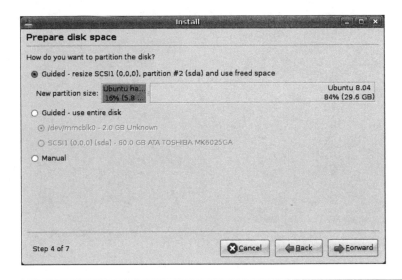

Figure 2-4 Main partitioning view

want to give each operating system, and then click Forward. You are then asked to confirm the actions. Click Yes to continue.

Manual Partitioning   In either option, installing only Ubuntu or dual-booting with an existing operating system, you may not be satisfied with the suggestions guided partitioning makes. In this case you will want to manually set the partitions. To do this, click the Manual option, and click Forward to continue. You will see the screen shown in Figure 2-5.

The main part of this screen displays available drives and configured partitions. Clicking on a drive or partition will change the actions available to you below the list. Select the relevant disk to add partitions to. The disks are listed by device name in the order they are connected within your computer.

QUICK TIP   The name of the device indicates how it is connected to your computer. For example, hda is the first IDE drive, and sdb is the second SCSI or SATA drive.

Before you begin, you should prepare the disk for your partitions. If you want to completely wipe a disk, right-click on the name of the device (/dev/sda in Figure 2-5), then click New Partition Table. You'll be asked if

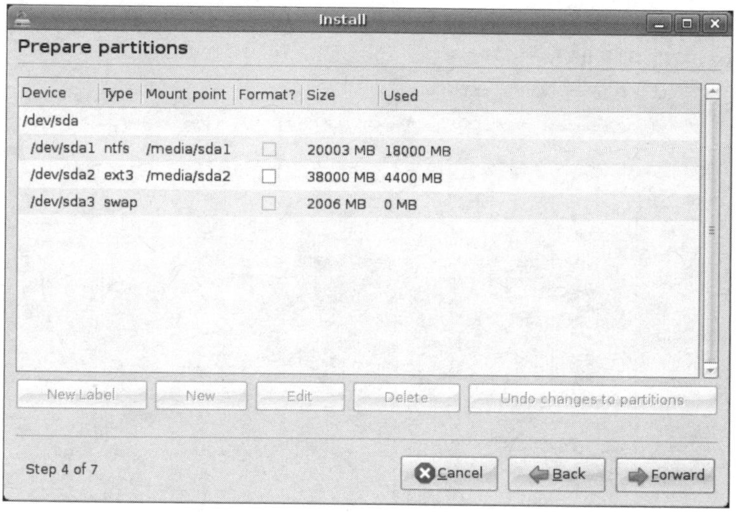

Figure 2-5 Manual partition view

you're sure, so click Continue. The disk is now filled with unallocated data. Now you can add your Ubuntu partitions.

To add a partition, click a free space entry in the list and then click the New button. A new window appears like that shown in Figure 2-6.

Set the values according to your requirements. The Use As combo box lets you select which one of the many filesystem types you want the partition to use. The default filesystem included with Ubuntu is ext3, and it is rec-

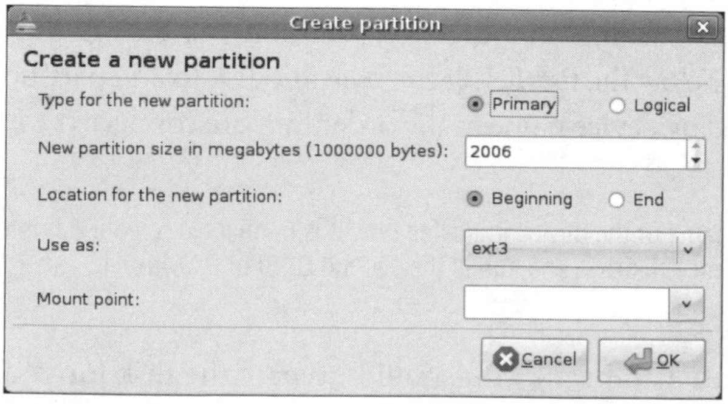

Figure 2-6 Configuring a partition

ommended that you use ext3 for any Ubuntu partitions. Although ext3 is a good choice for Ubuntu, you cannot read an ext3 partition in Windows. If you need to create a partition that is shared between Windows and Ubuntu, you should use the FAT32 filesystem.

Use the Mount Point combo box to select one of the different mount points, which tells Ubuntu where the partition should be used. You need to have a root partition, which has a mount point of /. Click OK to finish configuring this partition.

Once you've completed configuring all your partitions, click Forward to proceed with the installation.

Identification

The next step is to enter some details about you that can be used to create a user account on the computer (Figure 2-7).

In the first box, enter your full name. The information from this box is used in different parts of the system to indicate who the user is behind the account.

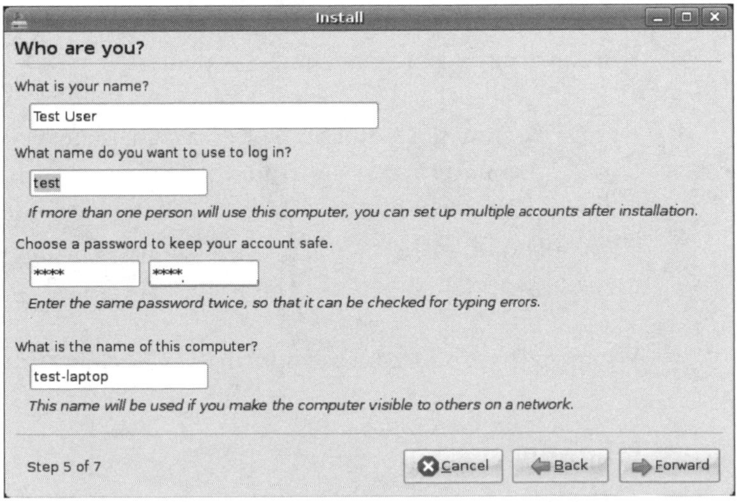

Figure 2-7 This user account is also used as the main system administrator.

In the next box, set a username for yourself (the installer will provide a suggestion based on your full name). Your username should be something easy to remember. Many people use either their first name or add an initial (such as jbacon or jonob). Each username on your computer must be unique—you cannot have two accounts with the same username.

In the next two boxes, add a password and then confirm it. This password is used when logging in to your computer with the username that you just created. When choosing a password, follow these simple guidelines.

■ Make sure you can remember your password. If you need to write it down, keep it somewhere secure. Don't make the *WarGames* mistake of putting the password somewhere easily accessible and known to others.

■ Try not to use dictionary words such as "chicken" or "beard" when choosing a password. Try to input numbers and punctuation and to not use "real words."

■ Your password should ideally be longer than six letters and contain a combination of letters, symbols, and numbers. The longer the password and the more it mixes letters, numbers, and symbols, the more secure it is.

Finally, add a hostname in the last box. The hostname is a single word that identifies your current machine. This is used on a local network so that you can identify which machine is which.

Believe it or not, hostnames can be great fun. Many people pick themes for their hostnames, such as superheroes, and name each computer on their network after a superhero (Superman, Batman, Spiderman, and so on). Think of a fun hostname theme you can use. For many people, this ends up being the hardest part of the install!

When you have added all the information, click Forward to continue.

Migration

Ubuntu also provides a migration assistant, which aims to ease your transition to your new OS. If a supported OS is found during installation, you

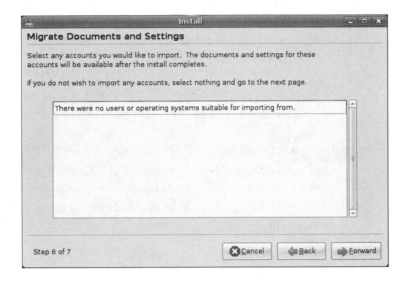

Figure 2-8 Migration assistant

will be presented with a list of accounts and the features that can be migrated. If you choose to migrate anything, you will need to provide details for the new user to whom the features will be migrated. Figure 2-8 shows a migration in progress.

Finishing Up

Before the installation is completed, you are given a summary of the choices you made. Once you confirm these choices by clicking Install, the Ubuntu software will be installed on your computer. At the end of this process, you are asked to reboot your computer. You are now finished!

TIP **Better Use of Your Valuable, Valuable Time**
One of the great benefits of the desktop CD installer is that while the files are being copied from the disk, you can still use the system. Instead of sitting at your computer staring at the progress bar, you can play a few games to while away the time.

Installing from the Alternate Install CD

Although the desktop CD is ideal for installing Ubuntu, you may want to use the traditional installer method to install the system. This method involves booting the alternate install CD, running through the installer, and then starting the system. This kind of installer is ideal for installation on older hardware.

To get started, put the CD in the drive, and restart your computer. When the CD boots, you will see the menu shown in Figure 2-9.

Select the Install Ubuntu option with the arrow keys, and press Enter. After a few moments, the installation process begins by asking you to choose a language. Select from the different languages by using the up and down arrow keys, and then use the Tab key to jump to the red buttons to continue through the setup.

TIP   **Installing a Server**
You can obtain a third version of Ubuntu that is especially tailored for server environments. For more information about this version, see www.ubuntu.com/server, or read Chapter 5 for more details about running Ubuntu as a server.

Choosing Your Spot in the World

Next you are asked to specify your location. First you need to choose your language (Figure 2-10).

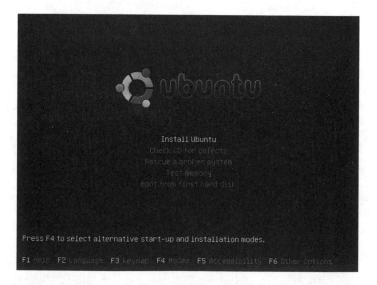

Figure 2-9 Alternate install CD menu

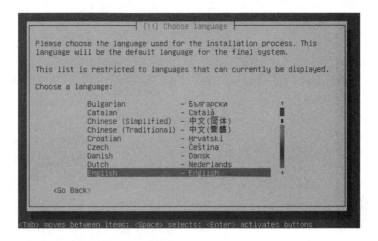

Figure 2-10 Select your language.

Then you need to pick which country you are in, again pressing Enter to accept your choice.

Now you need to select your keyboard layout. Keyboard layouts vary across the world to take into account the many and varied symbols and letters used in different countries. Even if you are using the typical Latin character set (as used in most European countries, America, Africa, and Australia), there are variations and additions (e.g., German umlauts). You can let Ubuntu detect your layout for you, or you can choose from a list of options. If you want your layout detected, you will be asked a series of questions until a guess can be made. If the guess is wrong, you can repeat the process. Otherwise, choose your keyboard layout from the options available.

Hardware

Next, the system will attempt to load the rest of the installer and to detect hardware. In most situations, this happens without prompting you for anything, although sometimes you might need to provide input such as choosing a primary network device. Once this is set up, your computer will also configure itself with your local network—if possible. If it cannot configure itself with a local network, it will tell you this and you'll have the option of configuring it manually or choosing to not configure it at that time. You can always come back and change things later once the installation is done.

Setting the Hostname and Time Zone

You are next asked for a hostname for the computer (Figure 2-11).

Use the text box to add your own hostname, or use the default Ubuntu hostname if required. Feel free to let your imagination go wild, and create a theme for your hostnames (such as superheroes).

After choosing a hostname, you will be asked to select your time zone. Choosing this should be a fairly straightforward operation.

Creating Partitions

The system will then read your disks to find out the current partition information. You will be asked to create or select partitions for Ubuntu to install on to. Creating partitions is the most challenging part of the installation routine. You will see the screen shown in Figure 2-12. Before you partition your disk, think about how your partitions should be organized.

You are given a number of partition options:

- Guided—Use Entire Disk
- Guided—Use Entire Disk and Set Up LVM
- Guided—Use Entire Disk and Set Up Encrypted LVM
- Manual

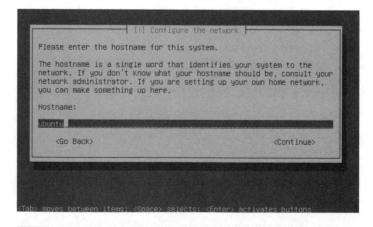

Figure 2-11 The hostname is used to identify you on your local area network.

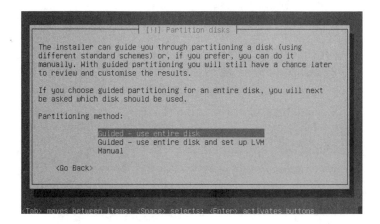

Figure 2-12 Partitioning disks

In most cases, you probably want to use the Guided—Use Entire Disk option. This will erase everything on the hard drive in your computer and set everything up for you. The second option, Guided—Use Entire Disk and Set Up LVM, allows you to use the Logical Volume Manager (LVM). The third is identical to the second option but also employs disk encryption, which will make your data safer and more secure in some circumstances. Finally, if you want to set up specific partitions, use the Manual option.

Let's look at each of these options in turn and how they are used.

Guided—Use Entire Disk   When you select this option, your entire disk is partitioned automatically. The installer will tell you that a primary and logical partition will be created, and then it asks if you want to go ahead and create the partitions. Click Yes, and you are done.

Guided—Use Entire Disk and Set Up LVM   Configuring LVM is covered in Chapter 5.

Guided—Use Entire Disk and Set Up Encrypted LVM   Configuring LVM is identical to the previous option except that it also uses a secure encryption layer to provide additional security and protection for your data.

Manual   Select this option if you want to create your own partitions manually. Here you can create a number of different types of partitions, set their sizes, and configure their properties. Creating these partitions is not done in the same graphical way as the live CD installer, so it is a little more complex. However, doing so is still largely a process of selecting something and pressing Enter.

Depending on your configuration (and the options you selected), you are given a number of options from which to choose:

▪ Configure Software RAID

▪ Configure the Logical Volume Manager

▪ Guided Partitioning

QUICK TIP   Discussion of software RAID and the Logical Volume Manager is covered in Chapter 5.

Your disk is listed below these options, and it may display a few existing partitions. If you want to delete the existing partitions, select each one, press Enter, and select Delete the Partition. When you have deleted some partitions, you should see a FREE SPACE line. The FREE SPACE line is used to create new partitions. If the disk was empty already and you don't see a FREE SPACE line, select the hard disk, and press Enter. When it asks if you want to create an empty partition table, click Yes. You should now see the FREE SPACE line.

To create a new partition, select the FREE SPACE line, and press Enter. In the next screen, click Create a New Partition, and press Enter. Now enter the size the partition should be. You can use gigabytes (GB) and megabytes (M) to indicate size. For example, 4.2GB is 4.2 gigabytes, and 100M is 100 megabytes. You can also use a percentage or just add max to use the entire disk. Add the size, and then press the Tab key to select Continue. Press Enter. You are next asked whether the partition should be primary or logical. It is likely that you will want a primary partition. Make your choice, and continue.

If this is the first partition, you are asked if the partition should be at the beginning or end of the disk. It is recommended that when creating the root partition (known as /) on older computers, it should be placed at the beginning of the disk. This gets around some potential BIOS problems on older hardware. On newer computers, this is no longer a problem, and you can put the partition where you like on the disk.

On the next screen to display (Figure 2-13), you can configure some settings for the partition.

Table 2-1 describes the settings.

When the partition is configured, choose the Done Setting Up the Partition option.

You can now select FREE SPACE again (if there is free space left, of course) to create another partition. When you have finished partitioning, click the Finish Partitioning and Write Changes to Disk option.

The system will now install the Ubuntu core to your newly partitioned disk. Depending on the speed of your computer and your CD drive, this installation could take some time.

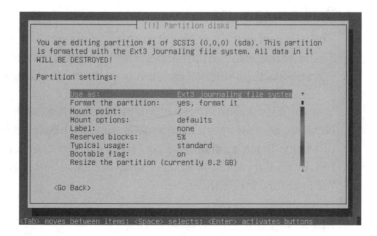

Figure 2-13 Setting partition options

Table 2-1 Partition Settings

Setting	Description	Example
Use as	This is the type of filesystem. For a normal Ubuntu system, ext3 is recommended.	ext3
Format the partition	This setting appears when editing an existing partition.	yes
Mount point	This specifies which part of the filesystem will live on the partition. See earlier in this chapter for details about the kind of partitions you should set up.	/
Mount options	A number of options can be passed to the mount point, although the default setting should be fine.	defaults
Label	A text label describes the partition. Usually it is set to the same value as the mount point.	/
Reserved blocks	This is the percentage of the filesystem reserved for the super-user; 5% is a good default.	5.00%
Typical usage	This option can be used to optimize how the filesystem is organized, although the standard setting is typically used.	standard
Bootable flag	Does this partition contain the kernel and bootloader? If this is the root partition (known as /), set this to *on*.	on

Configuring a User

The next part of the installation routine configures a user for the computer. This user role is important because it not only can be used as a normal user but also has the ability to use sudo to perform system administrator tasks.

You are first asked to enter a full name for the user (such as Alan Clement). Next you are asked for a username, or one will be picked for you from your full name (such as alanc). If you want another username, enter it there. Finally, you are asked to enter a password for the user and asked to repeat the password for verification.

Finishing Up

At this point, the installation routine will install the full system for you. After this, the computer will reboot, and the installation will be complete.

Installing from a USB Key

Some computers lack CD drives, especially in the recently popular Netbooks. USB keys are also more flexible, allowing you to save your files and configuration and to update the key to the latest version of Ubuntu.

As with a CD, you need to get Ubuntu onto the USB key first. Fortunately, there is an easy way to do this in Ubuntu. Under the System > Administration menu, find the USB creator tool. Upon starting, you will see a window asking for an ISO file and a few other options.

NOTE You will need to have administrative privileges on your computer to use the USB Startup Disk Creator.

If there is an Ubuntu CD already in the CD drive, it will be automatically detected and used. If you have downloaded the ISO, click the Other button and select the ISO you want. Any mounted USB keys will be shown in the second window for you to select.

Finally, you must choose whether or not to have persistence. This means that you can save your files and configuration to the USB key. Finally, click Make Startup Disk.

Once the disk has been created, you must restart your computer and boot off the USB key. This might involve holding down a key at startup to select from a boot menu or might involve changes to your computer's BIOS. Consult your manual for how to do this.

Once you are booted, your USB key will work exactly like a Live CD and allow you to use Ubuntu from the key or to install it on the computer.

NOTE Once the size of the persistence section has been selected, it cannot be changed, so think carefully.

Summary

Congratulations on your new Ubuntu system. Whether you used the desktop CD or the traditional alternate install CD approach to get Ubuntu on your computer, you now have a powerful, extensible, and easy-to-use OS with a huge array of available software. Unlike other operating systems, Ubuntu includes a complete end-to-end software selection with a range of tools for office productivity, system configuration, Internet access, e-mail, and more. In addition to this impressive array of desktop software, your new system also includes an incredibly powerful underlying architecture that can be heavily customized. Those of you with a fondness for code and programming will also get a kick out of the millions and millions of lines of code that are freely available and spread among the different applications included. Ubuntu also provides extensive development tools for creating desktop applications, Web applications, and more.

You are at the start of an exciting journey, so let's get going.

CHAPTER 3

Using Ubuntu on the Desktop

WITH UBUNTU INSTALLED and ready to go, it's time to get started using your new desktop. The stock install of Ubuntu provides a very complete and flexible system. Unlike other operating systems, such as Microsoft Windows or Mac OS X, Ubuntu includes everything you need to get started, such as an office suite, media tools, a Web browser, a graphics package, an e-mail client, and more. Once the installation is complete, you are up and running right away without having to install any additional software. Different people use their computers in different ways, and every user has her own personal preference for look and feel. Recognizing this desire, Linux has the capability to use any one of a number of different graphical interfaces. This flexibility, combined with the ballooning popularity of Linux and open source, has resulted in literally hundreds of different graphical environments springing up, each covering these different types of users and ways of working.

Even though there is a huge range of different environments available, there are two clear leaders in KDE and GNOME. Each environment provides a good-looking, comprehensive, and easy-to-use desktop, but they differ in how that desktop is used as well as in how further personalization can take place. The KDE system is in many ways more akin to Windows but aims for complete configurability of the desktop. If an option exists, the user has easy access to it and can change the behavior and look of almost everything. The competing GNOME desktop takes inspiration from both Windows and Mac OS X and sets a priority on simplicity and ease of use. GNOME is still easy to customize, but the less common options are either eliminated or well hidden to prevent user overload. Luckily, Ubuntu users are blessed with the choice of either desktop—the default desktop in stock Ubuntu is GNOME, and the Kubuntu distribution uses the KDE desktop. Kubuntu is covered in Chapter 8.

In this chapter, you get started with GNOME and use it to do the normal things you face every day with your computer and a few not-so-normal things. This includes opening and running applications, managing your files, adjusting the look and feel, using applications, managing your media, and more. Buckle up and get ready to take your shiny new desktop for a drive!

TIP   **The Ubuntu Desktop Is GNOME**
When reading about Ubuntu, you often see the terms *Ubuntu desktop* and *GNOME* used interchangeably. Both of these terms refer to the same thing—the default Ubuntu desktop is

a version of GNOME itself. Of course, Ubuntu provides several other desktops, including KDE (in Kubuntu), Xfce (in Xubuntu), and a variety of others.

Taking Your Desktop for a Ride

When you start your Ubuntu system, you are asked for a username and password to log in with. In the last chapter you specified a user account when installing the system, so use that to log in. First type in your username and press Enter, then your password and press Enter.

TIP   **Language? Sprache? Langue? Lingua?**
Click the Options > Select Language button to change the language of the desktop. If you click the button and the selection does not include your language, jump to the Ubuntu in Your Language section on page 103 to learn how to add new language packs.

After a few seconds you will see the Ubuntu desktop appear (Figure 3-1). The desktop has three main areas.

1. At the top of the screen is the panel. This bar contains the desktop menu options and application shortcut icons on the left side as well as the notification area on the right side. You use this bar to load

Figure 3-1 The Ubuntu desktop is simple, uncluttered, and . . . brown.

applications and to see the status of certain activities on your system. The panel is always visible when you use your desktop.

2. The large middle part of the screen is the desktop. This part of the screen is normally covered by the applications that you use, but you can also put icons and shortcuts on the desktop, too.

3. The bottom part of the screen is called the taskbar. This area displays a rectangle for each open application, just like in Windows.

You may have noticed that, unlike other operating systems, there are no icons on the desktop. The reason for this is that desktop icons typically get covered by applications, and, as such, you can't get at them. If you need to start applications, you typically use the Applications menu or the shortcuts.

TIP   **Device Icons**
Although there are no application icons on the desktop, when you plug in USB devices such as portable music players, keyring drives, or digital cameras, a device icon will appear on the desktop.

Starting Applications and Finding Things

Starting applications is simple. Just click on the Applications menu on the left side of the panel. Inside this menu are a number of submenus for different types of applications. Hover your mouse over each category, and then click the application you want to load. As an example, click on Applications > Internet > Firefox Web Browser. After a few seconds the browser will pop up.

When applications are loaded, the brown window border has three buttons on the right-hand side:

- **Left button (thin white line):** This is used to minimize the application and put it in the taskbar.
- **Middle button (white square):** This maximizes the window to take up the full desktop area.
- **Right button (white cross):** This button closes the application.

Every application has an entry in the taskbar at the bottom of the screen. You can click these entries to minimize or maximize the application and right-click to see some other options.

Changing Your Menu Layout Although the main Applications, Places, and System menus are logical by default, you may want to further customize them by moving entries into different submenus, not displaying certain items, and making other tweaks. All of this is easily done with the built-in menu editor.

To edit the menus, open the option at System > Preferences > Main Menu. The menu editor will appear, as shown in Figure 3-2.

The menu editor is fairly intuitive. To adjust which items are shown, click on a submenu in the left-hand pane and change the Show checkbox for the items you want to show or hide. To add a new item, select the submenu the item should appear in, and then click the New Item button on the right-hand side. The box shown in Figure 3-3 will appear.

Menu items can be applications (the default), applications running in terminals, or files. Select the appropriate setting for the Type box for your menu item, or leave it as Application. Provide a name for your menu item in the Name box, the command to run in the Command box (or the location

Figure 3-2 The menu editor lets you easily change the Ubuntu menus.

Figure 3-3 Feel free to add your own menu items.

of your file in the Location box if you changed the type to File), and a brief description in the Comment box. You can also use the Browse button to select the application to run (or the file to open). Finally, click the default icon off to the side, and select an icon for the item. Click OK to finish adding the new menu item.

Finding Your Files and Folders

When using your computer, you often need to save and open files and folders, move them around, and perform other tasks. The Places menu contains a bunch of entries, including those listed here, to access different parts of your computer and the network.

- **Home Folder:** Your home folder is used to store the files and work for each user who is logged in. This is the most important folder on the system, and you can think of it as the equivalent of My Documents in Windows—virtually everything you save lives here. Each user has a separate home folder.

- **Desktop:** The Desktop folder is inside your home folder and contains files that visually appear on your desktop as icons. If you drag a file onto your desktop, it will appear in the Desktop folder. Similarly, moving a file out of this folder or deleting it will remove it from your desktop.

- **Computer:** Clicking this item displays the different drives attached to your computer as floppy drives, CD/DVD drives, and USB keys or sticks. This is the equivalent of the My Computer icon in Windows.

- **Network:** This option accesses servers that are available on your local network. This is the equivalent of the Network Neighborhood in Windows.

- **Connect to Server:** Click this to run a wizard to create a connection to a network server. You can use this to add an icon to the desktop that, when clicked, provides a list of remote files in the desktop file manager. You can then treat this window like any other file manager window and drag files back and forth. This is really useful for copying files to other computers.

- **Search for Files:** Use this to search for files on your computer.

- **Recent Documents:** Click this submenu to display the most recently used documents.

Configuring Your System

The third and final menu, System, is used to configure and customize your system, access help, and report problems. Inside the menu are a few options, including these:

- **Preferences:** This submenu contains items for customizing the look and feel of your desktop. Each of these settings applies only to the desktop of a user who is logged in. If you log in as another user, the settings change to that user's preferences.

- **Administration:** This submenu is used to configure systemwide settings such as networking, users, printing, and more. To use these menu items, you need to know the system administrator password.

- **Help and Support:** With this you can access the Ubuntu Help Center, which provides documentation and guides for your Ubuntu desktop.

TIP   Feel the Power

When you installed Ubuntu, you were asked for a username and password for the system. This password not only provides access to your normal user account but also accesses the all-powerful Administration features. As such, when you access the menu options and are asked for the password, just enter your normal password, and you can use those features.

This feature applies only to the first user account that you created on the system. If you add other accounts, those users cannot access the Administration options unless you explicitly give them access.

Shortcut Icons

On the panel are a number of shortcut icons next to the menus. These small icons are always visible and can be single-clicked to gain immediate access to your favorite applications. Ubuntu comes with several stock shortcuts on the panel, but you are welcome to add your own.

Adding your own icon is as simple as finding the application you want to add in the menu and then dragging it to the panel. You can then right-click the new shortcut icon and select Move to move it to the right place.

Applets

One simple yet powerful feature in Ubuntu is the ability to run small programs called *applets* on the panel. These small programs are useful for a variety of tasks and provide quick and easy access via the panel.

To add an applet, right-click the panel and select Add to Panel. The window shown in Figure 3-4 pops up. Select one of the many applets, and click Add. When the applet appears on the panel, you can press the middle mouse button (or the left and right buttons together) to move it around.

Figure 3-4 Ubuntu comes bundled with a selection of applets.

The Notification Area

In the right-hand part of the top panel is the notification area and the clock. The notification area is similar to the Windows system tray in that it provides a series of small icons that indicate something specific. A good example of this is Network Manager, which looks after your network connections—both wired and wireless—for you.

You can fiddle with the notification area items by right-clicking them to view a context menu. Some icons (such as the volume control) allow you to left-click on them to view them. As an example, try clicking the little speaker icon and adjusting the slider.

QUICK TIP   Right-click the volume icon and select Open Volume Control to access the mixer settings for your sound card. These settings configure the speakers, microphone, line-in, and any other sound card inputs or outputs.

The Clock

Next to the notification area is the clock. Click on the clock to view a calendar. Later, when you use Evolution, items that are added to your calendar appear in the clock applet too. Instead of opening up Evolution to find out when your dentist appointment is, just click on the clock to see it immediately.

QUICK TIP   Customize your clock by right-clicking it and selecting Preferences.

The Taskbar

The taskbar sits at the bottom of the screen. This small bar is always visible and indicates which applications are currently open. In addition to this, the taskbar also sneaks in a few other handy little features.

To the far left of the taskbar is the Hide/Show Desktop button. Clicking this button hides all of your open applications and shows the desktop. Clicking it again redisplays them. This button is useful when you need to quickly access something on your desktop.

Next to this button is the applications area, which shows each of the currently open applications. For each application, an entry is added, and you can right-click it to view a context menu. This menu can also be used to minimize, maximize, resize, close, and otherwise control applications.

QUICK TIP   You can switch between multiple applications in Ubuntu just like in Windows by pressing Alt-Tab. When you press this key combination, a small window appears that can be used to switch between active applications.

To the right of the applications area are two small rectangles called the workspaces. Each of these rectangles represents another screen in which you can view an application. As an example, you may be using your Web browser and e-mail client while talking to your friends in a chat client on the first desktop and working on a document on the second desktop. You can then just click each virtual desktop to switch to it to access your different applications. Another useful tip applies when you're moving applications between virtual desktops—if you have an application on the first desktop, just right-click the brown window or the taskbar entry, select Move to Another Workspace, and pick the relevant workspace number. The menu also has Move to Workspace Left and Move to Workspace Right options. This makes moving applications between your workspaces quite simple.

QUICK TIP   Although Ubuntu has only two workspaces configured by default, you can have as many— or few—as you like. To configure them, right-click on one of the workspaces in the bottom right-hand corner of your screen, and select Preferences from the menu.

To the right of the workspaces is the trash. Files that are dragged onto this icon are destined to be deleted. To fully delete these files, right-click the trash and select Empty Trash.

TIP   **Usability and the Ubuntu Desktop**
Throughout the development of the Ubuntu desktop, great care and attention have gone into usability. As an example, the four corners of the screen are established as areas that are simple to access—you don't need to carefully mouse over the area and can instead just throw your mouse to the corner. This is why each corner has an important feature. It makes accessing each feature that little bit easier.

Ubuntu is filled with tiny usability improvements such as this that help make it as intuitive and powerful as possible.

Shutting Down Your Computer and Logging Out

Now that you're becoming acquainted with Ubuntu, you'll want to keep using it as long as possible, but there will always come a time when you have no choice but to leave your computer and go do something else. As you have already seen, Ubuntu is extremely flexible, and this area is no exception. Click the icon in the top right of the screen by your username to see the various options (shown in Figure 3-5) for ending your current computing session.

There are a number of options available upon logout, however, the choices presented to you will depend on your installation (e.g., Suspend may not be available).

- **Guest Session:** This option lets you allow someone else to use your computer while keeping you logged in but your data and account secure by giving the guest a limited desktop to work with temporarily and requiring your password to return to your desktop.
- **Lock Screen:** This option locks the screen. This is useful when you need to use the bathroom or grab some lunch. It will lock the computer and ask for your password to reenable the desktop.
- **Log Out:** This option lets you log out of the current session and go back to the main login screen.
- **Suspend:** If your computer supports Suspend, this option will be included in the list, and you can click it to save the current state of your system in RAM. The next time your computer is turned on, the desktop will be resumed. This option continues to use battery power but only a minimal amount.

Figure 3-5 Who knew that shutting down had so many possibilities?

- **Hibernate:** When you click this option, the current state of the system is saved to the hard disk and can be switched off. This is like the Suspend option but slower.

- **Restart:** Click this to restart the computer.

- **Shut Down:** Click this to shut down your computer.

Using Your Applications

Now that you have become familiar with the desktop, let's explore some of the many applications included on your new system. By default, Ubuntu comes with a wide range of popular and established applications to listen to music, watch videos, create documents, browse the Web, manage your appointments, read your e-mail, create images, and much more. These applications have been vetted by the developers to ensure they are the best-of-breed Linux applications available.

Although Ubuntu includes a range of software applications, it is likely you will want to install extra applications and explore other available software. Fortunately, the Ubuntu system is built on a powerful foundation that makes software installation as simple as pointing and clicking. Click Applications > Add/Remove, and a dialog box appears that you can use to install new applications. Just browse through the different categories and check the applications to install. Click the Apply button, and the application is downloaded and installed for you.

This tool provides a simple way to access a limited core set of popular applications, but there are actually more than 20,000 packages available to your Ubuntu system. Software installation is discussed in detail in Chapter 4.

TIP   **Another Way to Run Applications**
Although you will most typically start your applications by selecting them from the Applications menu, you can also press Alt-F2 to bring up a box where you can type in the name of an application and run it.

Browsing the Web with Firefox

Firefox is the default Ubuntu Web browser and provides you with a simple, safe, and powerful browsing experience. Firefox has become one of the most successful open source projects in the world and continues to garner huge popularity. With hundreds of millions of downloads and rapidly increasing browser share, Firefox has been an unparalleled success.

Fire up Firefox by clicking its icon (the first one next to the System menu) on the panel or by selecting Applications > Internet > Firefox Web Browser. Before long, you'll be presented with the main Firefox window (Figure 3-6).

The Firefox window looks similar to most Web browsers and includes the usual back, forward, reload, and stop buttons, an address bar, and some menus. These familiar-looking elements help you become acquainted with Firefox, and if you have used Internet Explorer, Opera, Netscape, or Safari before, you are sure to pick it up in no time.

Navigating your way around the Internet is no different in Firefox than in any other browser—just type the Web address into the address bar and press Enter. Firefox also has a few nice features that make it easy to access your favorite sites. As an example, if you want to visit the Ubuntu Web site,

Figure 3-6 The Firefox interface is sleek but extensible.

you can just enter www.ubuntu.com (leaving off all that http:// nonsense). Alternatively, you can just type in "Ubuntu," and Firefox will do the equivalent of going off to Google, entering "Ubuntu" as the search term, and taking you to the first result for the search. This feature is incredibly handy for popular sites that are likely to be at the top of the search results page.

TIP   The search box next to the address bar can be used to do searches. By default, these searches are on Google. To do a Google search, just type in your search term and press Enter. You can also click the down arrow next to the "G" and select from a variety of other sites to search, including the Ubuntu software archive Web site and Wikipedia

This search box can be used to search just about anything. To add more search engines, click the small icon and then select Manage Search Engines.

Tabbed Browsing   If you are anything like any of the authors behind this book, you look at a number of different Web sites each time you use the Internet. It is not uncommon to have your Webmail open as well as Wikipedia, some discussion forums like the Ubuntu Forums, news sites, blogs, and more. Before long, your desktop is littered with browser windows, and your taskbar is full to the brim.

Firefox has a nimble solution to this problem in the form of *tabbed browsing*. If you are looking at your friend's Web site about raccoons and decide you want to check out your favorite sports player's Web site, just click File > New Tab or press Ctrl-T and—ta-da!—a new tab is unveiled in your browser window. You can now load another page inside this tab.

The tabbed browsing fun doesn't stop, though—oh no! When you are reading the Web and you see a link you are interested in viewing, right-click the link and select Open Link in New Tab. The page will load in the new tab, and you can continue reading the article and view the link afterward.

Bookmarking Your Favorite Sites   To bookmark the page you are viewing, click Bookmarks > Bookmark This Page. In the dialog box that pops up, use the combo box to select the folder to store the bookmark in. You also have the option to add "tags" to your bookmark, which are like keywords that can be used to sort and search for your bookmarks in the future. When you have finished naming and tagging your bookmark, click Done to save the bookmark.

Save Time with Live Bookmarks   Firefox also includes a special feature called *live bookmarks* that automatically grabs content from a Web site without your needing to visit it. As an example, go to http://fridge.ubuntu.com (a popular Ubuntu news site), and you will see a small orange icon—which indicates that this site has feed available—on the right side of the address bar. Click this orange square, and you will be taken to a new page that previews the feed and gives you the option of what you would like to use to subscribe to it. Use the default option (Live Bookmarks), and click Subscribe Now. A dialog box will pop up. Use the default values provided and click OK. A new toolbar button is added, and when you click on it, a list of the items from the Web site are displayed. Each time you start Firefox, it will quietly go away and update this list so that you don't need to visit the site yourself.

TIP   **If You Liked the Fridge**
You may also like Planet Ubuntu at http://planet.ubuntu.com. This site collects the personal blogs of a number of different Ubuntu developers and other community members. Planet Ubuntu gives a unique insight into what the developers are working on and/or interested in.

Bolt It On, Make It Cool   Although Firefox is already a powerful and flexible Web browser, it can be extended even further using special plug-in extensions. These extensions cover not only typical browsing needs but also other more specialized extras that extend the browser itself.

To install normal Web plug-ins, just visit a site that requires the plug-in. A yellow bar will appear at the top of the page, indicating that you are missing a plug-in necessary to fully take advantage of the page you are visiting. Click the Install Missing Plug-ins button to grab the required plug-in. For example, Ubuntu does not come with the Macromedia Flash plug-in because it does not live up to Ubuntu software freedom requirements. As a result, you will have the option to install either Macromedia Flash or the free software version Gnash if you want to use Flash.

To extend the browser itself with additional features, go to https://addons. mozilla.org and browse for an extension that you are interested in. When you find something you would like to install, click the Install link. A dialog box will pop up asking you to confirm the installation. Click Install Now. Your new extension will now download and install automatically. Typically, this requires a restart of Firefox, and then your extension is available.

TIP   **Be Careful Where You Download**

It is recommended that you download extensions only from http://addons.mozilla.org. If you do need to install an extension from another site, make sure it is a site you trust. Otherwise, the extension may contain unsafe software, viruses, or spyware.

Creating Documents with OpenOffice.org

Included with Ubuntu is a full office suite called OpenOffice.org. This comprehensive collection contains applications for creating word processing documents, spreadsheets, presentations, databases, drawings, and mathematical equations. The suite provides an extensive range of functionality, including reading and writing Microsoft Office file formats, and can also export documents as Web pages, PDF files, and even animations.

Let's give OpenOffice.org a whirl by creating a letter with it. Start OpenOffice.org word processor by selecting it from the Applications > Office menu. When it has loaded, you will be presented with the interface shown in Figure 3-7.

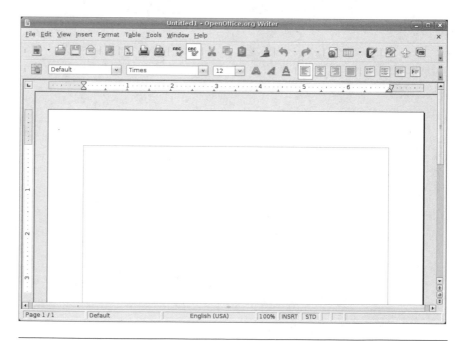

Figure 3-7 OpenOffice.org looks similar to Microsoft Office and is therefore quite simple to adjust to.

If you have used a word processing program before, many of the common interface elements, such as the buttons for setting font type and size, bold, italic, underline, and alignment, look and behave the same. The OpenOffice.org developers have designed the suite to be easy to migrate to if you have used a program like Microsoft Office before. After a few minutes playing with OpenOffice.org, you will be confident that you can find the functions you need.

Start your letter by first choosing a nice font. In the font combo box, you should see Times selected as the default. Click the box and instead choose the lovely Bitstream Vera Sans font. Change the font size by clicking the combo box to the right of the font box and selecting 10 as the size. With the cursor on the left side of the page, add your home address to the letter.

Now press Enter to leave a blank line under the address, and click the Align Right toolbar button (the icon looks like some lines aligned to the right). If you are unsure of what a button does, hover your mouse over it to pop up a tool tip. Now add to your letter the address of the recipient.

Press Enter again to leave a blank line, and type the main body of the letter. Feel free to use the bold, italic, and underline buttons to add emphasis to your words. You can also use other toolbar buttons to add items such as bullet points and numbered lists and to change the color of the font. If you want to add features such as graphics, tables, special characters, and frames, click the Insert menu and select the relevant item. You can customize each item added to the page by right-clicking the item and using the options shown in the context menu.

When your letter is complete, you can save it by selecting File > Save, by clicking the floppy disk toolbar icon, or by pressing Ctrl-S. The default file format used by OpenOffice.org is the OpenDocument Format. This file format is an official open standard and is used across the world. The file format is slightly different for different types of applications (.odt for word processor files, .ods for spreadsheets, and so on), but each format provides an open standard free from vendor lock-in. You can also save in a variety of other formats, including the default formats for Microsoft Office.

TIP   Vendor Lock-In?

In the proprietary software world, it is common for each application to have its own closed
file format that only the vendor knows how to implement. When a person uses the software
to create documents, the closed format means that only that specific tool can read and write
the format. As long as you want to access your documents, you need that tool. This is
known as vendor lock-in.

To combat this problem, the OpenOffice.org suite (and the vast majority of other open
source applications) uses an open file format that is publicly documented. In fact, the format
is a published standard under ISO/IEC 26300:3006. This means that other applications can
implement the OpenDocument file format, and you can be safe in the knowledge that your
documents will always be available and you are not locked in to any specific tool.

Another useful feature wedged into OpenOffice.org is the capability to
save your documents in the Adobe PDF format. PDF files have been
increasingly used in the last few years and are useful for sending people
documents that they should not change (such as invoices). PDF files provide a high-quality copy of the document and are well supported across all
operating systems. This makes PDFs ideal for creating catalogs, leaflets,
and flyers. To save a document as a PDF file, click the PDF button on the
main toolbar (next to the printer icon). Click the button, enter a filename,
and you are done. Simple.

Managing Your E-mail and Calendars with Evolution

Evolution has been modeled around the all-in-one personal information
management tool. Within Evolution you can read your e-mail, manage
your schedule, store contact details, organize to-do lists, and more in a
single place. This makes Evolution useful for both businesspeople and regular users who want easy access to this information.

Setting Up Your E-Mail Account   To use Evolution to read your e-mail, you
need to find out the following settings for connecting to your e-mail server
(you can get these details from your ISP or system administrator):

- Your type of e-mail server (such as POP or IMAP)
- Your mail server name (such as mail.chin.com)
- Your mail account's username and password
- Authentication type (typically by password)

- Your outgoing mail server type (typically SMTP)
- Your outgoing mail server name

TIP   **Evolution and Webmail**

You can't use Evolution to read Webmail such as Yahoo! Mail, or Hotmail unless you configure your Webmail to output as POP and use SMTP to send e-mail. Consult your Webmail provider for more details on if and how you can access the mail with a local client like Evolution.

Load Evolution by clicking the envelope and clock shortcut icon from the panel (hover your mouse over the shortcuts to see what they are) or by clicking Applications > Internet > Evolution Mail. When the application loads, you are taken through a wizard to set up your e-mail server (as shown in Figure 3-8).

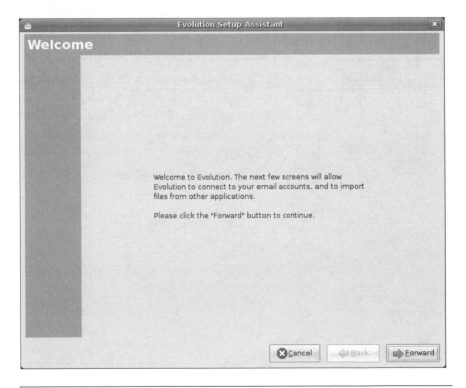

Figure 3-8 Setting up Evolution is simple as long as you know the details for your mail server.

Click Forward to continue the setup, and after choosing to not restore from a backup, you will be asked for your identity. Fill in your e-mail address in the E-Mail Address box, and add the optional information if you want to. The additional details are not essential for using Evolution. Click Forward to continue.

You are next asked to choose what kind of e-mail server you have from the drop-down box. When you make your selection, some additional settings are displayed. Fill in the server name and the username. You may need to adjust the Security and Authentication Type settings, but for most accounts the default settings should be fine. Click Forward to continue.

The next page configures some options for receiving your e-mail. None of these options are essential, although you may want to check the first box to automatically check for new mail. Click Forward to continue. The next screen configures the settings for sending e-mail. In the combo box select the Server Type (typically SMTP) and add the server name to the Server box. Click Forward to continue.

In the next screen enter a name to describe the account. The default entry (your e-mail address) is fine, but you may want to add something more meaningful such as "Work E-Mail" or "Home E-Mail." When you have added this, click Forward to continue. Finally, select your location from the map. If you click on your area of the world, the map will zoom in. Once you have done this, click Apply to complete the process and close the wizard.

With the wizard completed, the main Evolution interface will appear, as shown in Figure 3-9.

On the left sidebar you can see a number of buttons to access the mail, contacts, calendars, memos, and tasks components in Evolution. When you click each button, the interface adjusts to show you the relevant information about that component.

Working with Your E-Mail   Inside the e-mail component you can see the e-mail folders in the left panel and the list of messages in the top pane. When you click on a message, it is displayed in the bottom pane, where you can read it. With your new account set up, you will first want to go and

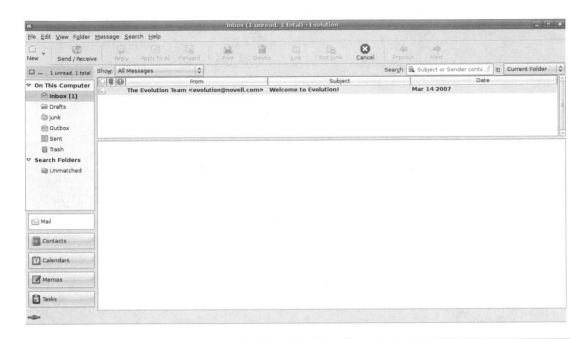

Figure 3-9 Those of you who have used Microsoft Outlook should find the interface very similar.

grab the e-mail from your mail server. Click Send/Receive, and the mail is retrieved from your server and any unsent mail is sent.

TIP   Problems?
If you cannot connect to your mail server, there may be an error in your account configuration. To edit your account settings again, click Edit > Preferences, select the account from the list, and click Edit.

With your messages loaded, new e-mails are shown in bold in the top pane. Move through the different e-mails using the up and down arrow keys, and each message will be displayed. You can reply to a message by clicking the Reply or Reply To All toolbar buttons. New e-mails can be created by clicking the New toolbar button. By default, new e-mails and replies are sent automatically when you click the Send button in the compose window. This way you don't need to click the Send/Receive button to deliver them.

Managing Your Calendar   Inside calendar mode, Evolution provides a convenient way to manage your schedule, add new events, and view your calendar in different ways. When you click the Calendars button to switch to this mode, you can see the timetable for today as well as the month view. The month view shows a couple of months in which the bold dates have events.

You can add two types of events to your calendar.

- **Meetings:** These are events with a specific group of people.

- **Appointments:** These are general events.

To add a new appointment, navigate to the date you require using the calendar, then right-click a time slot in the day view, and select New Appointment. Alternatively, simply click the New toolbar item. In the box that pops up, fill in the Summary, Location, Time (adjusting the date if necessary), and Description boxes. You can also select which calendar the event appears on if you have multiple calendars configured.

TIP   **Multiple Calendars**
Evolution supports multiple calendars. This is useful if you want different calendars for different types of events such as personal and work-related activities. To create a new calendar, right-click the calendar list in the left sidebar and select New Calendar.

To add a new meeting, again find the date, right-click the day view, and select New Meeting. Inside the dialog box that pops up, you need to add the participants who are attending the meeting. You can add participants in two ways: Use the Add button if they are not in your address book, or use the Attendees button if they are in your address book.

When you click Attendees, a new dialog pops up with a list of attendees down the left. You can use the Add and Remove buttons to add contacts to (or remove them from) the different categories of Chairpersons, Required Participants, Optional Participants, and Resources. Now, you probably don't have any contacts in there as you are just starting to use Evolution, so use the main Contacts button on the left side of the main Evolution window to add some.

You can view your calendar in lots of different ways by clicking the different toolbar buttons such as Week, Month, and List. Play with them and see which ones are most useful to you.

QUICK TIP   Remember, you can access your appointments without opening Evolution by clicking on the clock in the panel.

Creating Graphics with GIMP

The GNU Image Manipulation Program, affectionately known as GIMP to its friends, is a powerful graphics package. GIMP provides a comprehensive range of functionality for creating different types of graphics. It includes tools for selections, drawing, paths, masks, filters, effects, and more. It also includes a range of templates for different types of media such as Web banners, different paper sizes, video frames, CD covers, floppy disk labels, and even toilet paper. Yes, toilet paper.

Unlike Adobe Photoshop, GIMP does not place all of its windows inside a single large window; instead, GIMP has a number of separate child windows. This can be a little confusing at first for new users—especially those used to Photoshop. To get you started, let's run through a simple session in GIMP.

An Example   Start GIMP by clicking Applications > Graphics > GNU Image Manipulation Program.

When GIMP loads, you will see a collection of different windows, as shown in Figure 3-10.

Close the Tip of the Day window, and you are left with two other windows. The one on the left in the screenshot is the main tool palette. This window provides you with a range of different tools that can be used to create your images. The window on the right provides details of layers, brushes, and other information. GIMP provides a huge range of different windows that are used for different things, and these are just two of them.

To create a new image, click File > New. The window shown in Figure 3-11 will appear.

The easiest way to get started is to select one of the many templates. Click the Template combo box and select 640 × 480. If you click the Advanced

Figure 3-10 GIMP does not put everything in one window like Adobe Photoshop.

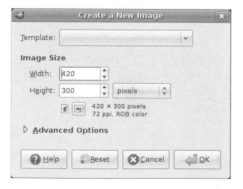

Figure 3-11 Lots of templates are available, including one for toilet paper!

Options expander, you can also select the type of color used in the image with the Colorspace box and the background fill. The Fill combo box is useful for either selecting a fill color or having a transparent background.

Click OK, and you will see your new image window (Figure 3-12).

To work on your image, use the tool palette to select which tool you want to use on the new image window. Each time you click on a tool in the palette, you see options for the tool appear at the bottom half of the palette window.

When you click the A button in the palette, it selects the text tool. At the bottom of the palette, you see the different options. Click the Font button that looks like an upper and lower case A (like Aa) and select the Sans Bold font. Now click the up arrow on the Size box, and select the size as 60.

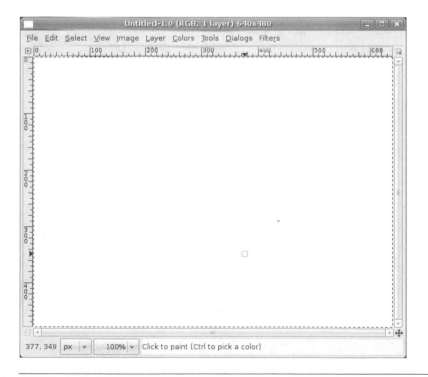

Figure 3-12 Use the right mouse button on the image to access lots of GIMP options and features.

Move your mouse over to the empty image window, and you will see the mouse pointer change to a text carat. Click in the image, and a box pops up in which you can enter the text to add to the image. Type in "Ubuntu." With the text entry still open, click the up arrow on the Size box so the text fills most of the window. As you can see, you can adjust the text while it is in the image. When you are happy with the formatting, click Close on the text entry box. Your image should look a little like Figure 3-13.

Now click the button in the palette with a cross with an arrow on each end. You can use this to move the text around. Click the black text, and move the mouse.

Let's now add an effect filter. GIMP comes with a range of different filters built in. You can access these by right-clicking the image and selecting the Filters submenu.

For our image, right-click the image and select Filters > Blur > Gaussian Blur. In the Horizontal and Vertical boxes select 5 as the value. Click OK,

Figure 3-13 Ubuntu comes with a range of attractive fonts for use in your images.

and the blur is applied to your text. Anything in GIMP can be undone by clicking Edit > Undo or typing Ctrl-Z. Your image should now look like Figure 3-14.

Now we are going to create another layer and put some text over our blurred text to create an interesting effect. In your image window, click Dialogues > Layers. The Layers window now appears (Figure 3-15).

Layers are like clear plastic sheets that can be stacked on top of each other. They allow you to create some imagery on one layer and then create another layer on top with some other imagery. When combined, layers can create complex-looking images that are easily editable because you can edit layers individually. Currently, our blurred text is one layer. We can add a new layer by clicking the paper icon in the Layers dialog box. Another window appears to configure the layer. The defaults are fine (a transparent layer the size of your image), so click OK.

Figure 3-14 Several filters and effects are bundled with GIMP in Ubuntu.

Figure 3-15 Layers are essential when creating complex images with lots of parts.

Now double-click the black color chip in the palette window and select a light color. You can do this by moving the mouse in the color range and then clicking OK when you find a color you like. Now click the text button from the palette and again add the "Ubuntu" text. When the text is added, it will be the same size as before. Now use the move tool and position it over the blurred text. Now you have the word "Ubuntu" with a healthy glow, as shown in Figure 3-16!

The final step is to crop the image to remove the unused space. Click Tools > Transform Tools > Crop, and use the mouse to draw around the Ubuntu word. You can click in the regions near the corners of the selection to adjust the selection more precisely. Click inside the selection, and the image will be cropped. To save your work, click File > Save, and enter a filename. You can use the Select File Type expander to select from one of the many different file formats.

Communicating with Pidgin

With the Internet steamrolling its way across the world, the ubiquitous global network has become a part of everyday life and something you can reasonably assume people have access to. This has in turn spawned a range of Web-based services and, interestingly, a variety of methods for communicating with each other.

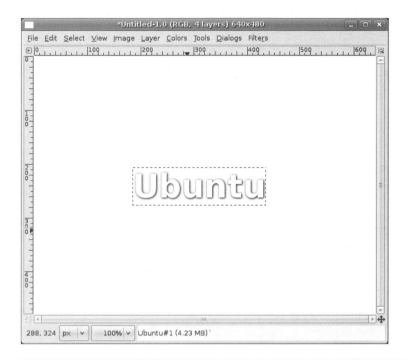

Figure 3-16 Combining steps as we have done can result in interesting effects such as this.

Included with Ubuntu is Pidgin (formerly known as Gaim), a cornucopia of different methods for instantly messaging your friends from within a single program. Instead of having to install a separate client application to talk to your friends on MSN, AIM, ICQ, and Jabber, Pidgin can do it all in one place. Pidgin is available by clicking Applications > Internet > Pidgin Instant Messenger.

Setting Up Your Accounts When you start Pidgin for the first time, you will be asked if you want to add an account, as none have been configured yet. Click the Add button to add a new account, and the Add Account box appears (Figure 3-17).

QUICK TIP To add or edit accounts at a later date, click Accounts > Add/Edit within Pidgin to access your account list.

Figure 3-17 Pidgin supports many different types of accounts (MSN, AIM, Jabber, ICQ, IRC, and so on).

This window adjusts which text boxes are available depending on the protocol chosen. The different networks available are listed as options in the Protocol box. To create an account, you will need to have an existing account on one of the networks. Pidgin allows you to have different accounts on different networks running together—you just create a new account for each protocol—or even multiple accounts on the same network.

When you have selected a protocol, fill in the remaining boxes. The Screen Name box needs to contain your registered username (or e-mail address for MSN), and the Password box needs the respective password to be added. You can also use the Local Alias box to add an interesting name that is displayed when other people see you online. If you want to configure any other options, click the Advanced tab.

Using Instant Messaging   With your account(s) set up, Pidgin will automatically sign you in. When you are logged in, your list of contacts (known as buddies in Pidgin) is displayed (Figure 3-18). Additionally, a little icon will appear in the notification areas that will show that Pidgin is running, your status, and if you have received any messages.

Figure 3-18 Pidgin provides quick and easy access to your buddies—just click them to talk!

You can use the Buddies menu option to add more buddies to the list with the Add Buddy option. To speak with a buddy, double-click the name, and a window will pop up. To change your status or sign out, click the status box at the bottom of your Buddy List and select the appropriate option.

Using IRC   Included in Pidgin is support for IRC channels, and it has a very nice interface for IRC discussion. To use the IRC feature, first create an account. Next, sign on, and then click Buddies > Add Chat and enter the IRC channel name in the Channel box. Finally, double-click on the channel name to go to it.

Cutting-Edge Voice Over IP with Ekiga

Included with Ubuntu is a simple-to-use yet powerful Internet phone called Ekiga. Formally known as GNOME Meeting, Ekiga lets you make voice and video calls with other people across the Internet. In addition to the traditional Microsoft Netmeeting support, Ekiga now supports SIP, a protocol commonly used to allow people with software phones such as Ekiga to communicate with people using hardware Voice Over IP phones. SIP is an industry standard that many hardware phones, software phones, services, and providers support.

If you choose to use SIP, calls from one phone to another across the Internet are free. In addition, many providers allow you to make calls to normal landline phones for very little cost. Ekiga offers you the possibility to call anyone in the world directly from your computer with little fuss.

You can access Ekiga by clicking Applications > Internet > Ekiga Softphone.

Setting Up   When you first start Ekiga, you are guided through a setup wizard (Figure 3-19).

Click Forward to get started, and you see the next page (Figure 3-20).

In this box, enter your first and last name (such as Frankie Banger). Click Forward to continue.

You can now configure an Ekiga.net account (Figure 3-21).

At Ekiga.net, a free SIP service is offered. If you don't have an account (which is likely if this is the first time you have used Ekiga), click the Get an Ekiga.net SIP Account button. Firefox is then loaded, and you can use the

Figure 3-19 Setting up Ekiga is simple with the setup wizard.

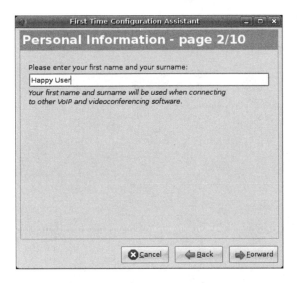

Figure 3-20 Adding your name makes it easier for people to find you online.

Figure 3-21 Ekiga.net offers a free SIP service.

online form to sign up. If you don't want an account, just select the check-box in the wizard saying you don't want to sign up. If you do sign up, add your username and password, and then click Forward.

Now you can configure your connection type (Figure 3-22).

Figure 3-22 Be honest here—selecting a faster speed won't make it any quicker!

Select the type of connection you have, and then click Forward.

Traditionally, one of the problems in the past with Internet phones has been that you need to modify your firewall (if you are running one) to get the phone working. This typically involved configuring your Network Address Translation (NAT) settings. Luckily, Ekiga can detect the type of NAT settings that you need (Figure 3-23).

After a few seconds of detecting your type of NAT, Ekiga will propose an option. Click Yes to continue, and then click Forward.

Next, configure your audio (Figure 3-24).

Select ALSA from the box, and click Forward to continue.

You can now select the audio input and output devices (Figure 3-25).

These settings are used to ensure that you can hear and record the audio. To test your settings, click Test Settings. If all is fine, click Forward to continue.

Next select the type of video manager (Figure 3-26).

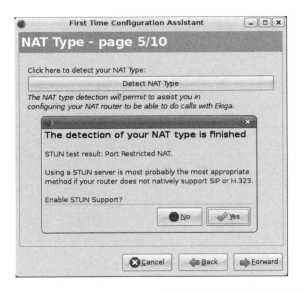

Figure 3-23 Traditionally, setting up NAT with Internet phones was a pain—until now.

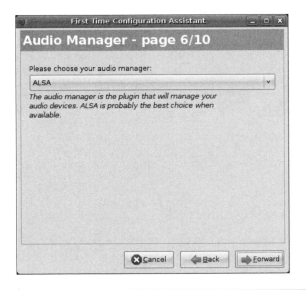

Figure 3-24 Ubuntu supports different types of audio frameworks, but the Advanced Linux Sound Architecture (ALSA) is the most common.

Figure 3-25 Make sure you get these settings right, or you won't hear anything.

Figure 3-26 Ubuntu supports different types of video, but V4L is the most common.

The video manager ensures that video is displayed correctly on your screen. Select V4L from the list, and click Forward to continue.

The final setting to configure is your Web camera (Figure 3-27).

Ensure that your camera is plugged in, and select a device from the combo box. If you can't see any options, you will need to configure your camera driver first. When you have selected a device, click Test Settings to verify that it works.

Finally, a summary of your options is displayed (Figure 3-28).

Ekiga is now configured. Click apply!

Making a Call   With the configuration wizard complete, the main Ekiga window is displayed (Figure 3-29).

Figure 3-27 Remember to look your best online!

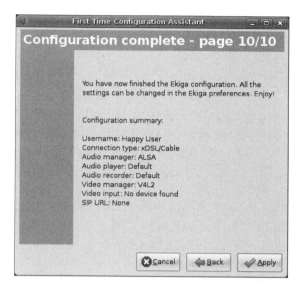

Figure 3-28 Now you are all set to make calls.

Figure 3-29 The Ekiga window is simple and sleek.

You are now ready to make a call. Simply enter the phone number or SIP address of the person you want to call, and click the Connect button next to the address bar. The call is then connected, and you can begin talking.

On the left side of the window are a number of icons that do different things.

- **Text Chat:** When in a chat, click this icon to open the text chat window. You can use this to send text messages to the user.

- **View Mode:** Click this icon to select which view mode Ekiga is in. You typically need this when in a video chat with someone.

- **Address Book:** Click this icon to access the address book. Here you can save your contacts, and you can also access the Ekiga.net online white pages to see who else is online.

- **View Webcam:** This icon switches on the Webcam so that you can see the person you are speaking to.

In addition to these icons, there are some tabs located below the numeric keypad. Click these tabs to configure the audio and video settings for Ekiga.

Exploring the Ubuntu Landscape

Unlike many other operating systems, Ubuntu includes a comprehensive suite of applications right inside the system. This range of tools has been selected to allow you to install Ubuntu and get your work done, communicate with other people, read and create documents, watch and/or listen to media, and more. Unfortunately, due to space restrictions, this book can only skim over the surface of available applications.

To help remedy this a bit, here is a quick summary of many of the applications included on the Applications menu in Ubuntu, including how to find the applications and a brief description.

- **Text Editor**

  Applications > Accessories > Text Editor

  This simple, yet powerful, text editor is ideal for editing documents, making quick notes, and programming. Included is a range of plug-ins for spell checking, statistics, file listings, and more.

- **Calculator**

  Applications > Accessories > Calculator

  For those times when you need to figure out a percentage or calculate whether you are getting a raw deal from your employer, the calculator is there. It provides a range of functionality for simple and scientific calculations.

▪ **Terminal**

Applications > Accessories > Terminal

Underpinning the desktop is an incredibly powerful command-line core. This application puts a window around a command-line interface and allows you to configure transparency, fonts, behavior, and more. Essential for the command-line junkies among you.

▪ **Gnometris**

Applications > Games > Gnometris

If you have too much time on your hands, a surefire way to waste it is to play this version of Tetris. If you decide that single-player Tetris is not enough, go and download gtetrinet with the Add/Remove programs.

▪ **Nibbles**

Applications > Games > Nibbles

The classic worm game comes to Ubuntu. Another surefire way to while away an afternoon.

▪ **Mahjongg**

Applications > Games > Mahjongg

For those of you who actually understand the rules of Mahjongg, this application provides a great implementation of the game.

▪ **FreeCell Solitaire**

Applications > Games > FreeCell Solitaire

There is a body of thinking that suggests that FreeCell may be responsible for untold hours of lost productivity. If you are impatient about playing Patience, select FreeCell Solitaire.

- **Movie Player**

  Applications > Sound & Video > Movie Player

  Although listed as a movie player, this application actually plays a range of different types of media, including both video and audio.

- **Sound Recorder**

  Applications > Sound & Video > Sound Recorder

  If you need to record something, such as your voice for a podcast or audio message, you can use this simple tool.

- **System Monitor**

  System > Administration > System Monitor

  To get an idea of the current performance or load on your computer, click on this tool. The System Monitor lets you know which applications are running and how much memory/processing power they are using, and it also allows you to kill or restart processes that are hogging the resources.

- **Sudoku**

  Applications > Games > Sudoku

  The increasingly popular logic game arrives on Ubuntu.

- **Disk Usage Analyzer**

  Applications > Accessories > Disk Usage Analyzer

  Bits and bytes never looked so good! In case you were wondering exactly where all your disk space had gone, this will help solve the mystery.

- **F-Spot Photo Manager**

  Applications > Graphics > F-Spot Photo Manager

  Manage your photos, download off your camera, and send them up to Flickr and other online photo sites.

Other Applications to Try   There are literally thousands of available packages that can be installed on your Ubuntu computer. These packages span a range of different areas, and this section covers some of the popular ones. Coverage of software installation appears in Chapter 4. Try the following useful applications.

■ **Blender**

Package to install: blender

Blender (Figure 3-30) is an incredibly powerful 3D modeling, animation, rendering, and production studio. Blender amasses an impressive range of functionality for creating photorealistic scenes, animations, and real-time virtual walkthroughs. Blender is also fully scriptable in Python.

■ **Inkscape**

Package to install: inkscape

Inkscape (Figure 3-31) is a drawing package for creating Scalable Vector Graphics (SVG). Ever since the SVG format was introduced, it

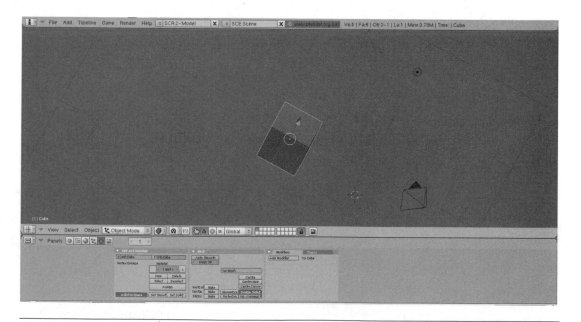

Figure 3-30 Blender

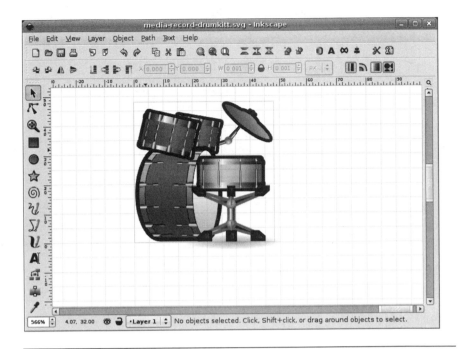

Figure 3-31 Inkscape

has taken the design world by storm. SVG allows the creation of graphics that can scale to any size. Inkscape is a hugely flexible tool for creating such graphics, and a huge range of icons and artwork in open source projects are made in Inkscape.

- **Beagle**

  Package to install: beagle

  Beagle (Figure 3-32) is a search system that indexes virtually everything. After you install Beagle, you can search for "campfire," and it will return documents, images, Web pages, blog entries, instant messaging conversations, and more that contain that term. Beagle is still very much in development but is an incredibly useful tool.

- **Bluefish**

  Package to install: bluefish

  For those of you who want to create Web pages but prefer to write code, Bluefish (Figure 3-33) is an excellent Web editor. Bluefish is a

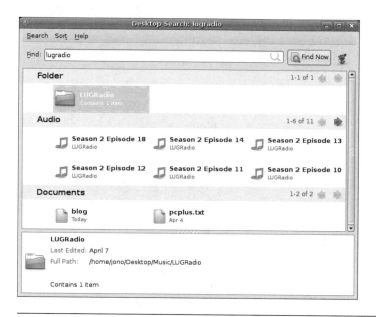

Figure 3-32 Beagle

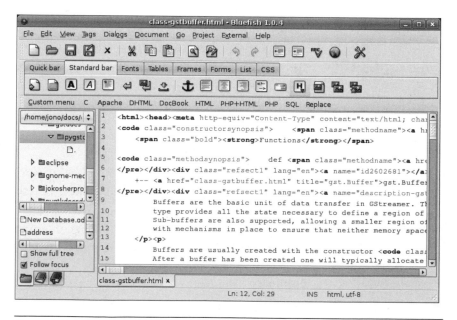

Figure 3-33 Bluefish

lightweight but feature-rich editor with support for a range of languages as well as HTML and CSS.

- **Audio CD Extractor**

Package to install: sound-juicer

Many of us have legally purchased compact disks that we would like to listen to using our computer or portable music player. Audio CD Extractor (Figure 3-34) will help you record the songs to your hard drive so you may do so.

Figure 3-34 Sound Juicer: An Audio CD Extractor

The Ubuntu File Chooser and Bookmarks

One area in which the GNOME developers have worked hard is in creating an intuitive and useful file chooser that is accessed in applications with File > Open. You may be wondering why they have spent so much time on such a small and seemingly insignificant part of the desktop. In reality, however, finding files is one of the most frustrating aspects of using computers and often involves digging through folder after folder to find what you need. Luckily, the GNOME file chooser (Figure 3-35) helps cut down much of this file hunting significantly.

The listing of files on the right-hand side is used to find the file you need, and you can click on folders in this listing to traverse deeper into your sub-folders. Note how each folder is displayed above the listing in a series of buttons. You can click these buttons to easily jump back to parent folders when needed.

Aside from enabling you to manually pick files, the chooser also supports bookmarks. On the left side of the chooser is a list of devices and bookmarks labeled Places. These include your home directory (shown as your user-

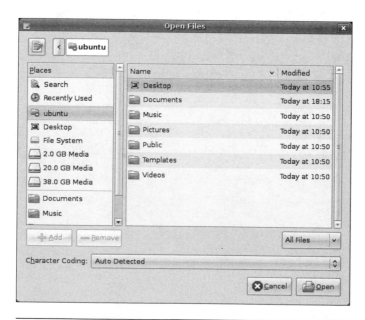

Figure 3-35 The file chooser has a number of subtle features such as bookmarks.

name), Desktop (the files on your desktop), and File System (the entire hard drive), as well as devices such as CD drives, floppy drives, and USB sticks.

To create your own bookmark, use the listing on the right to find the folder that you want to bookmark, single-click it, and then click Add below the Places box. The folder now appears in your bookmarks. Now whenever you need to access that folder, just click the bookmark! In addition to putting the bookmark in the file chooser, it is also available in other parts of the desktop, such as the Places menu and in the file manager.

Ubuntu in Your Language

When you installed Ubuntu, you were asked which language the system should use. Although this sets the initial language for the system, you may want to change the language at a later date. To do this, click System > Administration > Language Support.

Ubuntu supports a huge range of different languages, and many applications include a Translate This Application menu option in the Help menu so that all Ubuntu users can contribute translations in their language(s). If you would like to help with this effort, it is a fantastic contribution to the Ubuntu project.

When the language selector first loads, it may ask you to update your language packs. Just click Yes to continue. Inside the dialog box a number of languages are listed, each of which has a Support checkbox listed next to it. For each language that you want available on the system, check the relevant boxes.

When you have selected the boxes, click the Apply button, and the appropriate language packs are downloaded and installed. Now use the Default Language combo box to choose the new language. You need to log out and log back in for the changes to take effect.

TIP   **Choosing a New Language**
When you see the login screen, you can use the Language button to choose a language for that specific login session. When you select the language, you are asked if you want to make it the default language or use it just for that specific session.

Customizing Ubuntu's Look and Feel

Whenever we put someone in front of Ubuntu for the first time, there seems to be a uniform natural desire to tweak the look and feel of the desktop. It can be fun tweaking our desktops so they look just right, and Ubuntu has great support for all kinds of adjustments. Do you want different-looking applications with a lime green background and crazy fonts? No problem; just don't show it to anyone else. . . .

Changing the Background

To change the background of your desktop, right-click it and select Change Desktop Background. Inside the dialog box that appears, choose your wallpaper by clicking on an image, and the desktop background will automatically change. Ubuntu comes with a limited range of pre-installed wallpapers, so it is likely that you will want to add your own wallpaper. To do this, save your wallpaper somewhere on your computer, and then use the Add Wallpaper button to select it. The new wallpaper can be selected from the list.

If you are not really a wallpaper kind of person and would prefer just a color for the background, you can use the Desktop Colors controls at the bottom of the dialog box. The combo box provides three different types of background: Solid Color, Horizontal Gradient, and Vertical Gradient. Next to the combo box, click on the color chip to select the relevant color(s).

Changing the Theme

When you are using your applications, the visual appearance of the buttons, scroll bars, widgets, and other bits and pieces are controlled by the theme. The built-in theming system can make your applications look radically different, and Ubuntu ships with a number of themes that you can try.

Choosing a New Theme   To choose a new theme, click System > Preferences > Appearance and then click on the Theme tab. Inside the tab that pops up are a number of themes that you can choose. Just click on a theme, and the desktop will be adjusted automatically. You can further customize your theme by clicking the Customize button. A new dialog box appears that has tabs for the different parts of the theme you can configure. Click each tab, and select an entry from the list to create your own perfect theme.

Installing New Themes   To install a new theme, first head over to http://art.gnome.org and find a theme that you like. You need to look for Application Themes when browsing the site. When you find a theme that you like, download it to your computer. Now Click System > Preferences > Appearance, and click the Install button in the Theme tab. Using the file chooser, find the theme that you just downloaded, and it will install automatically. Now select your new theme from the list.

Configuring a Screensaver

To choose a different screensaver, click System > Preferences > Screensaver. The screensaver configuration tool then loads (Figure 3-36).

On the left side of the window is a list of available screensavers. Click on a screensaver and you will see a preview appear in the space to the right of the list. You can then use the slider to select how long the computer needs to be idle before the screensaver kicks in.

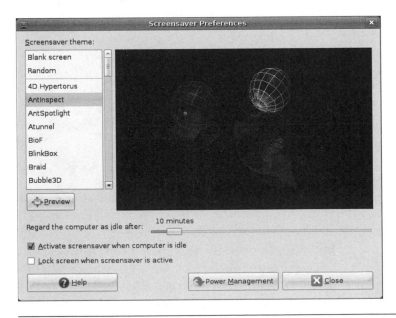

Figure 3-36 A number of screensavers are bundled with Ubuntu.

The Lock Screen When Screensaver Is Active checkbox can be selected to lock the screen when the screensaver starts and, as such, requires a user to enter the password to reactivate the desktop. This is useful if you work in an office and want to ensure that no one tampers with your computer when you are away.

Managing Your Files

Files are the tofu and potatoes of any computer, and they need to be managed, copied, moved, renamed, grouped, and loaded. Included with Ubuntu is a powerful yet simple file manager called Nautilus that integrates tightly into your desktop. You'll use it all the time even if you don't often see the name.

Nautilus makes extensive use of drag and drop. Unlike the kind of file manager used in Windows with its tree view and listing of files, Nautilus displays files in a series of windows in which you can drag files around easily. For those who just can't say goodbye to the tree view, Nautilus also supports that. Aside from providing a simpler user interface, Nautilus also includes a number of useful features such as video and image previews, emblems, bookmarks, permissions management, and more.

How Linux Stores and Organizes Files

Before we use Nautilus, it is worthwhile to have a crash course in how files and folders are organized on a Linux system. If you have not used Linux before, this is likely to be new to you because the layout is quite different from Windows and Mac OS X.

TIP   **Folders and Directories**
When reading about file management, don't get confused by the terms *folders* and *directories*—*both* words describe the same thing.

In the Windows world, each disk drive is labeled with an identifying letter such as C: for your hard disk and A: for the floppy drive. In the Linux world, however, everything is part of the same filesystem organization. As such, if you have two or three hard disks, a CD drive, and a USB stick all plugged in, they will all be part of the same folder structure.

The diagram shown in Figure 3-37 should give you an idea of how everything hangs together.

Right at the top of the tree is the root folder, referred to as /. Inside this folder are a number of special system folders, each with a specific use. As an example, the /home folder contains a number of home directories for each user on the system. As such, the mako user account has the home folder set to /home/mako.

Which Folder Does What?   The folder structure in a modern Linux distribution such as Ubuntu was largely inspired by the original UNIX foundations that were created by men with large beards. Although you don't really need to know what these folders do, since Ubuntu looks after the housekeeping for you, some of you may be interested in the more important folders. For your pleasure, we present the Linux folder hit list in Table 3-1.

Configuration Files   In Table 3-1, /etc is described as storing systemwide configuration files for your computer. Aside from these files that affect everyone, there are also configuration files for each specific user. Earlier, when you customized Ubuntu's look and feel, the settings were applied only to your current user account. So where are those settings stored?

Inside your home directory are a number of folders that begin with a dot (.), such as .gnome2 and .openoffice2. These folders contain the configuration settings for specific applications for that specific user. By default,

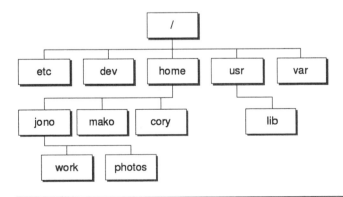

Figure 3-37 Linux filesystem organization

Table 3-1 Linux Folders

Folder	Use
/boot	This folder contains important files to boot the computer, including the bootloader configuration and the kernel.
/dev	Each device on your system (such as sound cards, Webcams, etc.) has an entry in this folder. Each application accesses the device by using the relevant items inside /dev.
/etc	Systemwide configuration files for the software installed on your system are stored here.
/home	Each user account on the system has a home directory that is stored here.
/lib	Important system software libraries are stored here. You should never need to delve into this world of the unknown.
/media	Media devices such as CD drives and USB sticks are referenced here when they are plugged in. More on this later.
/mnt	Other devices can be mounted, too. Again, more on this later.
/opt	Optional software can be installed here. This folder is usually used when you want to build your own software. If you don't build your own software, you ignore this folder.
/proc/sys	Information about the current running status of the system is stored here.
/root	This is the home directory for the main superuser.
/sbin	Software that should be run only by the superuser is stored here.
/usr	General software is installed here.
/var	This folder contains log files about the software on your computer.

these dot folders are hidden in Nautilus because you rarely need to access them. For future reference, you can view these hidden files and folders by clicking View > Show Hidden Files.

You can start Nautilus from a number of different places, but the easiest way to launch Nautilus is from the Places menu. Click on Places > Home Folder to load your home folder. When the folder loads, you should see something similar to what Figure 3-38 shows.

The Nautilus window is split into two parts. The sidebar shows categories of information such as bookmarks, folders, emblems (more on these later), and more. In the main part of the window, you can see the subfolders and

Figure 3-38 Accessing your home folder files is as simple as clicking Places > Home Folder.

files in the current folder. By default, Nautilus displays your bookmarks in the left sidebar and displays the contents of your home folder.

So, let's play with Nautilus and see what you can do with it. The first important skills to learn involve general file management. Many of the tasks you need to do can be achieved by right-clicking your file/folder and selecting the relevant option. There are also a number of options in the Edit menu.

First, create a folder right-clicking the main part of the window and selecting Create Folder. A folder is added, and you can type in the name of it. If you change your mind about the name, rename it by right-clicking and selecting Rename. If you double-click on a folder, you can access it and perform the same operations within that folder.

QUICK TIP   Just as folders and directories are the same thing, so are folders and subfolders . . . well, almost. When we refer to subfolders, we are referring to folders contained within another folder. For example, /home is a folder, while we can refer to /home/mako as a subfolder of /home.

Nautilus is also flexible in how your files are displayed. You can view the files and folders as either the default collection of icons or as a list. To switch to the list view, select View > View As List. You can also configure the organization of how your files and folders are displayed by right-clicking the main part of the window and selecting one of the options in the Arrange Items menu. Play with each of these options to see which ones work best for you.

QUICK TIP   Just like in the file dialog, Nautilus displays each of the different parts of the path as different buttons. As an example, /home/mako/work would have three buttons: home, mako, and work.

Selecting, Copying, and Moving Files and Folders

Copying and moving files and folders are simple tasks with Nautilus and can be done in a number of different ways. To test this, create two folders called Work and Invoices in your home directory. Save some files inside each folder. You can quickly create empty files by double-clicking the folder to go into it, right-clicking, selecting Create Document > Empty File, and renaming the file to something useful. With a couple of folders now complete with files in them, let's move them around.

One method is to use two windows. Right-click the Work folder, and select Open in New Window. You now have two windows open, one with the contents of Work and one with the contents of your home directory. Now copy the Invoices folder to the Work folder by clicking it and dragging it over to the second window (which shows the contents of Work). By default, dragging from one window to another copies the item.

Another option is to select what you want to copy and paste it. Selecting items can again be done in a number of ways. One method is to click each file/folder while holding down the Shift or Ctrl keys to make multiple selections. The difference between the two keys is that Shift allows you to select a number of files and folders next to each other, and Ctrl selects independent files and folders from anywhere in the folder-listing view. When you have selected what should be copied, right-click and select Cut or Copy. Cut will copy the original files but remove them, and Copy will just copy them while leaving the original files intact. Now go to the destination folder, right-click it, and select Paste. The files/folders are now added.

Using the Sidebar

The sidebar in Nautilus can be changed to a variety of views that should cater to virtually all tastes. Each of these different sidebar views has a range of functions. Table 3-2 explains each one.

Although you will probably stick with one in particular, it is not uncommon to switch between options to achieve a particular task. For this reason, the flexibility provided by the range of sidebar options is useful.

TIP   **Drag and Drop**
If you want to put something in the Places view, drag and drop the item. The Ubuntu desktop is filled with drag-and-drop shortcuts like this. If you think something could be dragged and dropped, try it!

Using Emblems

Emblems give you the ability to tag files and folders to indicate something. These small graphical icons are used to say that the file/folder falls into a particular category, visually signified by the emblem. As an example, you may want to tag a file to indicate it is a draft.

When you select the Emblems sidebar, a range of different emblems appears. To apply an emblem to a file/folder, just drag the emblem onto it. You can drag multiple emblems onto the files to indicate multiple things.

Table 3-2 The Different Nautilus Sidebar Options

Option	Feature
Places	(Default view) Includes the devices and bookmarks in the sidebar that you typically see in the file chooser.
Information	Displays some limited information about the current folder.
Tree	Displays a tree view similar to Windows/Mac OS X. Those of you who love the way Windows/Mac OS X works may want to use this.
History	Displays a history of the folders you have clicked on.
Notes	Allows you to write notes in the sidebar that are stored in the folder. This is handy when you need to explain or make comments about the current folder.
Emblems	Lists the files and folders that have specific emblems attached.

Ubuntu and Multimedia

In recent years, multimedia has become an essential part of computing. Watching DVDs and videos and listening to CDs and music have become part and parcel of the modern desktop computer experience. These multimedia capabilities have been further bolstered by the huge popularity of legal music downloading. With a range of online stores for a variety of different types of music, it is not uncommon to listen to most of your music without ever seeing a little shiny silver disk.

Installing Codecs

Multimedia files and disks come in a variety of different types, and each type uses a special codec to compress the content to a smaller size while retaining a particular level of quality. To play this media, you need to ensure that you have the relevant codecs installed. Ubuntu now makes this easier by suggesting packages that provide a suitable codec when you open a file that isn't supported by the ones that are currently installed. Simply double-click the file you want to open, and you should be provided with a list of packages that you can install to enable support for the file you have tried to open. Select the packages that seem appropriate, and click Install.

QUICK TIP   If you double-click a file but no packages are suggested, you may need to change the package filter in the top right-hand corner to All Available Applications.

Codecs still remain a problem for open source software because of the legal restrictions placed upon them. Certain codecs (including MP3, Windows Media Format, QuickTime, and RealMedia) are proprietary and as such have restrictions placed on their use, distribution, and licensing.

Although developers in the open source community have gone away and created free implementations of some of these codecs, the licensing that surrounds them conflicts with the legal and philosophical position that Ubuntu has set. These codecs are not included not only because they are legally dubious but also because they disagree with Ubuntu's ethic of creating a distribution that is entirely comprised of free software in the freest sense of the word.

QUICK TIP   If you want to find out more about installing these codecs, see https://wiki.ubuntu.com/RestrictedFormats.

To work toward resolving these problems, a number of developers are working on free codecs such as Ogg Vorbis and Ogg Theora that provide high-quality results and open licensing. The Ogg Vorbis codec is used on audio and can provide better results than MP3 at a smaller file size. The Ogg Theora codec is used for video and competes with the MPEG-4 codec. Ubuntu includes the Ogg Vorbis and Ogg Theora codecs by default, and you can encode and play back any media that uses those codecs out of the box.

Although the world would be a better place if all codecs were free, the reality is different, and many Ubuntu users still want to play media compressed with proprietary codecs. Table 3-3 shows the most typical codecs used to encode and play back media and lists their support in Ubuntu.

Listening to Audio Files

Ubuntu includes a powerful music player called Rhythmbox to organize and play your music file collection. By default, Ubuntu will look for music in the Music directory accessible in the Places menu.

Table 3-3 Codec Support

Codec	File Type	Included	Supported
MP3	.MP3	No	Yes
Ogg	.ogg	Yes	N/A
Windows Media Audio	.wma	No	Yes*
Wave	.wav	Yes	N/A
MPEG-1	.mpg	No	Yes
MPEG-2	.mpg	No	Yes
Raw DV	.dv	Yes	N/A
Quicktime	.mov	No	Yes*
Windows Media Video	.wmv	No	Yes*

* These codecs involve the installation of nonfree software that may or may not be legal in your country.

Using Rhythmbox   Load Rhythmbox (Figure 3-39) by clicking on Applications > Sound & Video > Rhythmbox Music Player. The Rhythmbox window is split into a number of different panes, each displaying different details about your music collection. The left pane (Source) lets you select the source of the music, such as your media library, podcasts, and Internet radio. Each of these options has a browser pane available to display the source of the content. As an example, when you use the Library, one pane displays the artists and one displays the albums. You can use this to navigate your music.

Listening to Podcasts   Podcasts are audio shows that you can subscribe to, and they are increasingly becoming the new way to listen to audio and music. When you subscribe to a podcast, each new release is automatically downloaded for you. This makes it extremely convenient to regularly listen to audio shows.

If you are new to podcasting, you should grab yourself a podcast feed of something you like. A site such as www.podcast.net is a good place to start.

Figure 3-39 Rhythmbox is a great place to look after your music collection.

Go to the site in Firefox, and when you see a link that indicates a podcast feed or RSS feed, right-click it and select Copy Link Location.

Rhythmbox has good support for Podcast feeds, and subscribing to a feed is simple. In the sidebar, right-click the Podcasts entry and click New Podcast Feed. Paste in the feed by right-clicking the box and selecting Paste. The files are automatically downloaded, and you can listen to them by double-clicking on them. Each time you start Rhythmbox, a check is made to see if any new episodes exist, and if so, they are downloaded.

NOTE   **Rhythmbox and iPods**
Rhythmbox can also read songs from your iPod—just plug it in and it will display in Rhythmbox. Rhythmbox can read from the iPod but may not be able to write to all iPods..

Playing and Ripping CDs

When you pop a CD into your CD drive, Audio CD Extractor (Sound Juicer) automatically loads to play your CD. If you are connected to the Internet, the CD is looked up on the Internet, and the album details and song titles are displayed.

Ripping Songs as Oggs   Sound Juicer is not just a CD player but a ripper too. Using a ripper you can convert the songs on the CD into files that you can play on your computer. By default, Sound Juicer rips the files in the Ogg format, which provides better sound quality than MP3 at a smaller size. By default, the ripped files are stored in the format discussed earlier, with each artist as a folder and albums as subfolders.

To rip the songs, just select the checkboxes of the songs you want ripped (by default, all songs are selected), and then click Extract. Each song is then stored in your Music folder, and the song titles are used as the names of the files.

Ripping Songs as MP3s   Although the default Ogg support is recommended in most situations, you may prefer to rip MP3 files if you have a digital audio player that does not support Ogg files. To do this, you need to configure Sound Juicer to enable MP3 support.

You should first install the gstreamer0.10-plugins-ugly-multiverse package (see Chapter 4 for more details on installing packages). Next, in Sound Juicer, click Edit > Preferences and choose the CD Quality, MP3 (MP3 audio) profile from the Output Format options.

Watching Videos

To watch videos in Ubuntu, you need to ensure that you have the correct codecs installed. As discussed earlier, some of these codecs are available separately due to the legal implications of including them with the Ubuntu system. Although the new process for suggesting and installing codecs should cover most popular types of files, you should still refer to the Ubuntu wiki at http://wiki.ubuntu.com for details of how to install ones that are not recognized.

Using Totem   To watch videos in Ubuntu, you use the Totem media player (Figure 3-40). Load it by clicking Applications > Sound & Video > Movie Player.

Figure 3-40 Totem is a simple and flexible media player.

To watch a video on your hard disk, click Movie > Open, and select the file from the disk.

TIP **Another Way to Load Files into Totem**
You can also load multimedia files into Totem by double-clicking them on your desktop or in the file manager.

Totem also supports video streams. To watch a stream, click Movie > Open Location, and enter the Internet address for the stream. The video feed is then loaded and displayed.

Getting DVDs to Work Ubuntu comes with DVD support for unencrypted DVDs. With the DVD industry being what it is, the majority of DVDs come encrypted, and if you want to watch them, you need to ensure that a library that can decrypt these DVDs is installed. Unfortunately, this library needs to be installed separately and is not included with Ubuntu. Refer to the Ubuntu wiki restricted formats page at https://wiki.ubuntu.com/RestrictedFormats for details.

With the library installed, insert a disk into your computer, and Ubuntu will automatically start Totem to view the disk. Alternatively, fire up Totem, and click Movie > Play Disk to play the DVD. Totem doesn't support DVD menus but you can still use it to play a DVD.

If you are settling down to watch a movie, you may want to configure a few other settings. First click View > Aspect Ratio to select the correct aspect ratio for your screen, and then select View > Fullscreen to switch to full screen mode. To exit full screen, just move your mouse, and some on-screen controls will appear.

TIP **Control Totem with a Remote Control**
Totem supports the Linux Infrared Control (LIRC) library so you can use a remote control while watching your media.

Summary

In this chapter you've learned how to start using the core features of your new desktop. These concepts should allow you to perform most of the day-to-day tasks when using your computer and provide a base from which to explore the other applications installed on your system. This solid grounding in the desktop paves the way for you to meander through the rest of the book, learning about the more advanced uses of your new system and exploring the enormous flexibility that Ubuntu provides.

Always remember that there is a wealth of help and documentation available online. If you ever find yourself stuck, take a look at the Ubuntu Web site at www.ubuntu.com or the Ubuntu documentation at http://help.ubuntu.com and make use of the forums, wiki, mailing lists, and IRC channels.

CHAPTER 4

Advanced Usage and Managing Ubuntu

- Adding and Removing Programs and Packages
- Keeping Your Computer Updated
- Moving to the Next Ubuntu Release
- Using and Abusing Devices and Media
- Configuring a Printer in Ubuntu
- Graphically Accessing Remote Files
- The Terminal
- Backup Stategies
- Working with Windows
- Summary

AS YOU'VE SEEN SO FAR, Ubuntu is relatively straightforward to set up and use for the common day-to-day tasks. With time, though, most users want to change their software, add and experiment with other software options available in Ubuntu, install and use hardware devices like printers, access remote files, use the famous (and sometimes feared) terminal, and maybe even run some Windows programs. Ubuntu provides many ways to do each of these things. While they are a little more complex than the material covered in previous chapters, the Ubuntu community has worked hard to make them as easy as possible, and this chapter gets you started with each of them and more.

Adding and Removing Programs and Packages

While Ubuntu already includes the things most people need, sometimes you want or need something extra, such as a desktop publishing application for school or a game to pass the time. The easiest way to add these is with Add/Remove Applications, which is extremely simple to use but has a few limitations.

Installing and Using Add/Remove Applications

Like Synaptic and the other tools discussed later in this chapter, Add/Remove Applications installs software from the same online Ubuntu software repositories. Using one tool to add or remove software will be recognized by the other, related tools.

To launch Add/Remove Applications, simply click on the Add/Remove entry at the bottom of the Applications menu. When it is run for the first time, and occasionally afterward, it will take a few moments to initialize itself and the list of available and installed applications. Once this is complete, you will see the main screen shown in Figure 4-1.

The interface is divided into three parts. On the left is a list of all the various types of applications, laid out in the same way as the menu. Select a category to see a list of all the applications in that category in the upper right. Selecting an application in the upper right section will display a description in the lower right section of what that program does.

In addition to the categories, Add/Remove Applications also allows you to filter the list with searches. Search results are based on the program name,

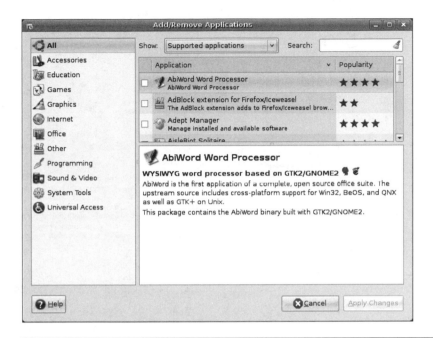

Figure 4-1 Add/Remove Applications main screen

the package name, or the description of the program. Enter the search term into the text box in the upper right, and it will search as you type. Figure 4-2 shows an example of search bar results.

By default, Add/Remove Applications will show only applications that are supported by Ubuntu. While this is a large list, there are even more to find. By changing the option in the box labeled Show in the top, you will be able to see all the programs available to you.

Additionally, Add/Remove Applications can list proprietary applications, those applications that are not released under a free software or open source license. Change the Show option accordingly, and they will become visible both via the listing and through search. As with any other application, they can be clicked to install, although similar to community-supported applications, you may be asked to confirm your intention to install the application. When you attempt to install an application that is community supported or has a restricted license, you will be asked to confirm your intention to do so (Figure 4-3).

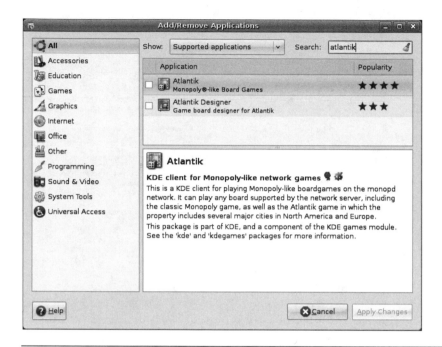

Figure 4-2 Search bar with results

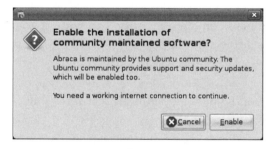

Figure 4-3 Confirming your intention to install a community-supported package

Terminology

You might need to know a few terms before you start, such as words used to describe how the software gets installed on your machine as well as how the system works.

- **APT:** Advanced Package Tool, or APT, describes the entire system of online repositories and the parts that download them and install them.

- **Repositories or software channels:** In the Ubuntu world, these giant online warehouses of software are divided between official Ubuntu repositories and nonofficial ones.

- **Packages:** Applications are stored in packages that not only describe the program you want to install but also tell your package manager what the program needs to run and how to safely install and uninstall it.

Installing with Synaptic

Synaptic is a powerful graphical tool called a package manager. While Add/Remove Applications deals with packages that contain applications, Synaptic deals with all packages, including applications, system libraries, and other pieces of software. Changing the system on this level is more difficult but allows more detailed control. For instance, you can choose to install a specific library if you need it for a program that is not available in a package format.

To find Synaptic, look under the System menu and then the Administration menu. It is listed as Synaptic Package Manager. Launch the task by clicking on the icon, and you will see the main window, as shown in Figure 4-4.

TIP **What's in a Name?**
Why the name Synaptic? *Synaptic* is a play on words, based on the word *apt*, which is the Debian package management system. Ubuntu is based on Debian and also uses APT.

Synaptic works a little differently from Add/Remove Applications. Unlike Add/Remove Applications, Synaptic deals directly with packages, which allows for a greater level of control while exposing the details of how package management works.

Installing a Package As with Add/Remove Applications, installing packages with Synaptic is fairly easy. After you find the package you wish to install, click the checkbox to the right of the name of the package and select Mark for Installation. A dialog box may pop up (Figure 4-5) showing you what else needs to be installed—if anything—which you can

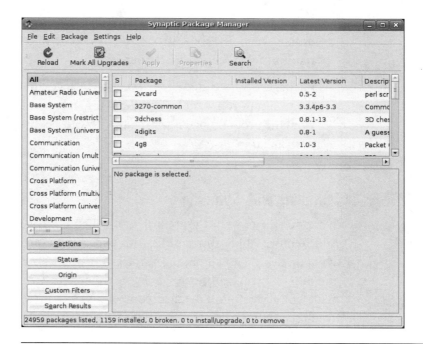

Figure 4-4 Synaptic main window

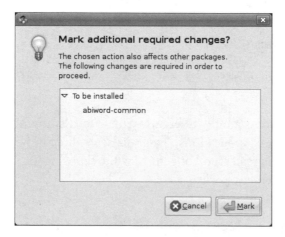

Figure 4-5 Pop-up on Mark for Installation

accept by clicking the Mark button. After you have selected the package(s) you wish to install, click Apply on the Synaptic toolbar to begin installation.

Removing a Package To remove a package, click on the green box, and choose Mark for Removal. As with installing a package, you may be asked to mark additional packages for removal (Figure 4-6). If you wish to remove all the configuration files too, choose Mark for Complete Removal. After you have selected the packages you wish to remove, click Apply on the toolbar to start the actual process of removing the package.

Finding That Package So you are looking for a package but don't know where to start? The fastest and easiest way is to simply click the Search button on the toolbar or type Ctrl-F. That will launch a search dialog box. By default, it searches both the package name and the description, but it can also search just by name or a number of other fields.

If you know what section the package is in, select it in the left pane (you may need to go back to the Sections pane). Select the button in the lower right labeled Sections, and browse through the packages in that section. The upper right pane also has a neat feature called Type-ahead (Figure 4-7).

Figure 4-6 Pop-up on Mark for Removal

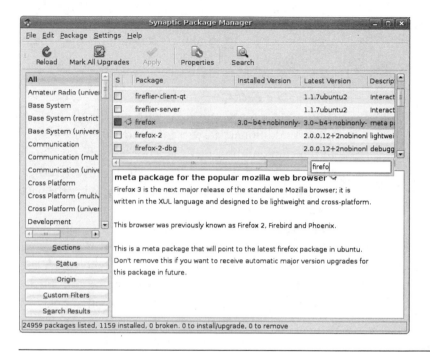

Figure 4-7 Type-ahead

Simply select any package, and then start typing the first few letters of the package name. The cursor should jump right to that section.

Keeping Your Computer Updated

No OS or piece of software is perfect. This means that Ubuntu developers release a number of security and other updates. These come as needed and are quite easy to install.

Most of the updates to your machine will be security related. This means that the developers have found a weakness in a particular program in Ubuntu and have released a fix for it. There will also be a small number of updates to fix some critical bugs. For a home user, there is generally no reason not to install these right away, as not installing them might leave your computer open to security breaches, virus infection, or worse. Ubuntu developers also have a very strict policy about not putting new versions of programs into stable versions of Ubuntu, which keeps your system more stable by not introducing new problems.

Installing Updates

Helpfully, Ubuntu will tell you when you need to update your machine.

Ubuntu 9.04 handles package updates by launching update-manager directly instead of displaying a notification icon in the GNOME panel as was done in earlier versions. Users are still notified of security updates on a daily basis, but for updates that are not security-related, users will only be notified once a week.

Learning about What Was Updated

The update window, shown in Figure 4-8, will also show you specifically what is going to be fixed. In the details pane, it will show you what got fixed and how. It might also list a CVE number. The CVE number is a unique identifier for a security vulnerability. You can look it up on

Figure 4-8 The update window

http://cve.mitre.org to see what the exact flaw was. However, most people don't need to worry (and really don't care) about these details.

Using Synaptic to Check for Updates

You can use Synaptic not only to manage packages but also to check for updates. When you launch Synaptic, it will ask you for your password. After it starts, first click on the Reload button in the upper left. This will prompt Synaptic to check the repositories for new updates. After it has finished, click Mark All Upgrades. This will prompt Synaptic to mark all software upgrades as those you want to install. If Synaptic does not tell you there are any updates to be made, everything is already up-to-date. If something requires updating, it will tell you which packages need to be updated. Close the window, and then click Apply. This will install any needed upgrades.

Sometimes the updater will tell you that it cannot update certain programs. This is because updating those programs would require the removal or addition of certain packages on the system. This is where Synaptic comes in. Synaptic can do what is called a smart update, which will figure out what needs to be added or removed. Synaptic will perform smart updates by default, and then you can just update as described in the previous paragraph. You can confirm that this feature is activated by going to Settings > Preferences (Figure 4-9). Make certain that the System Upgrade option is set to Smart Upgrade.

Moving to the Next Ubuntu Release

So now your system is up to date, but Ubuntu doesn't like to let the grass grow. One of the original goals for Ubuntu was to have frequent releases, and with only one notable exception (the 6.06 LTS release, which was delayed by two months), there have been six months between each release since 4.10. This book has been revised for the latest version—9.04—but another one will be along soon. Release 8.04 and the earlier 6.06 are both Long Term Support (LTS) versions of Ubuntu, supported for three years on the desktop and five on the server. All other versions are supported for eighteen months and are superseded by a new version every six months. Essentially, if you are running the LTS version, you might not be too interested in moving to the latest and greatest until the next LTS version comes out.

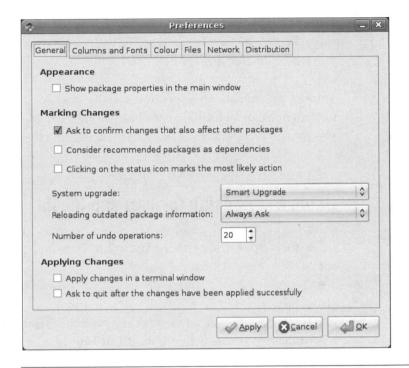

Figure 4-9 Synaptic preferences

Doing the Actual Upgrade

Since Ubuntu 6.06 was released, upgrading is far easier because of a graphical tool that tells you when a new version of Ubuntu is available and walks you through the upgrade process. Note that if you already know or want to learn the manual method, that is fine, too. Both means will achieve the same result.

When a new release is available, the update manager will tell you that a new version is available. All you need to do is click on the Upgrade button to start the process. You will first be shown the release notes, which mention new features or any outstanding bugs. After you click on the Upgrade button on this screen, the necessary changes to your software repositories are made, and then the program will download and install the new distribution. You may be prompted if you have changed any configuration files. After the actual installation is complete, you will be told which, if any, packages are no longer officially supported by Ubuntu (have moved to the universe repository). Last, all you need to do is restart your computer when prompted, and you will begin enjoying the new release.

You can also initiate an upgrade simply by inserting a CD that contains a newer version of Ubuntu than the one you are currently running. Follow the prompts for an upgrade experience similar to using the update manager.

Using and Abusing Devices and Media

With the increasingly cheap prices of hardware and media, typical computer users are burning more and more CDs and using USB memory sticks.

Using these kinds of devices in Ubuntu is simple and intuitive. In the vast majority of cases, you just plug them in and they work. Each device needs to be mounted before it can be used, but Ubuntu automatically mounts it for you. The main point to remember is to always unmount the device before you remove it. Even floppy disks should be properly unmounted before they are removed. Unmounting a device ensures all data has been copied to it before you pull it out.

> **TIP** **Problems Unmounting**
> If you have problems unmounting a device, make sure that you are not currently using it. As an example, if you have an open file manager window looking at the files on the device, it is currently being used and, as such, cannot be unmounted. As a general rule, just make sure you close everything down from the device and everything will be fine.

If at any time you are unsure which devices are plugged into your computer, click Places > Computer to see a list of the drives available.

Using USB Keyring Drives

In the last few years, USB keyrings, pens, and sticks have taken over as the common method for moving files between different computers. These cheap and often high-capacity little devices offer a simple and efficient way to carry your files with you. Although they come in many different shapes and forms, they all basically work the same way in Ubuntu.

Using USB storage devices in Ubuntu is a piece of cake. Just plug them in and a moment or two later, an icon representing the device appears on your desktop. A file manager window also appears to display the contents of the device. You can interact with the device and the files as you would with the files on your hard disk.

When you have finished using your USB device, right-click the device icon that appeared on your desktop and select Unmount. When the icon disappears from your desktop, you can safely remove it from the USB port.

TIP   **Copy Your Files to the Hard Disk**
USB comes in two major forms: USB1 and USB2, with the latter being much faster. If you have a multimedia file like an audio or video clip or another large file, you may want to copy it to a hard disk before you load it. Hard disks provide far faster load times than these other media.

Burning CDs

Burning files is simple in Ubuntu with its built-in support for CD writers. Simply place a writable CD into the drive, and an icon appears on the desktop. Double-click the icon, and an empty file manager window appears. Now drag the files to be burned into this window. When you are ready to burn the CD, click File > Write to Disk.

A dialog box appears, and you can configure a few items before the disk is burned. Enter a name for the disk in the Disk Name box, and use the Write Speed combo box to select the best write speed for your drive. If you have an old or unreliable CD writer, you may want to select a slower speed to prevent a burn error. Finally, click the Write Disk button to start the burn.

QUICK TIP   You can also access the burner by clicking Places > CD/DVD Burner.

Burning a CD from an Image   With more and more people downloading open source software, installation disks are often released as downloadable

.iso files. When you burn these files to a CD, the files from the disk image are restored and the resulting CD looks just like a normal CD.

To burn an .iso file to a CD, simply right-click it and select Write to Disk.

TIP   **More Complex Burning**
If you are looking for a complete application to cater to virtually all CD burning needs, install the GNOME Baker application using Synaptic or Add/Remove Applications.

Using Floppy Disks

To use a floppy disk in Ubuntu, insert the disk in the drive and then select Places > Computer. Now double-click on your floppy drive to mount it and display the files. When you have finished using the disk, right-click the floppy drive and select Unmount.

Using Digital Cameras

When you plug a digital camera into your computer, a device icon automatically appears on your desktop, and Ubuntu pops up a window asking if you want to view the photos from your camera. You can then view the photos and drag them from the photo viewer window over to a file manager window to save the photo.

Always remember that the majority of digital cameras are just USB devices, and you can access the photos like any other USB device from within the file manager.

TIP   **Ubuntu and Digital Photography**
Ubuntu is a fantastic platform for digital photography and photo manipulation. F-Spot tool provides a complete solution for managing your photo collection and can be started by clicking on Applications > Graphics > F-Spot Photo Manager.

For photo manipulation, GIMP provides a comprehensive tool and is installed by default. Load it by clicking Applications > Graphics > GIMP Image Editor.

Configuring a Printer in Ubuntu

In the Linux world, configuring a printer has traditionally been a challenge. For years, newcomers to Linux have been repeatedly challenged and even bludgeoned with terms, commands, and phrases such as CUPS, lpd, and "edit/etc/cups/printers.conf as root." Users often had to edit fairly complex text files by hand and spend a good deal of time learning how to insert arcane instructions just to get a printer to work. However, things have changed with Ubuntu.

Making It Easier with Printer Configurations

Although you may encounter some challenges, Ubuntu has made configuring a standard home printer much easier with the Printer configuration application. Using the application, you can usually configure both locally attached printers and those that reside on a remote networked system quickly and easily. You can run this application by pointing your mouse to the System > Administration menu, and then clicking on the Printing option, as shown in Figure 4-10.

Selecting this option will bring up the Printers window, as shown in Figure 4-11.

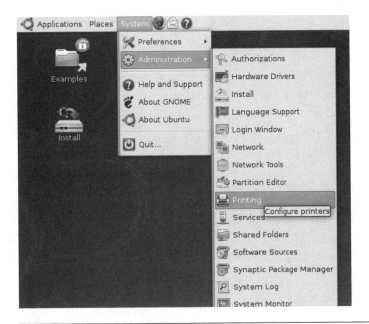

Figure 4-10 Selecting the Printing application from the System > Administration menu in Ubuntu

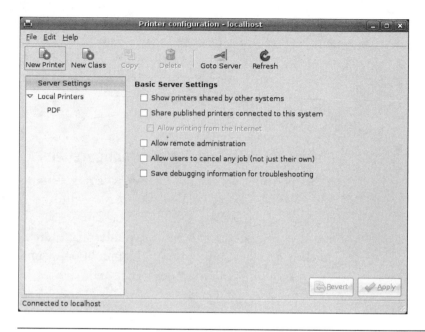

Figure 4-11 The GNOME Printers dialog box

Notice that no printers are defined. You are about to change this.

The Printer configuration application allows you to add printers, as well as modify their settings. You can also use this application to add and configure your printers. In the upcoming example, you will add a new printer and then view its settings.

Gathering Information

The most important thing to remember when configuring a printer is to not get ahead of yourself. Before you start clicking on icons and running anything, make sure that you have completed the following steps.

1. Obtain the make and model of the printer. In our example, we add a Lexmark Z33.

2. Plug in the printer, and turn it on.

Launching the Wizard

Once you have properly prepared to install your printer, click on the New Printer icon. The system will then automatically search for any new connected printers and will launch a New Printer wizard, shown in Figure 4-12.

In most cases, the wizards will be able to detect an attached printer automatically and will include it in a list of devices on the left. Select the device with your printer's name, and then hit forward.

At this point, you will have to choose a printer manufacturer. If your printer has been automatically detected, the wizard will choose a manufacturer. Click forward.

In the next screen, you'll be asked to choose both a model and a driver. For autodetected printers, both should be automatically selected, and the default driver should work. You can always change it later. If no driver is selected, scroll through the list of options by manufacturer. Figure 4-13 shows that a driver for the Lexmark Z33 (using the Z32 driver) has been selected.

Sometimes you may not find the exact model or driver for your exact printer, as this case shows. For example, the printer being used is a Lexmark Z33, but the Z32 driver is selected because no Z33 driver exists.

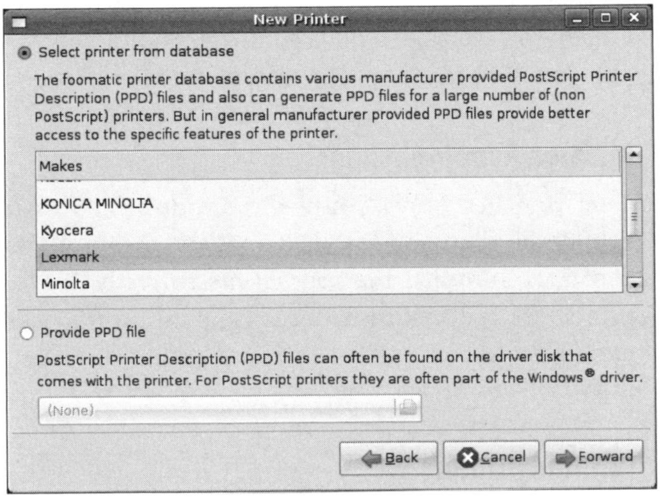

Figure 4-12 Step 1, selecting a printer

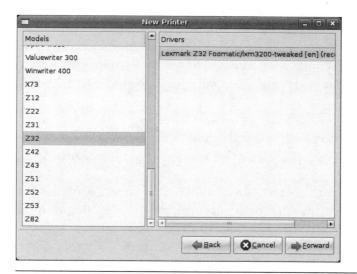

Figure 4-13 Step 2, selecting a driver

Generally, if the driver does not exist for your exact model, choose the closest one, and then test it. If that doesn't work, try other drivers.

Click Forward to proceed with the installation. If you need to install a custom driver, click the Install Driver button. You can see this button in Figure 4-13.

Finally, you can enter a description and location for your printer, as shown in Figure 4-14. Click Apply to complete the process and set up your printer.

Mission Accomplished!

After you click Apply, you will see your printer's name under the Local Printers heading. You can click on it and then print out a test page. Do so, and make sure that the page prints correctly. If you find that the page prints well, you are finished. You can now print from the applications you have installed. For example, you can print from OpenOffice.org, Mozilla, or even the command line.

Remote Printing

You can also configure your Ubuntu system to send print jobs to a remote print server. If, for example, you have a Windows system with a printer

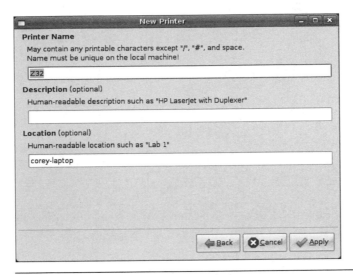

Figure 4-14 Step 3, entering printer location and description

attached on your network, simply choose the Network Printer radio button and specify the host name or IP address of the Windows system. You will then have to specify a connection protocol.

If your Windows system is sharing a printer, you will have to specify Samba, which is the standard way to get Linux and Windows systems to communicate with each other. You will still have to specify a print driver, as described earlier.

Graphically Accessing Remote Files

Within the Ubuntu desktop, you can use the same powerful file manager to manage files that are on a remote server, either on your local network or in far-flung parts of the world via the Internet. This feature is incredibly useful when you need to transfer lots of files around, such as when you work on Web pages or need to make your work remotely available to someone else. To access these files, you can connect to the server in various ways, each of which requires a connection profile. This profile configures the connection, and you will need to gather your server's settings to create it.

To set up the connection, click Places > Connect to Server, and you will see the dialog shown in Figure 4-15.

Figure 4-15 Access your remote server's files graphically on your desktop.

When the dialog box appears, select the type of connection from the combo box. The box then adjusts to display the settings required, and you should make sure the Name to Use for Connection box contains a descriptive name for the connection, such as "Work Server" or "Web Site." When you have added the settings, click the Connect button to continue.

An icon now appears on your desktop for the connection. Double-click the icon, and you are asked for a password to the server. Enter this password, and you are then asked if you would like to store your passwords in the keyring. The desktop keyring provides a convenient place to store all of your connection passwords, and you need to remember only the password for the keyring itself. If you choose to store the password in the keyring, you are asked for a password for it. In the future, whenever you double-click the icon to access the server, you will be asked for the keyring password.

When you have been authenticated to access the server, your files appear in a file manager window, and you can use the file manager as normal.

The Terminal

Although Ubuntu is a desktop-driven OS, the system is running on a powerful and incredibly flexible command-line core. Inspired by more than 30 years of UNIX heritage, the command-line environment present on Linux systems enables you to perform some incredibly powerful tasks by stringing together different commands in different ways.

The philosophy behind UNIX is to create a large number of small tools, each of which is designed to do one task but do it incredibly well. As a quick example to whet your appetite, there is a command called ls that does nothing more than list files in a folder. Although listing files is its singular function in life, it has every option imaginable for listing files.

Now, ls is limited by itself, but it can be combined with other commands that have equal levels of flexibility to create impressively powerful combinations. To do this, a *pipeline* is created using the | symbol to connect these different commands. Pipelines can be constructed in any number of different ways, and once the user has even a basic knowledge of what a few different commands do, stringing together a pipeline of commands can solve virtually any task you can imagine in quick and powerful ways.

It should be made 100 percent clear that using the command line is *not* an essential skill required to use Ubuntu, but it is a skill that can increase the flexibility of your computer for more advanced, customized tasks. Rather than cover the use of the terminal here, we have included an excellent introduction in Appendix A.

Backup Strategies

Everyone who has used a computer for any length of time has heard the advice, "Backup, backup often, test the backups, repeat." Few people actually do it. Ignoring this advice is dangerous and can cause the loss of important documents, files, pictures, and more.

To prevent this loss, prudent computer users, regardless of operating system, will pick a method of copying their files to a safe location for storage and will use that method on a regular basis. To help you devise a strategy that best suits you, we have come up with a few options to consider. This topic is a big one, and how you deal with it is a very personal decision. Rather than give step-by-step instructions, we mention a few options to consider and leave it to you to research them further and decide on one that looks appropriate and inviting.

Some users find that the easiest thing for them to do is copy all of their files to a CD-R or DVD-R every week or two. Others buy an external hard drive and do the same thing. Either of these methods is effective and easy enough for anyone to do.

Others will look at this and think to themselves, "There has to be a better way." Perhaps they noticed that these methods require every single file to be copied every time, even if the file has not changed in ages. In these cases, an incremental backup is ideal, where the computer is told to compare the files in the original location with stored files in a backup location (like an external hard drive) and copy only new or changed files.

For these users, we recommend looking into the following graphic user interface programs from the Ubuntu repositories: pybackpack, sbackup, or grsync. Each comes with a basic and useful graphic interface that is easy to figure out and use, and each is configurable to allow you to do full or incremental backups.

For those users who are a little more advanced (or a little braver) and who love the raw power available from learning a command-line program, the best two programs for backups are rar and rsync, which are both available from the Ubuntu repositories. Once they are installed, you can read the manual page and learn how to use them by typing man rar or man rsync from a terminal. They are complicated but are also fast and amazingly effective both at making the backups and restoring them.

Unfortunately, this quick mention in a small section of a very diverse chapter can only get you thinking about the need for good backups and help guide you in your search for the perfect method for you. However you decide to back up your data, we strongly encourage you not to ignore the need but to find a way to do it. If you have any questions about this or other topics, the Ubuntu community has a large number of very helpful people you can ask for help, and we recommend you start by searching or asking questions in the Ubuntu Forums at http://ubuntuforums.org/.

Working with Windows

Although the Linux platform offers an increasingly compelling platform for the desktop, there are sometimes situations when there is just no alternative application available. This is often the case with specific business applications, some educational tools, and games. Luckily, you can run many of these applications right on top of your Ubuntu desktop.

For the last twelve years, the members of the Wine project have been beavering away to create a free software implementation to run Windows applications on Linux. They have made great strides in getting more and more applications to run. Although there are still quirks here and there, many programs run perfectly under Wine. It is recommended that you try the applications you want to run before you use them for important work.

Install the Wine package with the Add/Remove Applications menu option or the Synaptic package manager. When the package has downloaded and installed, run the `winecfg` tool. To do this, press Alt-F2, and type `winecfg`. This small program sets up your Wine environment and provides some options for configuring how your Wine system is run. The default settings should be suitable for most applications.

Running Applications

To run an application, right-click it, and select Open with Wine Windows Emulator. Most Windows applications need to be installed before use, so first right-click the setup program, and run it under Wine. When the program is installed, you can find it in the .wine/c_drive/Program Files folder in your home folder. Navigate to that directory (making sure you turn on hidden file viewing in Nautilus), and run any files with an .exe extension.

Using Windows Files on Another Partition

For those of you with a considerable amount of your life present on Windows partitions, you may want to be able to access these partitions from Ubuntu. This is no problem, although you will need to edit a special configuration file to do this. Luckily, you need to edit this file only once, and then everything will be set up.

Ubuntu should automatically recognize any Windows partitions you have on your computer and set them up for you; however, you may need to modify them or add your own. You should first load System > Administration > Disks and write down the partition numbers and filesystem for your Windows partitions. The partition number will look something like /dev/hdb1 or /dev/sdb1, and the filesystem will be either FAT, VFAT, or NTFS.

The next step is to create some mount points. When your Windows partitions are enabled, they are accessed via a particular folder in Ubuntu. This is called a mount point. So, as an example, if you have a mount point as /media/win1 and on your Windows partition you want to access your Work folder, you would access it from Ubuntu as /media/win1/work.

Mount points usually live in the /media folder. Create a different mount point for each windows partition. As an example, if you have three Windows partitions, run the following commands:

```
foo@bar:~$ sudo mkdir /media/win1
foo@bar:~$ sudo mkdir /media/win2
foo@bar:~$ sudo mkdir /media/win3
```

Now open up the following configuration file:

```
foo@bar:~$ sudo gedit /etc/fstab
```

The /etc/fstab file maps partition numbers to mount points. At the bottom of the file add a line like this for each mount point:

```
/dev/hdb1 media/win1 vfat users,rw,owner,umask=000 0 0
```

You will need to change the partition number (the first column), mount point (second column), and filesystem (third column) for your relevant partitions.

Now reload /etc/fstab to enable the partitions:

```
foo@bar:~$ sudo mount -a
```

Some hard disk icons for the new partitions now appear.

Summary

In this chapter we looked at a variety of different advanced subjects related to running and managing your Ubuntu system. Installation, removal, and upgrade of software using the Add/Remove Applications dialog and using Synaptic were discussed. We also discussed the installation and use of several different types of hardware devices, including an in-depth look at printing. We perused some of the methods of accessing remote files and mentioned the powerful Ubuntu terminal and the need for learning how to back up your data regularly. Finally, we looked at a possibility of running certain programs written for Microsoft Windows under Ubuntu.

CHAPTER 5

The Ubuntu Server

- **What Is Ubuntu Server?**
- **Installing Ubuntu Server**
- **Ubuntu Package Management**
- **Ubuntu Server Security**
- **Advanced Topics**
- **Summary**

UBUNTU 4.10, LOVINGLY KNOWN AS WARTY WARTHOG, was the first public version of Ubuntu. Its installation media provided no obvious way to install the bare-bones OS without a full desktop environment. The system administrator crowds, easily irritable and feisty by nature, were greatly annoyed: They proclaimed Ubuntu was just a desktop distribution and sauntered back to their caves in contempt.

The next release of Ubuntu that came out, Hoary Hedgehog, rectified the problem and allowed for trivial installation of a minimal Ubuntu version suitable for servers. Yet the myth of Ubuntu as a purely desktop-oriented distribution stuck.

Luckily, the sentiment is just that—a myth. Ubuntu is a world-class server platform today, providing everything you'd expect from a server OS and with the human flavor that makes Ubuntu different. The dedicated hackers on the Ubuntu Server Team tend to the minutiae of hardware support and testing, mercilessly beat on the latest version of server software to make sure it's up to snuff for inclusion in the distribution, look for ways to push innovation into the server field, and are available to users like you to field feedback, questions, and cries of anguish.

That said, setting up a server is no small task. Server administrators constantly deal with complex issues such as system security, fault tolerance, and data safety, and while Ubuntu makes these issues more pleasant to deal with, they're not to be taken lightly. The aim of this chapter is thus not to teach you how to be a system administrator—we could easily fill a dozen books attempting to do that—but to give you a quick crash course. We'll also highlight the specific details that set Ubuntu Server apart from other server platforms, offer tips on some of the most common server uses, and give you pointers on where to find other relevant information.

What Is Ubuntu Server?

By far the most common reaction from users first encountering Ubuntu Server is one of utter and hopeless confusion. People are foggy on whether Ubuntu Server is a whole new distribution or an Ubuntu derivative like Kubuntu (only for servers) or perhaps something else entirely.

Let's clear things up a bit. The primary software store for Ubuntu and official derivatives is called the Ubuntu archive. The archive is merely a collection of software packages in Debian "deb" format, and it contains every single package that makes up distributions such as Ubuntu, Edubuntu, Xubuntu, Kubuntu, and Ubuntu Server. What makes Kubuntu separate from Ubuntu, then, is only the set of packages from the archive that its installer installs by default and that its CDs carry.

Ubuntu Server is no different. It depends on the very same archive as the standard Ubuntu distribution, but it installs a distinctive set of default packages. Notably, the set of packages comprising Ubuntu Server is very small. The installer will not install things such as a graphical environment or many user programs by default. But since all the packages for Ubuntu Server come from the same official Ubuntu archive, you can install any package you like later. In theory, there's nothing stopping you from transforming an Ubuntu Server install into a regular Ubuntu desktop installation or vice versa (in practice, this is tricky, and we don't recommend you try it). You can even go from running Kubuntu to running Ubuntu Server. The archive paradigm gives you maximum flexibility.

We've established that Ubuntu Server just provides a different set of default packages than Ubuntu. But what's important about that different set? What makes Ubuntu Server a server platform?

The most significant difference is a custom server kernel. This kernel employs an internal timer frequency of 100Hz instead of the desktop default of 250Hz, uses the deadline I/O scheduler instead of the desktop's CFQ scheduler, and contains a batch of other minor tweaks for virtualization, memory support, and routing. We'll spare you the OS theory: The idea is to offer some extra performance and throughput for server applications. In addition, the server kernel supports basic NUMA, a memory design used in some multiprocessor systems that can dramatically increase multiprocessing performance.

So what else is different in Ubuntu Server? Other than the server kernel and a minimal set of packages, not too much. Though Ubuntu has supported a minimal installation mode for a number of releases, spinning off Ubuntu Server into a separate product that truly stands on its own is still a young effort, but one that's moving along very quickly.

Starting with Ubuntu Server 6.06 LTS, known as Dapper Drake, Ubuntu Server offers officially supported packages for the Red Hat Cluster Suite, Red Hat's Global File System (GFS), Oracle's OCFS2 filesystem, and the Linux Virtual Server utilities: keepalived and ipvsadm. Combined with the specialized server kernel, these bits already let you use your Ubuntu Server for some heavy lifting. And there's a growing lineup of compelling features, including built-in virtualization, interoperability with Windows machines on the network through Samba, automatic version control for configuration files, support for LDAP directory services, hard drive replication over the network, and even a healthy dose of the latest buzzword—cloud computing.

Installing Ubuntu Server

So you've downloaded your Ubuntu Server CD from http://releases. ubuntu.com/9.04/ and burned it, eagerly placed it in your CD drive, and rebooted the machine to be greeted by the friendly Ubuntu menu. The first option, Install Ubuntu Server, marks the beginning of a journey toward your very own system administrator cave.

Until recently, the process of installing Ubuntu Server was identical to installing a desktop. Both installations were performed with a textual installer, a charmingly quaint combination of red and blue screens with text all over. Since then, the desktop version's installer has been replaced by a beautiful graphical environment that lets you play with a fully usable Ubuntu setup right off the install CD. But the Server CD retained its red and blue colors; because the textual installer doesn't rely on automatically detecting finicky graphics cards, it's just about certain to work on most any piece of hardware you can get your hands on. And when you're installing a server, that's worth more than all the eye candy in the world.

Here, we look at some of the advanced textual installer gadgetry that is particularly geared toward server users.

The neat stuff begins when you arrive at the partitioning section of the installer. With a desktop machine, you'd probably let the installer configure a basic set of partitions by itself and go on its merry way. But with servers, things get a bit more complicated.

A Couple of Installer Tricks

As we'll explore below, in terms of partitioning and storage, server installations can be quite a bit more complex than desktop ones. There's a small bag of useful tricks with the installer that can help when things get hairy.

The installer itself runs on virtual console 1. If you switch to console 2 by pressing Alt-F2, you'll be able to activate the console by hitting Enter and land in a minimalistic (busybox) shell. This will let you explore the complete installer environment and take some matters into your own hands if necessary. You can switch back to the installer console by pressing Alt-F1. Console 4 contains a running, noninteractive log file of the installation, which you can inspect by pressing Alt-F4. Finally, it's sometimes useful to be able to connect to another server during installation, perhaps to upload a log file or to gain access to your mailbox or other communication. By default, the shell on console 2 will not provide you with an ssh client, but you can install one by running `anna-install openssh-client-udeb` after the installer has configured the network. Now you can use the `ssh` and `scp` binaries to log in or copy data to the server of your choice.

Partitioning Your Ubuntu Server

Deciding how to partition the storage in your server is a tricky affair and certainly no exact science. Generally, it's a good idea to have at least three partitions separate from the rest of the system:

- /home: where all the user files will live

- /tmp: temporary scratch space for running applications

- /var: mail spools and log files

TIP   Partition Security and Separating Logs and Spools
There are several options that you can turn on for specific system partitions that afford you extra security. We'll explain them later in this chapter, in the section dealing with security.

As an aside, if your server will keep extensive mail and news spools, you might want to further separate /var into partitions for /var/log and /var/spool. Having them both on the same partition might cause severe I/O congestion under heavy use.

Keeping data on separate partitions gives you, the administrator, an expansive choice of filesystems you use for particular purposes. For instance, you might choose to put /tmp on ReiserFS for its superior handling of many files in a directory and excellent performance on small files, but you might keep /home and /var on ext3 for its rock-solid robustness.

In addition, a dedicated /home partition lets you use special options when mounting it to your system, such as imposing disk space quotas or enabling extended security on user data. The reason to keep /tmp and /var separate from the rest of your system is much more prosaic: These directories are prone to filling up. This is the case with /tmp because it's a scratchpad, and administrators often give users very liberal quotas there (but have a policy, for example, of purging all user data in /tmp older than two days), which means /tmp can easily get clogged up. /var, on the other hand, stores log files and mail spools, both of which can take up massive amounts of disk space either as a result of malicious activity or due to a significant spike in normal system usage.

Becoming a system administrator means you have to learn how to think like one. If /tmp and /var are easy to fill up, you compartmentalize them so that they can't eventually consume all the disk space available on your server.

The Story of RAID

If you've got only one hard drive in your server, feel free to skip ahead. Otherwise, let's talk about putting those extra drives to use. The acronym RAID stands for redundant array of inexpensive disks, although if you're a businessperson, you can substitute the word *independent* for *inexpensive*. We forgive you. And if you're in France, RAID is short for recherche assistance intervention dissuasion, which is an elite commando unit of the National Police—but if that's the RAID you need help with, you're reading the wrong book. We think RAID is just a really awesome idea for data: When dealing with your information, it provides extra speed, fault tolerance, or both.

At its core, RAID is just a way to replicate the same information across multiple physical drives. The process can be set up in a number of ways, and specific kinds of drive configurations are referred to as RAID levels. These days, even low- to mid-range servers ship with integrated hardware RAID controllers, which operate without any support from the OS. If your new server doesn't come with a RAID controller, you can use the software RAID functionality in the Ubuntu kernel to accomplish the same goal.

Setting up software RAID while installing your Linux system was difficult and unwieldy only a short while ago, but it is a breeze these days: The Ubuntu installer provides a nice, convenient interface for it and then handles all the requisite backstage magic. You can choose from three RAID levels: 0, 1, and 5.

RAID 0   A so-called striped set, RAID 0 allows you to pool the storage space of a number of separate drives into one large, virtual drive. The important thing to keep in mind is that RAID 0 does not actually concatenate the physical drives—it actually spreads the data across them evenly, which means that no more space will be used on each physical drive than can fit on the smallest one. In practical terms, if you had two 250GB drives and a 200GB drive, the total amount of space on your virtual drive would equal 600GB; 50GB on each of the two larger drives would go unused. Spreading data in this fashion provides amazing performance but also significantly decreases reliability. If any of the drives in your RAID 0 array fail, the entire array will come crashing down, taking your data with it.

RAID 1   This level provides very straightforward data replication. It will take the contents of one physical drive and multiplex it to as many other drives as you'd like. A RAID 1 array does not grow in size with the addition of extra drives—instead, it grows in reliability and read performance. The size of the entire array is limited by the size of its smallest constituent drive.

RAID 5   When the chief goal of your storage is fault tolerance, and you want to use more space than provided by the single physical drive in RAID 1, this is the level you want to use. RAID 5 lets you use n identically sized physical drives (if different-sized drives are present, no more space than the size of the smallest one will be used on each drive) to construct an array whose total available space is that of $n-1$ drives, and the array tolerates the failure of any one—but no more than one—drive without data loss.

TIP   **The Mythical Parity Drive**
If you toss five 200GB drives into a RAID 5 array, the array's total usable size will be 800GB, or that of four drives. This makes it easy to mistakenly believe that a RAID 5 array "sacrifices" one of the drives for maintaining redundancy and parity, but this is not the case. Through some neat mathematics of polynomial coefficients over Galois fields, the actual parity information is striped across all drives equally, allowing any single drive to fail without compromising the data. Don't worry, though. We won't quiz you on the math.

Which RAID to Choose?   If you're indecisive by nature, the past few paragraphs may have left you awkwardly hunched in your chair, mercilessly chewing a No. 2 pencil, feet tapping the floor nervously. Luckily, the initial choice of RAID level is often a no-brainer, so you'll have to direct your indecision elsewhere. If you have one hard drive, no RAID for you. Do not pass Go, do not collect $200. Two drives? Toss them into RAID 1, and sleep better at night. Three or more? RAID 5. Unless you really know what you're doing, avoid RAID 0 like the plague. If you're not serving mostly read-only data without a care about redundancy, RAID 0 isn't what you want.

TIP   **Other RAID Modes**
Though the installer offers only the most common RAID modes—0, 1, and 5—many other RAID modes exist and can be configured after the installation. Take a look at http://en.wikipedia.org/wiki/RAID for a detailed explanation of all the modes.

Setting Up RAID

After carefully studying the last section, maybe reading a few books on abstract algebra and another few on finite field theory, you finally decided on a RAID level that suits you. Since books can't yet read your mind, we'll assume you chose RAID 1. So how do you set it up?

Back to the installer. When prompted about partitioning disks, you'll want to bravely select the last option, Manually Edit Partition Table.

Below the top two options on the screen (Guided Partitioning, and Help), you'll find a list of the physical drives in your server that the Ubuntu installer detected.

TIP **Avoiding the "Oh, No!" Moment**
We've said this before, and we'll say it again: It's very easy to mistakenly erase valuable data when partitioning your system. Since you're installing a server, however, we'll assume you're comfortable deleting any data that might already exist on the drives. If this is not the case, back up all data you care about now! We mean it.

Indented below each drive, you'll find the list of any preexisting partitions, along with their on-disk ordinal number, size, bootable status, filesystem type, and, possibly, their mount point. Using the arrow keys, highlight the line summarizing a physical drive (not any of its partitions), and hit Enter—you'll be asked to confirm replacing any existing partition table with a new one. Select Yes, and the only entry listed below that drive will be FREE SPACE. In our fictional server, we have two 80GB drives—hda and hdb—so we'd follow this process for both drives, giving each a fresh partition table. Say we've decided on a 20GB /home partition. Arrow over to FREE SPACE, hit Enter, and create the partition. Once you've entered the size for the new partition, you'll be brought to a dialog where you can choose the filesystem and mount options. Instead of plopping a filesystem on the raw partition, however, you'll want to enter the Use As dialog and set the new partition to be a physical volume for RAID.

Still with us? Now rinse and repeat for the other drive—create the exact same partition, same size, and set it as a RAID volume. When you're done, you should be back at the initial partitioning screen, and you should have an identically sized partition under each drive. At this point, choose Configure Software RAID at the top of the screen, agree to write out changes to the storage devices if need be, and then choose to create an MD (multidisk) device. After selecting RAID 1, you'll be asked to enter the number of active devices for the array. In our fictional two-drive server, it's two. The next question concerns the number of spare devices in the array, which you can leave at zero. Now simply use the spacebar to put a check next to both partitions that you've created (hda1 and hdb1), and hit Finish in the Multidisk dialog to return to the basic partitioner.

If you look below the two physical drives that you used to have there, you'll notice a brand new drive, the Software RAID device that has one partition below it. That's your future /home partition, sitting happily on a RAID array. If you arrow over to it and hit Enter, you can now configure it just as you would a real partition.

The process is the same for any other partitions you want to toss into RAID. Create identical-sized partitions on all participating physical drives, select to use them as RAID space, enter the multidisk configurator (software RAID), and finally, create an array that uses the real partitions. Then create a filesystem on the newly created array.

TIP   **Array Failure and Spare Devices**
When a physical drive fails in a RAID array that's running in a level that provides redundancy—such as 1 or 5—the array goes into so-called degraded mode (never verbally abuse or be cruel to your RAID arrays!). Depending on the number of devices in the array, running in degraded mode might just have performance downsides, but it might also mean that another physical drive failure will bring down the whole array and cause total data loss. To recover the array from degraded mode, you need to add a working physical drive to the system (the old one can be removed) and instruct the array to use the new device to "rebuild."

In order to minimize the amount of time an array spends in degraded mode, and to prevent having to power off the machine to insert new physical drives if the server doesn't support hot-swapping, you can put extra physical drives into the machine and flag them as hot spares, which means the system will keep them active but unused until there's a drive failure. Cold spares, as the name implies, are just extra drives that you keep around on a shelf until there's a failure, at which point you manually add them to the array.

That's it! The Ubuntu installer will take care of all the pesky details of configuring the system to boot the RAID arrays at the right time and use them, even if you've chosen to keep your root partition on an array. Now let's look at another great feature of the Ubuntu installer: logical volume management (LVM).

The Story of the Logical Volume Manager

Let's take a step back from our RAID adventure and look at the bigger picture in data storage. The entire situation is unpleasant. Hard drives are slow and fail often, and though abolished for working memory ages ago, fixed-size partitions are still the predominant mode of storage space allocation. As if worrying about speed and data loss weren't enough, you also have to worry about whether your partition size calculations were just right when you were installing a server or whether you'll wind up in the unenviable position of having a partition run out of space, even though another partition is maybe mostly unused. And if you might have to move a partition across physical volume boundaries on a running system, well, woe is you.

RAID helps to some degree. It'll do wonders for your worries about performance and fault tolerance, but it operates at too low a level to help with the partition size or fluidity concerns. What we'd really want is a way to push the partition concept up one level of abstraction, so it doesn't operate directly on the underlying physical media. Then we could have partitions that are trivially resizable or that can span multiple drives, we could easily take some space from one partition and tack it on another, and we could juggle partitions around on physical drives on a live server. Sounds cool, right?

Very cool, and very doable via LVM, a system that shifts the fundamental unit of storage from physical drives to virtual or logical ones (although we harbor our suspicions that the term *logical* is a jab at the storage status quo, which is anything but). LVM has traditionally been a feature of expensive, enterprise UNIX operating systems or was available for purchase from third-party vendors. Through the magic of free software, a guy by the name of Heinz Mauelshagen wrote an implementation of a logical volume manager for Linux in 1998. LVM has undergone tremendous improvements since then and is widely used in production today, and just as you expect, the Ubuntu installer makes it easy for you to configure it on your server during installation.

LVM Theory and Jargon   Wrapping your head around LVM is a bit more difficult than with RAID because LVM rethinks the whole way of dealing with storage, which expectedly introduces a bit of jargon that you need to learn. Under LVM, physical volumes, or PVs, are seen just as providers of disk space without any inherent organization (such as partitions mapping to a mount point in the OS). We group PVs into volume groups, or VGs, which are virtual storage pools that look like good old cookie-cutter hard drives. We carve those up into logical volumes, or LVs, that act like the normal partitions we're used to dealing with. We create filesystems on these LVs and mount them into our directory tree. And behind the scenes, LVM splits up physical volumes into small slabs of bytes (4MB by default), each of which is called a physical extent, or a PE.

Okay, so that was a mouthful of acronyms, but as long as you understand the progression, you're in good shape. You take a physical hard drive and set up one or more partitions on it that will be used for LVM. These partitions are now physical volumes (PVs), which are split into physical extents (PEs) and then grouped in volume groups (VGs), on top of which you finally create logical volumes (LVs). It's the LVs, these virtual partitions, and not the ones on the physical hard drive, that carry a filesystem and are mapped and mounted into the OS. And if you're really confused about what possible benefit we get from adding all this complexity only to wind up with the same fixed-size partitions in the end, hang in there. It'll make sense in a second.

The reason LVM splits physical volumes into small, equally sized physical extents is that the definition of a volume group (the space that'll be carved into logical volumes) then becomes "a collection of physical extents" rather than "a physical area on a physical drive," as with old-school partitions. Notice that "a collection of extents" says nothing about where the extents are coming from and certainly doesn't impose a fixed limit on the size of a volume group. We can take PEs from a bunch of different drives and toss them into one volume group, which addresses our desire to abstract partitions away from physical drives. We can take a VG and make it bigger simply by adding a few extents to it, maybe by taking them from another VG, or maybe by tossing in a new physical volume and using extents from there. And we can take a VG and move it to different physical storage simply by telling it to relocate to a different collection of extents. Best of all, we can do all this on the fly, without any server downtime.

Do you smell that? That's the fresh smell of the storage revolution.

Setting Up LVM

By now, you must be convinced that LVM is the best thing since sliced bread. Which it is—and, surprisingly enough, setting it up during installation is no harder than setting up RAID. Create partitions on each physical drive you want to use for LVM just as you did with RAID, but tell the installer to use them as physical space for LVM. Note that in this context, PVs are not actual physical hard drives; they are the partitions you're creating.

You don't have to devote your entire drive to partitions for LVM. If you'd like, you're free to create actual filesystem-containing partitions alongside the storage partitions used for LVM, but make sure you're satisfied with your partitioning choice before you proceed. Once you enter the LVM configurator in the installer, the partition layout on all drives that contain LVM partitions will be frozen.

Let's look back to our fictional server, but let's give it four drives, which are 10GB, 20GB, 80GB, and 120GB in size. Say we want to create an LVM partition, or PV, using all available space on each drive, and then combine the first two PVs into a 30GB volume group and the latter two into a 200GB one. Each VG will act as a large virtual hard drive on top of which we can create logical volumes just as we would normal partitions.

As with RAID, arrowing over to the name of each drive and hitting Enter will let us erase the partition table. Then hitting Enter on the FREE SPACE entry lets us create a physical volume—a partition that we set to be used as a physical space for LVM. Once all three LVM partitions are in place, we select Configure the Logical Volume Manager on the partitioning menu.

After a warning about the partition layout, we get to a rather spartan LVM dialog that lets us modify VGs and LVs. According to our plan, we choose the former option and create the two VGs we want, choosing the appropriate PVs. We then select Modify Logical Volumes and create the LVs corresponding to the normal partitions we want to put on the system—say, one for each of /, /var, /home, and /tmp.

You can already see some of the partition fluidity that LVM brings you. If you decide you want a 25GB logical volume for /var, you can carve it out of the first VG you created, and /var will magically span the two smaller hard drives. If you later decide you've given /var too much space, you can shrink the filesystem and then simply move over some of the storage space from the first VG to the second. The possibilities are endless.

Last but not least, recent Ubuntu versions support encrypting your LVM volumes right from the installer, which is music to paranoid ears: It means you can now have full-disk encryption from the moment you install your machine. Encrypted LVM is offered as one of the "guided" options in the partitioning menu, but you can also accomplish the same result by hand.

TIP   **LVM Doesn't Provide Redundancy**

The point of LVM is storage fluidity, not fault tolerance. In our example, the logical volume containing the /var filesystem is sitting on a volume group that spans two hard drives. Unfortunately, this means that either drive failing will corrupt the entire filesystem, and LVM intentionally doesn't contain functionality to prevent this problem.

Instead, when you need fault tolerance, build your volume groups from physical volumes that are sitting on RAID! In our example, we could have made a partition spanning the entire size of the 10GB hard drive and allocated it to physical space for a RAID volume. Then, we could have made two 10GB partitions on the 20GB hard drive and made the first one also a physical space for RAID. Entering the RAID configurator, we would create a RAID 1 array from the 10GB RAID partitions on both drives, but instead of placing a regular filesystem on the RAID array as before, we'd actually designate the RAID array to be used as a physical space for LVM. When we get to LVM configuration, the RAID array would show up as any other physical volume, but we'd know that the physical volume is redundant. If a physical drive fails beneath it, LVM won't ever know, and no data loss will occur. Of course, standard RAID array caveats apply, so if enough drives fail and shut down the array, LVM will still come down kicking and screaming.

Encrypted Home and Software Selection

After you have partitioned the disk, the installer will install the base system and ask you for user information, much like with the desktop install. You'll then be asked a question you might not have seen before: Do you wish to encrypt your home directory?

If you answer in the affirmative, your account password will take on a second purpose. Rather than just allowing you to log in, it will also be used to transparently encrypt every file in your home directory, turning it into gibberish for anyone without the password. This means that if your computer gets stolen, your data remains safe from prying eyes as long as your password isn't too easy to guess. If this sounds familiar, it's because this functionality exists as FileVault on Apple's Mac OS X and is also a subset of the BitLocker system that debuted in Windows Vista. (The directory encryption system used in Ubuntu is called ecryptfs, which is a decidedly less punchy name. We're working on it.)

TIP   **Encrypted Swap and Remote Login**
If you use a swap partition, protecting your home directory isn't enough; sensitive data can get swapped out to disk in the clear. The solution is to use encrypted swap, which you can manually enable with the `ecryptfs-setup-swap` command, but this will presently take away your computer's ability to enter the hibernate power-saving mode. Suspend mode is unaffected.

Note also that encrypting your home directory makes all the data in it, including special directories such as .ssh, unavailable until after you log in. If you're logging into a machine where your home directory is encrypted and hasn't yet been unlocked, and the machine only allows SSH public key authentication, there is no way for the system to consult your authorized_keys file, and you're locked out. You can fix this by physically logging in, unmounting your encrypted home directory with `ecryptfs-umount-private`, then creating a .ssh directory in your "underlying" home directory left behind by ecryptfs. Stick your public keys into an authorized_keys file under that .ssh directory as normal, and you'll be all set to log in remotely, at which point you can use `ecryptfs-mount-private` to enter your password and unlock your actual home directory.

After the installer downloads some updated software sources, though, you will see a new menu that lists a number of common server types, including DNS, LAMP, Mail, OpenSSH, PostgreSQL, Print, and Samba servers. Select one or more of these options and the installer will automatically download the standard set of packages you will need for that server as well as perform some basic configuration of the services for you. For instance, if you wanted to install a LAMP environment, but you also wanted to make sure you could ssh into the machine from another computer, you could select both LAMP and OpenSSH server from the menu.

TIP   **Software Installer Prompts**
Depending on which servers you select, you may be asked a number of questions as the packages install. For instance, when you select the LAMP environment, the installer will recommend you choose a password for the root MySQL user.

You're Done—Now Watch Out for Root!

Whew. With the storage and software stuff out of the way, the rest of your server installation should go no differently than installing a regular Ubuntu workstation. And now that your server is installed, we can move on to the fun stuff. From this point on, everything we do will happen in a shell.

When your Ubuntu server first boots, you'll have to log in with the user you created during installation. Here's an important point that bites a number of newcomers to Ubuntu: Unlike most distributions, Ubuntu does not enable the root account during installation! Instead, the installer adds the user you've created during installation to the admin group, which lets you use a mechanism called sudo to perform administrative tasks. We'll show you how to use sudo in a bit. In the meantime, if you're interested in the rationale for the decision to disable direct use of the root account, simply run man sudo_root after logging in.

TIP   **Care and Feeding of RAID and LVM Arrays**
If you've set up some of these during installation, you'll want to learn how to manage the arrays after the server is installed. We recommend the respective how-to documents from The Linux Documentation Project at

www.tldp.org/HOWTO/Software-RAID-HOWTO.html and

www.tldp.org/HOWTO/LVM-HOWTO.

The how-tos sometimes get technical, but most of the details should sound familiar if you've understood the introduction to the subject matter that we gave in this chapter.

Ubuntu Package Management

Once your server is installed, it contains only the few packages it requires to boot and run properly plus whatever software you selected at the software select screen. In the comfort of the GNOME graphical environment on an Ubuntu desktop, we could launch Synaptic and point and click our way through application discovery and installation. But on a server, we must be shell samurai.

The Ubuntu Archive

Before we delve into the nitty-gritty of package management, let's briefly outline the structure of the master Ubuntu package archive, which we mentioned in the introduction to this chapter. Each new release has five repositories in the archive, called main, restricted, backports, universe, and multiverse. A newly installed system comes with only the first two enabled plus the security update repository. Here's the repository breakdown.

- **Main:** This includes all packages installed by default; these packages have official support.

- **Restricted:** These are packages with restricted copyright, often hardware drivers.

- **Backports:** These are newer versions of packages in the archive, provided by the community.

- **Universe:** The universe includes packages maintained by the Ubuntu community.

- **Multiverse:** The multiverse includes packages that are not free (in the sense of freedom).

The term *official support* is a bit of a misnomer, as it doesn't refer to technical support that one would purchase or obtain but speaks instead to the availability of security updates after a version of Ubuntu is released. Standard Ubuntu releases are supported for 18 months, which means that Ubuntu's parent company, Canonical, Ltd., guarantees that security updates will be provided, free of charge, for any vulnerabilities discovered in software in the *main* repository for 18 months after a release. No such guarantee is made for software in the other repositories.

Of particular note is that certain Ubuntu releases have longer support cycles. These releases are denoted by the acronym LTS (Long Term Support) in their version number. The latest Ubuntu LTS, version 8.04 (Hardy), will be supported for five years on servers, while the next LTS is due out in 2010.

APT Sources and Repositories

You're now aware of the structure of the Ubuntu archive, but we didn't explain how to actually modify the list of repositories you want to use on your system. In Debian package management parlance, the list of repositories is part of the list of Advanced Package Tool (APT) sources. (Keep your eyes peeled: Many of the package tools we'll discuss below begin with the prefix *apt*.) These sources tell APT where to find available packages: in the Ubuntu archive on the Internet, on your CD-ROM, or in a third-party archive.

The APT sources are specified in the file /etc/apt/sources.list. Let's open this file in an editor. (If you're not used to vim, substitute nano for it, which is an easier-to-use, beginner-friendly editor.)

```
$ vim /etc/apt/sources.list
```

The lines beginning with a hash, or #, denote comment lines and are skipped over by APT. At the top, you'll see the CD-ROM source that the installer added, and following it these two lines (or something very similar):

```
deb http://us.archive.ubuntu.com/ubuntu/ jaunty main restricted
deb-src http://us.archive.ubuntu.com/ubuntu/ jaunty main restricted
```

We can infer the general format of the APT sources list by looking at these lines. The file is composed of individual sources, one per line, and each line of several space-separated fields. The first field tells us what kind of a source the line is describing, such as a source for binary packages (deb) or source code packages (deb-src). The second field is the actual URI of the package source, the third names the distribution whose packages we want (jaunty), and the remaining fields tell APT which components to use from the source we're describing—by default, main and restricted.

If you look through the rest of the file, you'll find it's nicely commented to let you easily enable two extra repositories: the very useful universe and the bleeding-edge backports. In general, now that you understand the format of each source line, you have complete control over the repositories you use, and while we strongly recommend against using the backports repository on a server, enabling universe is usually a good idea.

With that in mind, let's get you acquainted with some of the basic command-line package management tools on an Ubuntu system. Ubuntu inherits its package management from Debian, so if you're familiar with Debian, the utilities we'll discuss are old friends.

dpkg

Our first stop is the Debian package manager, dpkg, which sits around the lowest levels of the package management stack. Through a utility called dpkg-deb, dpkg deals with individual Debian package files, referred to as *debs* for their .deb filename extension.

dpkg is extensively documented in the system manual pages, so you can read about the various options it supports by entering man dpkg in the shell. We'll point out the most common dpkg operations: listing and installing packages. Of course, dpkg can also remove packages, but we'll show you how to do that with the higher-level tool called apt-get instead.

Listing Packages   Running dpkg -l | less in the shell will list all the packages on your system that dpkg is tracking, in a six-column format. The first three columns are one letter wide each, signifying the desired package state, current package status, and error status, respectively. Most of the time, the error status column will be empty.

The top three lines of dpkg output serve as a legend to explain the letters you can find in the first three columns. This lets you use the grep tool to search through the package list, perhaps to look only at removed packages or those that failed configuration.

Installing a Package Manually

There are more than 17,000 packages in the Ubuntu archive for each release. Only a small percentage of those are officially supported, but all the other packages are still held to reasonably rigorous inclusion requirements. Packages in the Ubuntu archive are thus almost universally of high quality and are known to work well on your Ubuntu system.

Because of this, the archive should be the very first place you look when you choose to install new software. On rare instances, however, the software you want to install won't be available in the archive because it's new or because redistribution restrictions prevent it from being included. In those cases, you might have to either build the software from source code, run binaries that the vendor provides, or find third-party Ubuntu or Debian packages to install.

TIP   **Practice Safe Hex!**
That's a terrible pun. We apologize. But it probably got your attention, so follow closely: Be very, very cautious when dealing with third-party packages. Packages in the Ubuntu archive undergo extensive quality assurance and are practically certain to be free from viruses, worms, Trojan horses, or other computer pests. If you install software only from the archive, you'll never have to worry about viruses again.

With third-party packages, you just don't know what you could be installing. If you install a malicious package, you've given the package creator full control of your system. So ideally, don't install third-party packages at all. And if you must, make absolutely sure you trust the source of the packages!

Impatience is a hallmark virtue of programmers and system administrators alike, so if you were too impatient to read the warning note, do it now. This is serious business. Let's continue: Say you've downloaded a package called myspecial-server.deb. You can install it simply by typing:

```
$ sudo dpkg -i myspecial-server.deb
```

dpkg will unpack the deb, make sure its dependencies are satisfied, and proceed to install the package. Remember what we said about the root account being unusable by default? Installing a package requires administrator privileges, which we obtained by prefixing the command we wanted to execute with sudo and entering our user password at sudo's prompt.

TIP   **A Quick Note on Shell Examples**
In the dpkg example, the dollar sign is the standard UNIX shell symbol, so you don't need to actually type it. We'll use it in the rest of the chapter to indicate things that need to be entered in a shell. On your Ubuntu system, the shell prompt won't be just a dollar sign but will look like this:

user@server:~$

user and *server* will be replaced by your username and the hostname you gave the server during installation, respectively, and the part between the colon and dollar sign will show your working directory. A tilde is UNIX shorthand for your home directory.

apt-get and apt-cache

Now let's jump higher up in the stack. Whereas dpkg deals mostly with package files, apt-get knows how to download packages from the Ubuntu archive or fetch them from your Ubuntu CD. It provides a convenient, succinct interface, so it's no surprise it's the tool that most system administrators use for package management on Ubuntu servers.

While apt-get deals with high-level package operations, it won't tell you which packages are actually in the archive and available for installation. It knows how to get this information behind the scenes from the package cache, which you can manipulate by using a simple tool called apt-cache. Let's see how these two commands come together with an example. Say we're trying to find and then install software that lets us work with extended filesystem attributes.

Searching the Package Cache and Showing Package Information   We begin
by telling apt-cache to search for the phrase "extended attributes."

```
$ apt-cache search "extended attributes"
attr - Utilities for manipulating filesystem extended attributes
libattr1 - Extended attribute shared library
libattr1-dev - Extended attribute static libraries and headers
python-pyxattr - module for manipulating filesystem extended
attributes
python2.4-pyxattr - module for manipulating filesystem extended
attributes
rdiff-backup - remote incremental backup
xfsdump - Administrative utilities for the XFS filesystem
xfsprogs - Utilities for managing the XFS filesystem
```

The parameter to apt-cache search can be either a package name or a phrase describing the package, as in our example. The lines following our invocation are the output we received, composed of the package name on the left and a one-line description on the right. It looks like the attr package is what we're after, so let's see some details about it.

```
$ apt-cache show attr
Package: attr
Priority: optional
Section: utils
Installed-Size: 240
Maintainer: Ubuntu Core Developers <ubuntu-deel-
discuss@lists.ubuntu.com>
Original-Maintainer: Nathan Scott <nathans@debian.org>
Architecture: i386
Version: 1:2.4.39-1
Depends: libattr1 (>= 2.4.4-1), libc6 (>= 2.6.1-1)
Conflicts: xfsdump (<< 2.0.0)
Filename: pool/main/a/attr/attr_2.4.39-1_i386.deb
Size: 31098
MD5sum: 84457d6edd44983bba3dcb50495359fd
SHA1: 8ae3562e0a8e8a314c4c6997ca9aced0fb3bea46
SHA256:
f566a9a57135754f0a79c2efd8fcec626cde10d2533c10c1660bf7064a336c82
```

```
Description: Utilities for manipulating filesystem extended
  attributes
  A set of tools for manipulating extended attributes on filesystem
  objects, in particular getfattr(1) and setfattr(1).
  An attr(1) command is also provided which is largely compatible
  with the SGI IRIX tool of the same name.
  .
   Homepage: http://oss.sgi.com/projects/xfs/
Bugs: mailto:ubuntu-users@lists.ubuntu.com
Origin: Ubuntu
```

Don't be daunted by the verbose output. Extracting the useful bits turns out to be pretty simple. We can already see from the description field that this is, in fact, the package we're after. We can also see the exact version of the packaged software, any dependencies and conflicting packages it has, and an e-mail address to which we can send bug reports. And looking at the filename field, the pool/main snippet tells us this is a package in the main repository.

Installing a Package   So far, so good. Let's perform the actual installation:

```
$ sudo apt-get install attr
```

apt-get will track down a source for the package, such as an Ubuntu CD or the Ubuntu archive on the Internet, fetch the deb, verify its integrity, do the same for any dependencies the package has, and, finally, install the package.

Removing a Package   For didactic purposes, we're going to keep assuming that you're very indecisive and that right after you installed the attr package, you realized it wasn't going to work out between the two of you. To the bit bucket with attr!

```
$ sudo apt-get remove attr
```

One confirmation later and attr is blissfully gone from your system, except for any configuration files it may have installed. If you want those gone, too, you'd have to instead run the following:

```
$ sudo apt-get --purge remove attr
```

Performing System Updates   Installing and removing packages is a common system administration task, but not as common as keeping the system up to date. This doesn't mean upgrading to newer and newer versions of the software (well, it does, but not in the conventional sense), because once a given Ubuntu version is released, no new software versions enter the repositories except for the backports repository. On a server, however, you're strongly discouraged from using backports because they receive a very limited amount of quality assurance and testing and because there's usually no reason for a server to be chasing new software features. New features bring new bugs, and as a system administrator, you should value stability and reliability miles over features. Ubuntu's brief, six-month development cycle means that you'll be able to get all the new features in half a year anyway. But by then they will be in the main repositories and will have received substantial testing. Keeping a system up to date thus means making sure it's running the latest security patches, to prevent any vulnerabilities discovered after the release from endangering your system.

Luckily, `apt-get` makes this process amazingly easy. You begin by obtaining an updated list of packages from the Ubuntu archive:

```
$ sudo apt-get update
```

and then you simply run the upgrade:

```
$ sudo apt-get upgrade
```

After this, `apt-get` will tell you either that your system is up to date or what it's planning to upgrade, and it will handle the upgrade for you automatically. How's that for cool?

Running a Distribution Upgrade

When a new Ubuntu release comes out and you want to upgrade your server to it, you'll use a new tool, `do-release-upgrade`. The upgrade tool will switch over your sources.list to the new distribution and will figure out what packages are needed and whether they have any known issues. After it has done this, it will ask you to confirm the update by pressing y or to view the updated packages by pressing d. If you choose to view the updates, merely type y to continue the update, as the tool will not prompt you again.

NOTE   The update process may take a couple of hours and should not be interrupted during that
time.

Building Packages from Source   The Ubuntu archive, unlike Debian's,
doesn't permit direct binary uploads. When Ubuntu developers want to
add a piece of software to the archive, they prepare its source code in a certain way and put it in a build queue. From there it's compiled, built automatically, and—if those steps succeed—pushed into the archive.

Why go through all the trouble? Why not just have the developers build
the software on their machines? They could upload binaries to the archive,
bypassing the build queue, which can take hours to build software. Here's
the catch: Ubuntu officially supports three hardware platforms (Intel x86,
AMD64/EM64T, and PowerPC). Without the build queue, developers would
have to build separate binaries of their software for each platform, which
entails owning a computer running on each platform (expensive!) or creating
complicated cross-compilation toolchains. And even then, sitting through
three software builds is an enormous waste of precious developer time.

The build queue approach solves this problem because the automatic
build system takes a single source package and builds it for all the necessary platforms. And it turns out that the approach provides you, the system administrator, with a really nifty benefit: It lets you leverage the
dependency-solving power and ease of use of apt-get and apply it to building packages from source!

Now that you're excited, let's backtrack a bit. Building packages from source
is primarily of interest to developers, not system administrators. In fact, as a
sysadmin, you should avoid hand-built packages whenever possible and
instead benefit from the quality assurance that packages in the Ubuntu
archive received. Sometimes, though, you might just have to apply a custom
patch to a piece of software before installing it. We'll use the attr package
example, as before. What follows is what a session of building attr from
source and installing the new package might look like—if you want to try
it, make sure you install the dpkg-dev, devscripts, and fakeroot packages.

```
$ mkdir attr-build
$ cd attr-build
```

```
$ apt-get source attr
$ sudo apt-get build-dep attr
$ cd attr-2.4.39
<apply a patch or edit the source code>
$ dch -i
$ dpkg-buildpackage -rfakeroot
$ cd ..
$ sudo dpkg -i *.deb
```

All of the commands we invoked are well documented in the system man pages, and covering them in detail is out of the scope of this chapter. To briefly orient you as to what we did, though, here's a quick description.

1. We made a scratch directory called attr-build and changed into it.

2. `apt-get source attr` fetched the source of the attr package and unpacked it into the current directory.

3. `apt-get build-dep attr` installed all the packages required to build the attr package from source.

4. We changed into the unpacked attr-2.4.25 directory, applied a patch, and edited the package changelog to describe our changes to the source.

5. `dpkg -buildpackage -rfakeroot` built one or more installable debs from our package.

6. We ascended one directory in the filesystem and installed all the debs we just built.

This is a super-compressed cheat sheet for a topic that takes a long time to master. We left a lot of things out, so if you need to patch packages for production use, first go and read the man pages of the tools we mentioned and get a better understanding of what's going on!

aptitude

Around the highest levels of the package management stack hangs aptitude, a neat, colorful textual front end that can be used interchangeably with apt-get. We won't go into detail about aptitude use here; plenty of information is available from the system manual pages and the online aptitude help system (if you launch it as aptitude from the shell). It's worth mentioning, though, that one of the chief reasons some system administrators prefer aptitude over apt-get is its better handling of so-called orphan packages. Orphan packages are packages that were installed as a dependency of another package that has since been removed, leaving the orphan installed for no good reason. apt-get provides no automatic way to deal with orphans, instead relegating the task to the deborphan tool, which you can install from the archive. By contrast, aptitude will remove orphan packages automatically.

Tips and Tricks

Congratulations. If you've gotten this far, you're familiar with most aspects of effectively dealing with packages on your Ubuntu server. Before you move on to other topics, though, we want to present a few odds and ends that will probably come in handy to you at one point or another.

Listing Files Owned by a Package   Sometimes it's really useful to see which files on your system belong to a specific package, say, cron. dpkg to the rescue:

```
$ dpkg -L cron
```

Be careful, though, as dpkg -L output might contain directories that aren't exclusively owned by this package but are shared with others.

Finding Which Package Owns a File   The reverse of the previous operation is just as simple:

```
$ dpkg -S /etc/crontab
cron: /etc/crontab
```

The one-line output tells us the name of the owner package on the left.

Finding Which Package Provides a File   Both dpkg -S and dpkg -L operate on the database of installed packages. Sometimes, you might need to figure out which—potentially uninstalled—package provides a certain file. We might be looking for a package that would install the bzr binary, or /usr/bin/bzr. To do this, first install the package apt-file (requires the universe repository), then execute:

```
$ apt-file update
$ apt-file search /usr/bin/bzr
```

Voila! apt-file will tell you that the package you want is bzr, with output in the same format as dpkg -S.

That's it for our package management tricks—it's time to talk about security.

Ubuntu Server Security

As a system administrator, one of your chief tasks is dealing with server security. If your server is connected to the Internet, for security purposes it's in a war zone. If it's only an internal server, you still need to deal with (accidentally) malicious users, disgruntled employees, and the guy in accounting who *really* wants to read the boss's secretary's e-mail.

In general, Ubuntu Server is a very secure platform. The Ubuntu Security Team, the team that produces all official security updates, has one of the best turnaround times in the industry. Ubuntu ships with a no open ports policy, meaning that after you install Ubuntu on your machine—be it an Ubuntu desktop or a server installation—no applications will be accepting connections from the Internet by default. Like Ubuntu desktops, Ubuntu Server uses the sudo mechanism for system administration, eschewing the root account. And finally, security updates are guaranteed for at least 18 months after each release (five years for some releases, like Dapper), and are free.

In this section, we want to take a look at user account administration, filesystem security, system resource limits, logs, and finally some network security. But Linux security is a difficult and expansive topic; remember that we're giving you a crash course here and leaving out a lot of things—to be a good administrator, you'll want to learn more.

User Account Administration

Many aspects of user administration on Linux systems are consistent across distributions. Debian provides some convenience tools, such as the useradd command, to make things easier for you. But since Ubuntu fully inherits Debian's user administration model, we won't go into detail about it here. Instead, let us refer you to www.oreilly.com/catalog/debian/ chapter/book/ch07_01.html for the basics. After reading that page, you'll have full knowledge of the standard model, and we can briefly talk about the Ubuntu difference: `sudo`.

As we mentioned at the end of the installation section (You're Done— Now Watch Out for Root!), Ubuntu doesn't enable the root, or administrator, account by default. There is a great deal of security benefit to this approach and incredibly few downsides, all of which are documented at the man pages for `sudo_root`.

The user that you added during installation is the one who, by default, is placed into the admin group and may use `sudo` to perform system administration tasks. After adding new users to the system, you may add them to the admin group like this:

```
$ sudo adduser username admin
```

Simply use `deluser` in place of `adduser` in the above command to remove a user from the group. (Adding the `--encrypt-home` option to `adduser` will automatically set up home directory encryption for the new user.)

One thing to keep in mind is that `sudo` isn't just a workaround for giving people root access. `sudo` can also handle fine-grain permissions, such as saying, "Allow this user to execute only these three commands with superuser privileges."

Documentation about specifying these permissions is available in the sudoers man page, which can be a bit daunting—feel free to skip close to the end of it, until you reach the EXAMPLES section. It should take you maybe 10 or 15 minutes to grok it, and it covers a vast majority of the situations for which you'll want `sudo`. When you're ready to put your new knowledge to use, simply run:

```
$ visudo
```

Be careful here—the sudoers database, which lives in /etc/sudoers, is not meant to just be opened in an editor because an editor won't check the syntax for you! If you mess up the sudoer's database, you might find yourself with no way to become an administrator on the machine.

Filesystem Security

The security model for files is standardized across most UNIX-like operating systems and is called the POSIX model. The model calls for three broad types of access permissions for every file and directory: owner, group, and other. It works in exactly the same way on any Linux distribution, which is why we won't focus on it here. For a refresher, consult the man pages for chmod and chown, or browse around the Internet.

We want to actually look at securing partitions through mount options, an oft-neglected aspect of dealing with system security that's rather powerful when used appropriately. When explaining how to partition your system, we extolled the virtues of giving, at the very least, the /home, /tmp, and /var directories their own partitions, mentioning how it's possible to use special options when mounting these to the filesystem.

Many of the special mount options are filesystem-dependent, but the ones we want to consider are not. Here are the ones that interest us.

nodev   A filesystem mounted with the nodev option will not allow the use or creation of special "device" files. There's usually no good reason to allow most filesystems to allow interpretation of block or character special devices, and allowing them poses potential security risks.

nosuid   If you read up about UNIX file permissions, you know that certain files can be flagged in a way that lets anyone execute them with the permissions of another user or group, often that of the system administrator. This flag is called the setuid (suid) or the setgid bit, respectively, and allowing this behavior outside of the directories that hold the system binaries is often unnecessary and decreases security. If a user is able to, in any way, create or obtain a setuid binary of his or her own choosing, the user has effectively compromised the system.

noexec   If a filesystem is flagged as noexec, users will not be able to run any executables located on it.

noatime   This flag tells the filesystem not to keep a record of when files were last accessed. If used indiscriminately, it lessens security through limiting the amount of information available in the event of a security incident, particularly when computer forensics is to be performed. However, the flag does provide performance benefits for certain use patterns, so it's a good candidate to be used on partitions where security is an acceptable tradeoff for speed.

Deciding which mount options to use on which partition is another fuzzy science, and you'll often develop preferences as you become more accustomed to administering machines. Here's a basic proposal, though, that should be a good starting point:

- /home: nosuid, nodev

- /tmp: noatime, noexec, nodev, nosuid

- /var: noexec, nodev, nosuid

System Resource Limits

By default, Linux will not impose any resource limits on user processes. This means any user is free to fill up all of the working memory on the machine, or spawn processes in an endless loop, rendering the system unusable in seconds. The solution is to set up some of your own resource limits by editing the /etc/security/limits.conf file:

```
$ sudoedit /etc/security/limits.conf
```

The possible settings are all explained in the comment within the file, and there are no silver bullet values to recommend, though we do recommend that you set up at least the nproc limit and possibly also the as/data/memlock/rss settings.

TIP   **A Real-Life Resource Limit Example**
Just to give you an idea of what these limits look like on production servers, here is the configuration from the general login server of the Harvard Computer Society at Harvard University:

```
*       -       as       2097152
*       -       data     131072
```

```
*       -      memlock    131072
*       -      rss        1013352
*       hard   nproc      128
```

This limits regular users to 128 processes, with a maximum address space of 2GB, maximum data size and locked-in-memory address space of 128MB, and maximum resident set size of 1GB.

If you need to set up disk quotas for your users, install the quota package, and take a look at its man page.

System Log Files

As a system administrator, the system log files are some of your best friends. If you watch them carefully, you'll often know in advance when something is wrong with the system, and you'll be able to resolve most problems before they escalate.

Unfortunately, your ability to pay close attention to the log files dwindles with every server you're tasked with administering, so administrators often use log-processing software that can be configured to alert them on certain events, or they write their own tools in languages such as Perl and Python.

Logs usually live in /var/log, and after your server runs for a while, you'll notice there are a lot of increasingly older versions of the log files in that directory, many of them compressed with gzip (ending with the .gz filename extension).

Here are some log files of note:

- /var/log/syslog: general system log
- /var/log/auth.log: system authentication logs
- /var/log/mail.log: system mail logs
- /var/log/messages: general log messages
- /var/log/dmesg: kernel ring buffer messages, usually since system bootup

Your Log Toolbox   When it comes to reviewing logs, you should become familiar with a few tools of choice. The `tail` utility prints, by default, the last ten lines of a file, which makes it a neat tool to get an idea of what's been happening last in a given log file:

```
$ tail /var/log/syslog
```

With the `-f` parameter, `tail` launches into follow mode, which means it'll open the file and keep showing you changes on the screen as they're happening. If you want to impress your friends with your new system administrator prowess, you can now easily recreate the Hollywood hacker movie staple: text furiously blazing across the screen.

Also invaluable are `zgrep`, `zcat`, and `zless`, which operate like their analogues that don't begin with a *z*, but on `gzip`-compressed files. For instance, to get a list of lines in all your compressed logs that contain the word "warthog" regardless of case, you would issue the following command:

```
$ zgrep -i warthog /var/log/*.gz
```

Your toolbox for dealing with logs will grow with experience and based on your preferences, but to get an idea of what's already out there, do an `apt-cache` search for "log files."

A Sprinkling of Network Security

Network security administration is another feature provided largely by the OS, so it's no different on Ubuntu than on any other modern Linux distribution. That means we won't cover it here but will leave you with a pointer.

The `iptables` command is the front end to the very powerful Linux firewall tables. Unfortunately, dealing with `iptables` can be rather difficult, particularly if you're trying to set up complex firewall policies. To whet your appetite, here's `iptables` in action, dropping all packets coming from a notorious time-sink domain:

```
$ sudo iptables -A INPUT -s www.slashdot.org -j DROP
```

Tutorials, how-tos, and articles about iptables are available on the Internet in large numbers, and the system man pages provide detailed information about all the possible options. Spending some time to learn iptables is well worth it because it'll let you set up network security on any Linux machine and will make it pretty easy for you to learn other operating systems' firewall systems if need be.

Final Words on Security

We've barely even scratched the surface of system security in this subsection, though we've tried to give you good pointers on where to start and where to get the information you need to learn more. But let us give you some sage advice on security in general, since it's a painful truth to learn: There is no such thing as a fully secure system. Securing systems isn't about making it impossible for a breach to occur. It's about making the breach so difficult that it's not worth it to the attacker. This definition is pretty fluid because if your attacker is a bored 14-year-old sitting in a basement somewhere chewing on cold pizza, you can bet that kid will leave your system alone if it's even marginally secure. But if you're keeping around top-secret information, it's a lot more difficult to have the system be secure enough that breaking into it isn't worth it, from a cost/benefit point of view, to the attackers.

Security is also neat because, as a concept, it permeates the entire idea space of computer science. Getting really good at security requires an incredibly deep understanding of the inner workings of computer systems, which has the nonobvious advantage that if you're trying to get a deep understanding of computer systems but don't know where to start, you can start with security and simply follow the trail. Use this to your advantage! Good luck.

TIP   **Getting In Touch**

If you want to tell us why you like Ubuntu Server, or why you hate it, or send us cookies, or just stalk us from a distance, come on in! Go to

https://lists.ubuntu.com/mailman/listinfo/ubuntu-server

to join the ubuntu-server mailing list, visit our page on Launchpad at

https://launchpad.net/people/ubuntu-server,

or jump on IRC. We're on the #ubuntu-server channel on FreeNode. Hope to see you there!

Advanced Topics

A single book chapter isn't the right place to go into great detail on all the features packed into Ubuntu Server. There isn't enough space, and many of the features are quite specialized. But that doesn't stop us from taking you on a whirlwind tour. Our goal here is to give just enough information to let you know what's there and interest you in finding out more about those features that may be relevant to how you use Ubuntu.

Virtualization

If there's been one buzzword filling out the server space for the past couple of years, it's *virtualization*. In August 2007, a virtualization company called VMware raised about a billion U.S. dollars in its initial public offering, and the term virtualization finally went supernova, spilling from the technology realm into the financial mainstream, and soon to CIOs and technology managers everywhere.

Fundamentally, virtualization is a way to turn one computer into many. (Erudite readers will note this is precisely the opposite of the Latin motto on the Seal of the United States, "E Pluribus Unum," which means "out of many, one." Some technologies match that description, too, like Single System Image, or SSI, grids. But if we talked about virtualization in Latin, it would be "Ex Uno Plura.") Why is it useful to turn one computer into many?

Back in the 1960s, servers were huge and extremely expensive, and no one wanted to buy more of them than they absolutely needed. It soon became clear that a single server, capable of running different operating systems at once, would allow the same hardware to be used by different people with different needs, which meant fewer hardware purchases, which meant happier customers with less devastated budgets. IBM was the first to offer this as a selling point, introducing virtualization in its IBM 7044 and IBM 704 models, and later in the hardware of its Model 67 mainframe. Since then, the industry largely moved away from mainframes and toward small and cheap rack servers, which meant the need to virtualize mostly went away: If you needed to run separate operating systems in parallel, you just bought two servers. But eventually Moore's law caught up with us, and even small rack machines became so powerful that organizations found many of them underutilized, while buying more servers (though cheap in itself) meant sizable auxiliary costs for cooling and electricity. This set the stage for virtualization to once again become vogue. Maybe you want to run different Linux distributions on the same machine. Maybe you need a Linux server side by side with Windows. Virtualization delivers.

There are four key types of virtualization. From the lowest level to highest, they are hardware emulation, full virtualization, paravirtualization, and OS virtualization. Hardware emulation means running different operating systems by emulating, for each, all of a computer's hardware in software. The approach is very powerful and painfully slow. Full virtualization instead uses a privileged piece of software called a hypervisor as a broker between operating systems and the underlying hardware, and it offers good performance but requires special processor support on instruction sets like the ubiquitous x86. Paravirtualization also uses a hypervisor but supports only executing operating systems that have been modified in a special way, offering high performance in return. Finally, OS virtualization is more accurately termed "containerization" or "zoning" and refers to operating systems that support multiple user spaces utilizing a single running kernel. Containerization provides near-native performance but isn't really comparable to the other virtualization approaches because its focus isn't running multiple operating systems in parallel but carving one up into isolated pieces.

The most widely used hardware emulators on Linux are QEMU and Bochs, available in Ubuntu as packages qemu and bochs respectively. The big players in full virtualization on Linux are the commercial offerings from VMware, IBM's z/VM, and most recently, a technology called KVM that's become part of the Linux kernel. In paravirtualization, the key contender is Xen; the Linux OS virtualization space is dominated by the OpenVZ and Linux-VServer projects, though many of the needed interfaces for OS virtualization have gradually made their way into the Linux kernel proper.

Now that we've laid the groundwork, let's point you in the right direction depending on what you're looking for. If you're a desktop Ubuntu user and want a way to safely run one or more other Linux distributions (including different versions of Ubuntu!) or operating systems (BSD, Windows, Solaris, and so forth) for testing or development, all packaged in a nice interface, the top recommendation is an open source project out of Sun Microsystems called VirtualBox. It's available in Ubuntu as the package virtualbox-ose, and its home page is www.virtualbox.org.

If you want to virtualize your server, the preferred solution in Ubuntu is KVM, a fast full virtualizer that turns the running kernel into a hypervisor. Due to peculiarities of the x86 instruction set, however, full virtualizers can work only with a little help from the processor, and KVM is no exception. To test whether your processor has the right support, try:

```
$ egrep '(vmx|svm)' /proc/cpuinfo
```

If that line produces any output, you're golden. Head on over to https:// help.ubuntu.com/community/KVM for instructions on installing and configuring KVM and its guest operating systems.

If you lack the processor support for KVM, you don't have great options. Ubuntu releases after Hardy (8.04) no longer offer kernels capable of hosting Xen guests (dom0 kernels aren't provided, in Xen parlance), which means if you're desperate to get going with Xen, you'll have to downgrade to Hardy or get your hands quite dirty in rolling the right kind of kernel yourself, which is usually no small task.

TIP   Point-and-Click Xen

One Xen-related project to point out is MIT's open source XVM (not to be confused with Sun Microsystems' xVM), which is a set of tools built on top of Debian that allow users to create and bring up Xen guests through a Web browser, complete with serial console redirection, ssh access, and a variety of other goodies. MIT uses the system to offer point-and-click virtual machines to any MIT affiliate; the project home page is http://xvm.mit.edu.

Disk Replication

We've discussed the role of RAID in protecting data integrity in the case of disk failures, but we didn't answer the follow-up question: What happens when a whole machine fails? The answer depends entirely on your use case, and giving a general prescription doesn't make sense. If you're Google, for instance, you have automated cluster management tools that notice a machine going down and don't distribute work to it until a technician has been dispatched to fix the machine. But that's because Google's infrastructure makes sure that (except in pathological cases) no machine holds data that isn't replicated elsewhere, so the failure of any one machine is ultimately irrelevant.

If you don't have Google's untold thousands of servers on a deeply redundant infrastructure, you may consider a simpler approach: Replicate an entire hard drive to another computer, propagating changes in real time, just like RAID1 but over the network.

This functionality is called DRBD, or Distributed Replicated Block Device, and it isn't limited to hard drives: It can replicate any block device you like. Ubuntu 9.04 ships with DRBD version 8.3.0, and the user space utilities you need are in the drbd8-utils package. For the full documentation, see the DRBD Web site at www.drbd.org.

Cloud Computing

Slowly but surely overtaking virtualization as the uncontested hottest topic in IT, cloud computing is just a new term for an old idea: on-demand or "pay-as-you-go" computing. Building and managing IT infrastructure aren't the core competencies of most organizations, the theory goes, and it's hard to predict how much computing capacity you'll need at any given time: If your company store transitions from wallowing in relative obscurity to becoming an overnight Internet sensation, what do you do? Buy up a truckload of new servers, ship them overnight, and work your IT staff to a pulp to bring all this new infrastructure up in as little time as possible? In the interim, your customers are overwhelming your existing capacity and getting frustrated by the slow response times. In the worst case scenario, by the time you have the new hardware running, customer interest has ebbed away, and you're now stuck having paid for a ton of extra hardware doing nothing at all. Cloud computing is the promise of a better way. Instead of dealing with IT infrastructure yourself, why not rent only the amount of it you need at any given moment from people whose job it is to deal with IT infrastructure, like Amazon or Google?

Cloud services like Amazon's S3 and EC2 and Google's App Engine offer exactly that. And Ubuntu is getting in on the action in two ways. As this book goes to press, Ubuntu is offering a beta program wherein Ubuntu images can be deployed to existing Amazon EC2 instances, allowing you to run Ubuntu servers on Amazon's infrastructure. It is expected that this functionality will become widely available in the foreseeable future. More interestingly, Ubuntu bundles a set of software called Eucalyptus (http://eucalyptus.cs.ucsb.edu) that allows you to create an EC2-style cloud on your own hardware while remaining interface-compatible with Amazon's. Such a setup offers savvy larger organizations the ability to manage their own infrastructure in a much more efficient way and makes it possible for even small infrastructure shops to become cloud service providers and compete for business with the big boys.

Summary

If you've never administered a system before, the transition from being a regular user will be difficult, regardless of which OS you choose to learn to administer. The difficulty stems from the wider shift in thinking that's required. Instead of just making sure your room is clean, now you have to run and protect the whole apartment building. But the difficulty is also educational and rewarding. (We realize they also told you this for your theoretical physics class in college, but we are not lying.) Learning to maintain Ubuntu servers is a great choice for you because you'll benefit from a vibrant and helpful user community, and you'll be working with a top-notch OS every step of the way.

Just as we were in the final editing stages of the first edition of this book, Ubuntu founder Mark Shuttleworth took the stage with then-new Sun Microsystems CEO Jonathan Schwartz in front of an audience of 15,000 at Sun's annual JavaOne conference. In 2001, Sun's previous CEO Scott McNealy famously compared running Linux on a mainframe to "having a trailer park in the back of your estate." But standing together in San Francisco, Schwartz and Shuttleworth announced that Sun plans to provide commercial support for Ubuntu Server on Sun's hardware. Meeting with reporters after his presentation, Schwartz called Ubuntu "one of the most important—if not *the* most important—Linux distribution out there," adding that "the odds are quite good that [Sun] will be aggressively supporting the work that Ubuntu is doing." Recent work with Sun has culminated with a version of Java shipped on Ubuntu servers and support for Sun's SPARC architecture. While it's still too early to know exactly how

Sun's collaboration with Ubuntu will play out in the long term, one thing is certain after the JavaOne announcement: The industry sees Ubuntu Server as a very powerful contender in the server OS arena.

If you're a seasoned administrator who came to see what all the Ubuntu Server fuss is about, stay tuned. The project, though rock solid as far as stability goes, is still in its feature infancy, and the Server Team is working very hard at making it the best server platform out there. We're emphasizing advanced features and we're being very fussy about getting all the little details just right.

In both cases, if you're installing a new server, give Ubuntu Server a try. It's a state-of-the-art system, and we're sure you'll enjoy using it. Get in touch, tell us what to do to make it better, and lend a hand. Help us make Ubuntu rock even harder on big iron and heavy metal!

CHAPTER 6

Support and Typical Problems

DESPITE THE FACT that the Ubuntu developers work tirelessly to make the Ubuntu user experience as fluid and problem-free as possible, there are always going to be bugs, glitches, and errors in software. This is nothing unique to Ubuntu; it is a characteristic that applies to all software. Anything created by humans is subject to error.

One of the many benefits of the open source development process is that errors and bugs are typically reported, found, and fixed in a far shorter time than is usually the case with proprietary software. This ensures that the software included with Ubuntu is far more solid and stable than some proprietary alternatives.

Although typical bugs are fixed quickly, there is still the case of user error. Even if a piece of software is completely bug-free, it can be used incorrectly, be misconfigured, or otherwise not work as expected. This is perfectly normal, and the aim of this chapter is to discuss some of the most common problems faced by users and to explore how to fix or otherwise resolve these issues.

This chapter is presented in a cookbook format, presenting each problem followed by a concise solution. If you have read through the other chapters in the book and not found the solution in this chapter, the next option is to try the superb Ubuntu forums at www.ubuntuforums.org. In recent years, the forums have proved to be a gold mine of useful information. Not only do they include discussion about problems and issues that other people have, they are also laden with community-contributed how-to articles that cover a wealth of different areas.

TIP   **Before You Begin**
As is the case with most books, there simply isn't room to cover everything in great detail. Part of the challenge when you face a problem lies in identifying what the cause is, which you can then explore using the forums, IRC, Web searches, and more. For many of the problems discussed in this chapter, we will point you to other resources that provide more information about fixing the problem.

The System

Your Ubuntu system is a little like an ecosystem. For certain things to work, other things must be already working. When you are new to any OS, it can often be a little difficult to get to know how some of these core system functions work.

In this section we cover the core system technology in Ubuntu and problems that can crop up when using it.

Ubuntu Won't Start!

When Ubuntu first starts, the GRUB bootloader loads an OS for you. If you have only Ubuntu installed on your computer, it is loaded automatically. Otherwise, if you have more than one OS (e.g., both Ubuntu and Microsoft Windows), you can pick the one you want from a menu. If you don't see the menu, restart your computer, wait until you see the word *GRUB*, and press Enter. Then use your arrow keys to select an option.

The core piece of software that is loaded when Ubuntu starts is the kernel, and sometimes there are a few different kernels installed on your system. On the menu, each kernel version (such as 2.6.28) has two options: the stock kernel and one called recovery mode. Try booting the newest kernel that is not a recovery mode one, and see if your system starts.

The Bootloader   If your system still fails to start, it is likely that your bootloader is broken. When you use a bootloader such as GRUB, a tiny file (called the *boot sector*) is copied into the very first part of your hard disk. If this file is broken or corrupted, your system often won't boot. Don't worry, though, you can fix this by reinstalling GRUB using a live CD, such as the regular Ubuntu installation CD! To reinstall GRUB, boot your computer using the Ubuntu CD. Go through the process using all the default options until you reach the disk partitioning step. Select Manual Partition. Mount your Linux partitions like /, swap, and /home. Do not format them, or you will lose all your data. You are merely telling the installer where your partitions are. Finish the manual partitioning step and save the changes. You will receive an error message saying that the system couldn't install. Ignore the message: You don't want the system to install itself. Instead, select Continue until you get to the Ubuntu install menu. From there, select Install Grub. When the process is complete, reboot the computer, removing the CD from the drive at the appropriate moment. You should boot normally using a fixed bootloader.

There is a lot more that may be done to configure GRUB, and there are other ways to repair or reinstall GRUB in the unlikely event that problems come up. Unfortunately, we don't have the space to cover GRUB configuration here, so we recommend that you consult the excellent documentation on the GRUB Web site at https://help.ubuntu.com/community/GrubHowto.

Backing Up and Restoring Your Boot Sector   When GRUB runs, the boot sector part of your hard disk contains information about which OS you can boot. This sector sometimes gets corrupted due to a system crash or power loss, and then your computer won't boot. Luckily, with a few carefully chosen commands, you can back up and restore this important sector.

Back it up using this command:

```
foo@bar:~$ sudo dd if=/dev/hda of=MBR-backup bs=512 count=1
```

The dd command copies the sector from the first disk (*/dev/hda*—change this to your disk) and saves it as MBR-backup in the current directory.

QUICK TIP   You may see references to boot sectors prefixed with MBR—this is short for *master boot record.*

To restore the sector, run this command:

```
foo@bar:~$ sudo dd if=MBR-backup of=/dev/hda bs=512 count=1
```

When you boot your computer in rescue mode, you can use these commands to manage your boot sector.

Ubuntu Loads but Keeps Restarting

If Ubuntu boots beyond GRUB but keeps rebooting, here are two issues you might be running into.

Memory Problems   One possible problem is that your computer has faulty memory in it. To test this, restart your computer, and at the GRUB screen, choose Memory Test. Let this run for at least several hours. If your memory has any problems, this test will bring them up.

Wrong Kernel   Sometimes you will get the wrong kernel with your computer. This might be because you have an older computer and are using a server kernel, which does not work with early Pentium computers. To fix this, install an appropriate generic kernel.

The Ubuntu Logo Appears Corrupted or Just Looks Odd While Booting

When your system starts, it uses a special splash image to make the boot process more attractive, as shown in Figure 6-1.

If you have problems with this splash screen, you can disable it. To do this, load the /boot/grub/menu.lst file into a text editor, and scroll to the bottom of the file. You should see a line such as this:

```
kernel    /boot/vmlinuz-2.6.20-9-generic root=/dev/hda1 ro quiet
          splash
```

Just remove the splash word from the line and restart your computer. Now plain-text boot messages are displayed when the system starts.

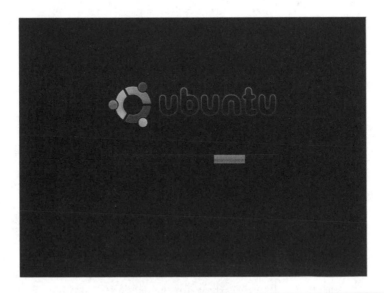

Figure 6-1 The graphical boot screen can be switched off if needed.

When I Start My Computer, I Get Text Instead of a Graphical Interface

The graphical interface used in Ubuntu comes in two parts: X and GNOME. The X server is an underlying chunk of software that ensures your graphics card and monitor work, and it provides a base for GNOME to run on. The GNOME desktop uses X as an engine to create the rich desktop platform you have been using. If you start your computer and can see only text and no graphical interface, this is a problem with X.

First restart your computer to see if that fixes the problem. If that doesn't work, restart your computer again and choose the recovery mode option in GRUB. You may have to hit Esc to enter GRUB. After the loading sequence, you will see a window with a number of options, as below. Choose the xfix option, which will change your video drive to a more generic one. You will then be returned to the same menu, where you can choose Resume normal boot to get back to the login window.

If this doesn't work, there is likely some deeper problem. Unfortunately, we don't have the space to cover X configuration in more detail, so please refer to http://help.ubuntu.com/community/DebuggingXAuto configuration for more help.

TIP   **Restricted Drivers**
Ubuntu ships with only fully free and open source graphics drivers. There are, however, closed source drivers available for ATI and NVIDIA cards. For more information about these drivers, visit the manufacturers' Web sites.

I Tried to Use a Word or PowerPoint Document, and the Fonts Are All Wrong

When loading Microsoft Office documents in OpenOffice.org, the documents may not look the way the author intended unless they are displayed with Windows fonts that are not on Ubuntu systems by default. While these fonts are proprietary, several of these are available online and can be downloaded with the msttcorefonts package from the multiverse repository.

When you install msttcorefonts, it automatically downloads and installs the following common Windows fonts:

- Andale Mono
- Arial (bold, italic, bold italic)
- Arial Black
- Comic Sans MS (bold)
- Courier New (bold, italic, bold italic)
- Georgia (bold, italic, bold italic)
- Impact
- Times New Roman (bold, italic, bold italic)
- Trebuchet (bold, italic, bold italic)
- Verdana (bold, italic, bold italic)
- Webdings

With the installation complete, restart X to make the fonts available.

I Want to Add TrueType Fonts to My Desktop Quickly

Fonts have a huge impact on how attractive and usable your desktop is. Although Ubuntu comes with a range of high-quality fonts, you may want to install some additional fonts. This is often the case when you need to use a specific company font. On modern operating systems, most fonts come in the form of TrueType fonts. Ubuntu offers full support for True-Type fonts, and it is simple to add new fonts.

To add a font, open your home directory using Nautilus and create a hidden directory called .fonts. Don't miss the . at the beginning because this is what makes a directory hidden. It is also the name that Ubuntu will expect for your personal font directory; if you use any other name, neither the directory nor your fonts will be found. Open .fonts and drag and drop your new font(s), as you can see in Figure 6-2. You may need to restart any applications, such as the GIMP, to use the new fonts.

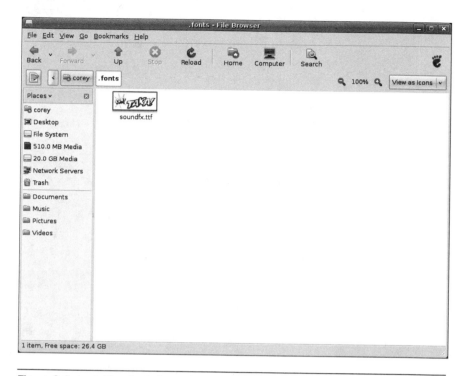

Figure 6-2 Installing fonts is as simple as dropping them into the font directory.

TIP **Nautilus and fonts:///**
In older versions of Ubuntu, you could open the font folder with fonts:/// in Nautilus. Due to changes in Nautilus, this no longer works in 8.04.

My Fonts Don't Look Good on My LCD Screen

If your fonts don't look good on your LCD screen, it is possible that a quick change to your configuration may make a large difference. LCDs use what is called *subpixel hinting* to make the fonts look best. Open the System > Preferences > Appearance tool, and under the Font tab, choose the Rendering option that looks best on your monitor. The Details button opens a further dialog to control DPI (dots per inch), smoothing, hinting, and pixel order. Try various options until you arrive at an optimal configuration.

How Do I Install a Package?

See the section Adding and Removing Programs and Packages in Chapter 4.

How Do I Install Another Desktop Environment?

By default, Ubuntu comes with the GNOME desktop environment. Other variants of Ubuntu come with different desktops; for example, Kubuntu comes with KDE and Xubuntu with Xfce. All of these desktop environments are easy to install on the other variants, via convenient metapackages. The Ubuntu package is called ubuntu-desktop, the Kubuntu one is kubuntu-desktop, and the Xubuntu one is xubuntu-desktop.

I Want to Install an Application That Is Not in the Repositories

Although the repositories contain a huge selection of packages, sometimes the package you need is not included. The first thing you should check is that you have enabled the additional repositories such as universe and multiverse. You can do this from your menu at System > Administration > Software Sources. In the Ubuntu Software tab, ensure that the boxes are checked for main, universe, restricted, and multiverse. (See help.ubuntu .com/community/Repositories/Ubuntu for more details.)

TIP   **The Repository Run-Down**

The *universe* repository contains the thousands of packages that are part of the Debian distribution, upon which Ubuntu is based. All of these packages are entirely free and supported by a community of Ubuntu contributors.

The *multiverse* repository contains a number of packages that are freely available to download but are not fully open source. If you want to run only open source software, you may not want to use this repository.

If you have enabled these extra repositories and your package is still not there, have a quick hunt around with a search engine to see if you can find a repository (known as a Debian or APT repository) for your package. If you find one, use the Repositories dialog box you have just played with to add the new repository, and then use Synaptic to install the package.

If no repository is available, look for a Debian package (.deb) for the application. If you find one, download it, and double-click it to install. If no

Debian package exists, look for an Autopackage. (An upcoming subsection, I Downloaded an Autopackage, but I Don't Know How to Run It, provides details about Autopackage installation.)

Finally, if all else fails, download the source code and compile it.

I Want a Local Copy of the Ubuntu Repositories

If you have a number of computers to administer or do a lot of package maintenance, having a local copy of the Ubuntu repositories can make your life a lot easier. There are two primary ways to do this: via debmirror and via rsync. Both are fairly lengthy processes to undertake, so the full recipe is hosted on the Ubuntu help wiki at http://help.ubuntu.com/community/Rsyncmirror and http://help.ubuntu.com/community/Debmirror.

The File Manager Is Slower Than I Would Like— How Can I Make It Run Faster?

You can deactivate a number of options to make using the file manager a faster process. First, click Edit > Preferences, find the tab marked Preview, and click on it. If Show Text in Icons (the first option) is enabled, it will preview some of the contents of text documents in their icons. Set this option to Never. Next, there's an option called Show Thumbnails. This option will preview image files as thumbnails. Set this option to Never to further improve the speed of the file manager's browsing. If enabled, the option Preview Sound Files will make it possible to preview sound files without actually opening them. Set this to Never as well. The last option, Count Number of Items, shows how many items are within the folders listed in the directory you're currently browsing. Set this to Never.

If you are still not satisfied with the speed of the file manager, you could check out some other file managers, such as Rox Filer or Thunar.

I Can't See the Hidden Files and Folders in the File Manager

Files and directories that begin with a dot (such as .bashrc) are typically used to store settings and configuration details for a particular application. By default, the file manager does not show these files. So how do you view, move, and copy them? Simple. Just click View > Show Hidden Files, or press Ctrl-H, and your hidden files are displayed, as shown in Figure 6-3.

TIP   **Warning!**
Don't ever mess around with hidden files and directories unless you know exactly what you are doing. Making the wrong move with one of these files or directories could break something!

How Do I Restore Something I Deleted in the File Manager?

When you delete something in Ubuntu, the files are not deleted immediately and are instead moved to the trash. If you accidentally deleted your important report and want to avoid limb removal by your boss, open the trash by double-clicking the small trash icon in the bottom right-hand corner of the screen, and then drag your files back into the file manager. The world now returns to the happy place it was before you accidentally deleted your files.

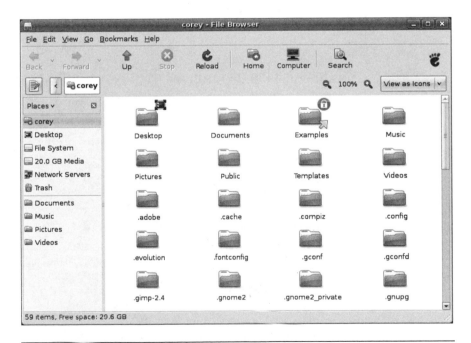

Figure 6-3 Displaying hidden files can be useful when you need to edit them.

How Can I Check If an .iso File Fully Downloaded?

Whenever you download a Linux distribution such as Ubuntu, you typically download an .iso file, a file that contains an image of a CD. You then use this file to create an installation CD for installing the distribution. After downloading the file, you may want to verify that the file you downloaded is the same as on the server. To test that you have the same file as on the server, you need to verify the .iso file. Open a terminal and run the following command:

```
foo@bar:~$ md5sum my_iso_file.iso
```

Wait a little while and Ubuntu will print a "word" that is 33 characters long. Now go to the site from which you downloaded the file, and compare this word with the md5sum given by the owner of the .iso file, usually a file named md5sums. The words should match. If they do not match, you should redownload the file and test it again.

NOTE   md5sum will work with just about any file, so it is a useful tool for quickly checking that two copies of the file are identical.

I Downloaded an Autopackage, but I Don't Know How to Run It

Autopackages are software packages that install on any Linux distribution, including Ubuntu. Autopackages offer a way to install software on your system that is not available via Synaptic. If you need something Synaptic can't offer, Autopackages are an alternative.

TIP   **Replacing an Application with an Autopackage**
If you are running an existing application that was installed via Synaptic and you want to replace it with an Autopackage, make sure that you uninstall the application first with Synaptic. Autopackages do not work in conjunction with Synaptic, so ensure that you remove any applications before you install the Autopackage.

When you find an Autopackage that you want to install, download it to your desktop. Now, right-click the package, and select Properties. In the

Permissions tab, select the Execute checkbox on the Owner row. Now close the dialog box, and double-click the package.

The installation program now begins, and you can just follow the on-screen instructions.

How Do I Compile an Application?

When a distribution package is not available, the source code is always available to compile with open source applications. Compilation is the process of converting programming code into a program that you can run and use. Although it sounds like a devilishly difficult process, it is typically fairly simple.

You should first have a look on the application's Web page, or in the INSTALL or README file included with the code, to see what software the application needs to run. When you know what is required, use Synaptic to search for the required tools. Many of the requirements will be software libraries (software that applications require to run), and these libraries typically have lib at the start of the package name. As an example, if you need to have the Ogg Vorbis audio codec installed, do a search in Synaptic for Ogg Vorbis, and libvorbis will be one of the packages. You should also install the package with -dev at the end of the name (such as libvorbis-dev). These packages allow you to compile software for that library.

The process of compiling software involves three steps: (1) configuration, (2) compilation, and (3) installation. Open a terminal, move into the directory from which you extracted the source code, and configure it:

```
foo@bar:yourapp$ ./configure
```

When you run /configure, it checks to see that you have all the required software. If it throws an error, it is likely that a required tool or library is missing. Find out what it is, and install it. Typically, configure will tell you what you need to install.

If the configure script works fine, compile the code with this command:

```
foo@bar:yourapp$ make
```

If a problem appears when compiling the software, it may be a bug or problem in the source code. It is best to refer your problem to the author of the code for further help.

If the compile process was successful, install the application with this command:

```
foo@bar:yourapp$ sudo make install
```

The software is now fully installed.

QUICK TIP   If you want to ensure that you have all the right tools installed to build your application, run the following command:

```
foo@bar:~$ sudo apt-get build-dep packagename
```

The Desktop Has Hung—What Do I Do?

If your computer still responds, you can press Ctrl-Alt-F1, which will show you a text login prompt. Login with your username and password, and then use top to find out if there is a program or process that is using all your processor power.

```
foo@bar:~$ top
```

You will be given some global stats at the top of the screen, and just under that will be a chartlike display of active programs and processes. The chart includes the pid (a number used by the processor to identify a specific process or program), the user running the process or program, and other great information. What you are looking for is the pid and the percentage of your CPU power each process is using. To make your task even easier, only the top several processes are listed, and they are listed in order of how much system resources they are consuming. You may find one that is using too many system resources. If so, note the pid, and use the number to replace <pid> in this command:

```
foo@bar:~$ sudo kill -9 <pid>
```

If that doesn't help, you can always restart your computer, but you may lose any unsaved work. To restart, enter:

```
foo@bar:~$ sudo reboot
```

NOTE   In previous versions of Ubuntu, you could press Ctrl-Alt-Backspace to restart the X server. This option has been disabled in Ubuntu 9.04 to prevent accidental data loss.

My Screen Resolution Is Wrong

If your screen resolution is incorrect, click System > Preferences > Display, and select a new resolution from the combo box.

How Can I Automatically Log In Without Having to Enter My Login Details?

If logging in is a drag for you, click System > Administration > Login Window. Under the Security tab, check the Enable Automatic Login and select the user who should be logged in automatically.

Be careful when automatically logging in—anyone will have access to the computer when it is started. If you would prefer that certain people not have access to the computer, automatically logging in may not be such a good idea.

TIP   **Avoid Automating a Root Login**
In the Security tab of the Login Screen Setup window, you can allow root to log in automatically. Although possible, this is *not recommended* due to the security implications. Automating a root login could allow anyone to tamper with your computer—so be careful!

I Tried to Upgrade My System, but I Got an Error

If you get an error when you try to install some software or upgrade your computer, the package manager may have tied itself in a knot. To try to resolve this, open a terminal, and run the following commands:

```
foo@bar:~$ sudo apt-get update
foo@bar:~$ sudo apt-get -f install
```

The first command updates your package list, and the second command tries to fix your package manager. If this is successful, the packages that failed will be installed correctly.

In addition to these commands, you can reconfigure any packages that have not yet been configured by running this command:

```
foo@bar:~$ sudo dpkg --configure --pending
```

I Am Running Out of Disk Space—How Do I Free Up Some Space?

If you are concerned that you may be running out of disk space, you can use a few techniques to clear some room. Before you do anything, you should get a report of how much disk space is available. Under the Applications > Accessories menu you will find a tool called Disk Usage Analyzer. After it has loaded, click on the Scan Home button. This will show you a graphical circular chart.

The center circle represents the root folder being scanned, in this case, your home directory. Each directory under that shows up as a ring. The larger the way around the ring, the greater the percentage of the total it is using. To find out specifically which directory is referred to, run your mouse over that segment. With the diagram, you can now explore to find the largest files and folders and clean them out as needed.

A new tool in 9.04 is the Computer Janitor, which clears out disk space and other accumulated "cruft" that exists on a well-used computer.

I Deleted Something in the File Manager, but I Don't See the Extra Disk Space

When you delete files in the file manager, they are copied to the trash. To finally delete them, right-click the trash in the bottom right-hand corner of the screen, and click Empty the Trash. A dialog box pops up asking you to confirm the deletion. Click the Empty the Trash button, and the files are removed.

Another Version of Ubuntu Is Out— How Do I Upgrade to It?

If a new version of Ubuntu is released, the update manager will notify you via an upgrade notification pop-up bubble. To upgrade, click the Upgrade button, and follow the instructions.

If you want to manually upgrade, you can also use the update manager. To update to an unstable version, run the update manager with the -d option, as follows:

```
foo@bar:~$ sudo update-manager   d
```

Applications

Applications are the lifeblood of any desktop computer, but they are also packed with configuration options, different types of functionality, and other things that could possibly trip you up. This section covers some of the common application-oriented problems in Ubuntu.

When I Click the Close Window Icon, My Program Doesn't Go Away

If your application seems to hang, and the window won't go away, keep clicking the X icon. After a few seconds, a dialog box should appear indicating that the program has become inactive and asking if you want to close it.

If this does not work, you can use xkill to stop it. Press Alt-F2, type xkill, and press Enter. Your mouse cursor changes to a small skull and crossbones. Click the offending application window, and it will finally be banished to that place where naughty applications wallow.

The Upgrade Notification Bubble Keeps Appearing, and I Want It to Stop

When your system detects new upgrades, a small bubble appears in the notification area. To switch this off, right-click the upgrades icon and deselect the Show Notifications option.

Extending the File Manager with Scripts

The file manager driving your Ubuntu desktop is called Nautilus. This comprehensive tool not only is packaged with features out of the box but also has the ability to be extended and improved with the use of special scripts.

A Nautilus script is just an executable shell script (usually using the default Ubuntu bash shell) that is placed in a special scripts directory so that the Nautilus graphical shell can find it. This is a really neat function of Nautilus because it allows you to extend the functionality of the file browser to do just about anything.

Scripts are invoked by selecting a file or group of files and right-clicking with the mouse to bring up a context menu. One of the options of this menu is the Scripts submenu, which allows you to select a script to invoke on the selected files.

Installing a Script   For a script to appear on the Scripts submenu, it must be placed in your scripts directory and be executable. If you place an executable script in your scripts directory, its name will not necessarily appear on the Scripts menu immediately. You first must visit the scripts directory with Nautilus by using the last option in the Scripts menu. Once the directory is visited, Nautilus will know about which scripts you have, and you will be able to use them. The current location of the scripts directory is .GNOME2/Nautilus-scripts in your home directory.

A Sample Nautilus Script   To get you started with Nautilus scripts, we look at an example script. This script pops up a window to ask for a folder location and then loads Nautilus at that location. It's a simple example, but it shows you how to create a script and run it.

Open your favorite text editor, and type the following code into a new file:

```
#! /bin/bash
#
# GoTo script for Nautilus scripts
# by ardchoille
```

```
# This script is released under the GPL
# February 20, 2006
#
mylocation='zenity --entry --text="Enter the desired location:"
--width=300 --title="Nautilus location"'
Nautilus --no-desktop --browser $mylocation
exit
```

Save the new file to your Nautilus scripts directory with the filename GoTo. (You can use any filename, really.) Now make the new script executable with this command:

```
foo@bar:~$ chmod a+x filename
```

Right-click in Nautilus, and choose Scripts > GoTo, and you will be presented with a dialog that asks for a valid path. After entering the path, click the OK button, and Nautilus will open with the specified path.

TIP   **For More Fun and Games . . .**
Install the Nautilus-actions package to add an extension to Nautilus for configuring programs to be launched depending on Nautilus selections.

I Went to a Web Site in Firefox, and the Macromedia Flash Plug-in Is Missing

If you visit a Web site in Firefox and the Flash plug-in is required, a small bar appears indicating that you need to install an additional plug-in. To do this, click the Install Missing Plug-ins button, and follow the instructions. When the program has downloaded and installed the plug-in, restart Firefox, and you are all set.

Java Is Not Installed on My System

To run a Java application on your system or access a Java Web site in Firefox, you need to install the Java libraries first. To install the Java plug-in, go to Applications > Add/Remove Applications, and search for Java. Install the Sun Java Plug-in. This will also install the Sun Java Runtime libraries.

My E-Mail Doesn't Work in Evolution

When you first run Evolution, it runs through the setup procedure to configure your e-mail address. To do this successfully, you need to have the following details available:

- Your type of e-mail server (such as POP or IMAP)
- Your mail server name (such as mail.server.com)
- Your mail account's username and password
- Authentication type (typically password)
- Your outgoing mail server type (typically SMTP)
- Your outgoing mail server name

If you have configured your account and your e-mail doesn't work, click Edit > Preferences, select the account from the list, and click the Edit button. Ensure that the settings are all correct. If you still cannot connect to your e-mail server, there is either a configuration problem or a network problem.

The latter problem would mean one of two things: Your computer is not connected to the network, or the mail server is not connected to the network. To test this, run the following command in a terminal:

```
foo@bar:~$ ping mail.server.com
```

Replace *mail.server.com* with the name of your mail server. The ping command sends a few pieces of information to the server to see if it responds. If it does respond, a series of lines will be displayed with a response time. If you get this, your network is running fine, and the problem is likely to be a configuration error.

A configuration error can be on either your computer or the mail server itself, with your computer being the far more likely candidate. You should get in touch with the person who runs the mail server and confirm that your settings are correct. Also check that the mail server is running fine. If the configuration error is on the mail server side, there is nothing you can do until it is corrected. In this case, ask the administrator to let you know when it is fixed.

When you find out the correct configuration settings, enter them into Evolution and try again.

Multimedia

Multimedia is playing an increasingly important role in modern desktops, and most people like to listen to music, watch movies, and watch videos on their desktops. Unfortunately, multimedia has had something of a checkered history in the Linux world due to the licensing problems with the all-important codecs required to view and hear media. This section explores some of the common problems faced with multimedia and your Ubuntu desktop.

TIP **Restricted Formats**
You can get further help and guidance on restricted media formats that don't ship with Ubuntu by visiting http://help.ubuntu.com/community/RestrictedFormats.

I Downloaded a Particular Media File, and It Won't Play

Included with Ubuntu are open source codecs such as Ogg Vorbis and Ogg Theora, but the vast majority of media on the Internet use restrictively licensed codecs such as MP3, Windows Media, QuickTime, and others.

Ubuntu does not ship these codecs for legal reasons. It's legally questionable to freely distribute most multimedia codecs because either the codec is patented or the player is reverse engineered and, as such, may fall afoul of the Digital Millennium Copyright Act (DMCA) in the United States. For most codecs, when you attempt to play the multimedia file, the movie or audio player will attempt to install the codecs as they are needed.

Ubuntu 7.04 began shipping a new tool to help address this problem. If you try to play a file without a necessary codec, Ubuntu will prompt you and allow you to automatically install any available codecs that can decode the file in question.

My DVD Won't Play

As with the previous problem, DVD playback is also a somewhat restricted process that requires special software to be installed. The software is available if needed. See http://help.ubuntu.com/community/ RestrictedFormats/PlayingDVDs for more details.

DVD Playback Is Jittery and Jumpy

When you watch DVD movies on your computer, you may find that they are jittery and unstable. In most cases the problem is that the direct memory access (DMA) mode in your DVD drive is not enabled. When you enable this mode, your problems should disappear.

Check whether DMA mode is enabled by running this command:

```
foo@bar:~$ sudo /sbin/hdparm /dev/hdc | grep dma
```

Most DVD drives are /dev/hdc, but change the final letter if yours is different. If DMA mode is not enabled, you will see this:

```
using_dma   = 1 (on)
```

To turn on DMA mode, run this command:

```
foo@bar:~$ sudo /sbin/hdparm -d1 /dev/hdc
```

Now try to play your DVD.

If this solves your problems, you should edit /etc/hdparm.conf and add the following block:

```
/dev/hdc {
    dma = on
}
```

When I Start Some Applications, I Hear No Sound on Playback

There are literally hundreds of thousands of applications for the Linux system, and many of them have different requirements and dependencies. One area in which this can be a problem is audio software. Each audio application relies on one of many sound servers: pieces of software that manage communication with the sound card. These sound servers come in many forms, including pulseaudio, JACK, and the now obsolete esd and aRts.

In Ubuntu, pulseaudio is the default sound server. Although the multimedia applications included with your desktop work fine, some other applications (such as Audacity) may fail to play with pulseaudio running. To solve this, go to Applications > System Tools > System Monitor. In the list of processes, click on pulseaudio, and click the End Process button. By stopping pulseaudio, you can now use the application.

TIP

But Remember . . .
Of course, by killing pulseaudio, those applications that require pulseaudio will not run. To use those applications (such as the default multimedia application included in Ubuntu), start pulseaudio by pressing Alt-F2 and typing pulseaudio into the text box. You will hear some beeps to indicate pulseaudio is now running.

My Microphone Doesn't Work

Although it seems like an obvious first point to check, make sure that you have plugged your microphone into the right socket. Many computers include a number of audio inputs/outputs, and they can be easily confused. In recent years, a number of hardware manufacturers seem to have gone out of their way to poorly mark these sockets, so don't worry if you get them mixed up. If in doubt, consult your manual.

With the microphone properly plugged in, load up the recording level monitor by clicking Applications > Sound & Video > Sound Recorder, press Record, and speak into your microphone. If you record nothing, you need to turn on and adjust the volume of your microphone. To do this, right-click the volume icon in the notification area, and select Open Volume Control. Inside the dialog that pops up, click the Capture tab, and make sure that the microphone sliders are near the top and that the small microphone icon does not have a red cross on it. Clicking this icon toggles whether devices are muted.

Now speak into the microphone, and you should see the recording level monitor flash.

My Sound Is Distorted

If you are experiencing distorted sound, one common cause is volume that is set too high. Open the Volume Control mixer by double-clicking on the Speaker in the upper right of your panel, beside the clock. Then set the PCM setting to around 70 percent. This might solve your problem.

How Do I Change the Visual Theme?

To change the way your Ubuntu desktop looks, click System > Control Center and choose Theme under the Look & Feel section. You will see a screen similar to that shown in Figure 6-4.

From there, you can select predefined themes or click Customize to create a custom theme. Changes are applied immediately. If you click Customize, you get a dialog box with three tabs. All themes are separated into three parts: the elements (buttons, text fields, and so on), the window frame (the

Figure 6-4 Changing themes is simple—click it, and it changes!

title bar), and icons. If you have downloaded new themes, drag them into the theme details window, and click Install Theme. When you are done, click Close.

How Do I Find and Install New Desktop Themes and Backgrounds?

We all love tweaking our desktops so they look individual to our own tastes and preferences. Luckily, the desktop is very flexible in how it can be visually configured. To make this as simple as possible, the GNOME Art Web site was created to host a huge array of wallpapers and themes. You can use the site to spruce up your desktop.

TIP   **Art Web Site**
In addition to GNOME Art, you can also use http://gnome-look.org to get themes.

To make this even easier, you can use the art manager tool to find new themes and backgrounds, but it is not installed by default. To install it, use Synaptic to install the gnomeart package. After it is installed, click System > Preferences > Art Manager.

To find desktop backgrounds, click Art > Backgrounds > All. If you don't want to see GNOME backgrounds, click Art > Backgrounds > Other. Alternatively, if you want only GNOME backgrounds, click Art > Backgrounds > GNOME. The art manager downloads thumbnails and descriptions of all available backgrounds. The latest backgrounds are at the bottom of the list. Select one from the list. To show the background in detail, click Preview. To install it, click Install. The Change Background window then shows the installed background. From there you can optionally change its style. When you're done, click Finish to get back to the art manager.

To find desktop theme elements, click Art > Desktop Themes > Application. The latest are at the bottom of the list. A sample window displaying the selected theme can be seen by clicking Preview. To install the theme, click Install. Then from the Theme window, choose the newly installed theme and then click the Close button to get back to the art manager.

Finding new window borders and icon themes works in a similar way. You can also install splash screens and login screens, but the former are not used by default in Ubuntu (though they can be enabled in the session manager), and the latter cannot be installed directly. GTK+ engines are seldom used. None of the applications installed by default use it.

How Do I Turn My Ubuntu Computer into a MythTV Box?

MythTV is a collection of applications that can convert a computer into a full-fledged media center with the ability to pause live TV, record shows, play music, play videos, play DVDs, access weather information, and more. More details about MythTV are available at www.mythtv.org. MythTV also goes to great lengths to look like a normal TV device and not like a computer plugged into a TV (see Figure 6-5 for an example).

To install a full MythTV system, install each of the mythtv packages available in Synaptic. You also need to install a few other packages:

- **xmltv:** This is used to grab TV listings in XML formatting.

- **DVD support:** To learn how to enable watching DVDs, you should refer to the Ubuntu wiki and install the relevant packages.

- **lirc:** Install this if you want to use a remote control.

MythTV comes in two major parts: the front end and the back end. The back end is used to perform the grunt work such as recording and process-

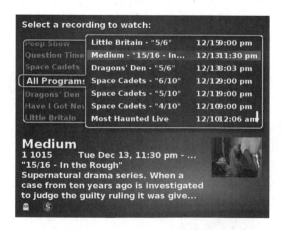

Figure 6-5 MythTV makes TV so much more fun!

ing shows, and the front end provides an attractive user interface. With this architecture, you could run the back end on a bulky, noisy machine elsewhere in the house and run the front end on a fanless, attractive little machine in your living room.

Fortunately, a new Ubuntu derivation, Mythbuntu has been created and makes the installation of MythTV on Ubuntu a breeze. Take a look at the Mythbuntu Web site at http://mythbuntu.org.

Networking

Few modern computers are not on the Internet now. With such an important feature, having a networking problem can feel like a crippling blow, particularly for those of us who spend extended periods of time staring at a Web browser. This section identifies some of the common problems with wired and wireless networking.

I Can't Access My Wired Local Area Network

First, check that the cables for your network are plugged in correctly. On many hubs, a small light appears when a cable is plugged into one of the sockets. Many Ethernet cards also display a connection light.

If the wired network is connected, Network Manager will show an icon of two computers. If that icon isn't showing, you can manually edit the network configuration by opening System > Preferences > Network Connections. You should see a line labeled Auth eth0 under the Wired tab. If there isn't one, you need to add one. If your network requires a static address, you can set one by pressing the Add button. In the dialog box that comes up, the static address information can be added under the Ipv4 Settings tab.

My Computer Says It Can't Resolve a Web Site

If the network is working but Web sites are not loading, you might have a problem with the incorrect name or DNS servers, which turn domain names such as google.com into IP addresses. To test this, you will need to know an IP address. You may have been given some IP addresses for different services from your ISP. Alternatively, you can use another computer to find an IP address with which to test. Try pinging the address, and if you get pings back, you know it's a name server problem. To resolve this, specify the correct name servers in the DNS tab.

How Do I Use SSH for Transferring Files Across a Network?

Secure Shell (SSH) is a protocol for connecting to remote computers in a safe way. To connect on the client side to a remote computer, click Locations > Connect to Server, and choose SSH as the service type. In the first field, enter the hostname or IP address of the remote computer.

The folder field can be left blank but can be used to go straight into a folder when you open the connection in the file manager. For instance, the home folder of user joe is typically /home/joe. Other folders are still accessible by clicking the up button on the toolbar. Enter the username of the user on the remote computer in the username field. If it's the same as the local username, just leave it blank. Both the folder field and the username field are case sensitive. Click Connect to proceed.

The first time you connect, a question appears that says the identity of the remote computer is yet unknown. This is normal. Click the Login Anyway button to proceed. If you are asked for a password, enter the password of the user on the remote computer. Click on remember password for this session and Connect. If the password was wrong or it took too long to enter the password, it is asked for again.

The connection appears on the desktop. If you chose not to remember the password for the session or in the key chain, you may be asked again. Now you can use the remote files the same way you use them locally. You can even copy files across different SSH connections and other network protocols such as FTP.

How Do I Use a Graphical Application Remotely with SSH?

To connect on the client side to the remote computer, first open a terminal. Click Applications > Utilities > Terminal. Now run this command:

```
foo@bar:~$ ssh host -X -l user
```

where *user* is the username on the remote computer, and *host* is the hostname or IP address. If the username is the same, leave out the -l *user* option. The -X option signals ssh that you want to run graphical applications. Make sure you use a capital X exactly as shown. Usernames are also case sensitive.

If it's the first time you are connecting, you will get a warning similar to the following:

```
The authenticity of host '251.152.123.101' (251.152.123.101)' can't
be established.
RSA key fingerprint is
01:12:23:34:45:56:67:78:89:9a:ab:bc:cd:de:ef:ff.
Are you sure you want to continue connecting (yes/no)?
```

Type yes, and press Enter. When asked for a password, enter the password of the user on the remote computer. Now you should have a shell on the remote computer, and it's possible to run commands remotely. For example, you can try Firefox to open up Mozilla Firefox, or Gaim to have a chat with yourself.

My Wireless Card Is Not Working

One of the greatest new features for laptop users in Ubuntu is Network Manager, an easy way to connect your Ubuntu system to any wireless network. Where previously you had to jump through hoops to do WPA or 802.1x authentication, Network Manager makes this completely transparent.

Simply click on the network icon in the upper panel by the clock to see all available wireless networks, and click on the network to connect to it. If wireless authentication is needed, be it WEP, WPA, or 802.1x, a dialog will pop up asking for your authentication details.

Of course, these improvements are not limited to laptop or even desktop users. Even for machines without a GUI, networking has been made easy by the Debian and Ubuntu developers who integrated WPA authentication into the standard network configuration system.

If Network Manager does not solve the problem, there are a few debugging steps you can take. First and most obvious to check is your laptop's hardware wifi switch (if it has one). Next, you should see if Ubuntu is finding your wireless card. Go to System > Administration > Network and see if a Wireless Connection exists. If it does, you will need to enable Roaming Mode to use Network Manager.

If Ubuntu does not see your wireless card, then you need to determine which driver your wireless card needs. Do a search for your card on Google and in the Ubuntu forums to find out. Next, you need to figure out what sort of wireless card you have. To do this, you need to install the gnome-device-manager package and then run Applications > System Tools > Device Manager, shown in Figure 6-6, and look for your wireless card. It will likely say Wireless or 802.11a, b, or g, or possibly WLAN.

After you have found out the card type, you will need to enable the driver. This may involve compiling code or can be as simple as enabling the driver that is already in Ubuntu. Check out the Ubuntu Forums or search Google for this information.

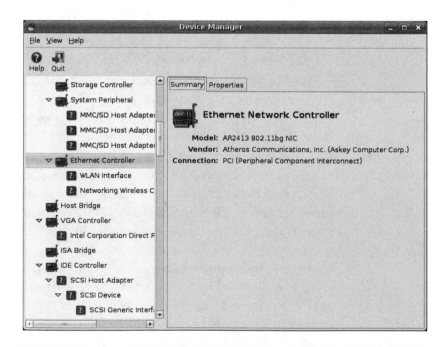

Figure 6-6 GNOME Device Manager is a tool to display information about and manage hardware, including wireless cards.

With the card identified, you now need to get connected, as we explained at the beginning of this question.

For more information, see https://wiki.ubuntu.com/HardwareSupportComponentsWirelessNetworkCards.

Hardware

There are many, many different types of hardware available for computers, including Webcams, network cards, hard disks, video cards, sound cards, and more. For each of these devices to work, a driver needs to be loaded by the Linux kernel. Unlike systems such as Windows, you don't need to install a special driver included with the device. Instead, the driver should already be included in Ubuntu and ready to work out of the box.

Of course, this is not always the case, and sometimes hardware can be something of a beast to get working. In this section, we tear apart some of the hardware-related problems and attempt to resolve them.

I Plug In My USB Stick and Nothing Happens

When a USB stick is plugged in, it must be mounted before you can access it. This normally happens automatically, and you should see an icon on your desktop similar to that displayed in Figure 6-7.

Unfortunately, in some rare cases it doesn't work. To fix this problem, first check that your system is set to automatically mount USB sticks. Click System > Preferences > Removable Drives and Media and look in the Storage tab. The following checkboxes should be selected:

- Mount removable drives when hot-plugged
- Mount removable media when inserted
- Browse removable media when inserted

When you have selected the boxes, click Close, and try plugging in your USB stick again.

Figure 6-7 To use a USB storage device, you just double-click the device icon that appears.

If you still have no luck, plug in the USB stick and then click Places > Computer. If there is an additional drive in the Computer window, right-click it, and select Mount Volume.

If you still have no luck, you need to manually mount the disk. First, click Applications > Accessories > Terminal, and then plug in your USB stick. Now run the following command:

```
foo@bar:~$ sudo mount -t vfat /dev/sda1 /mnt
```

To view your files, use the file manager to access the /mnt directory. Before you finish with the disk, unmount it with this command:

```
foo@bar:~$ umount /dev/sda1
```

TIP   **Drive Names**
On some computers you may need to use /dev/sdb1 or /dev/sdc1. Type in the following command when you have plugged in your disk to see which drives are available:

```
foo@bar:~$ ls -l /dev/sd*
```

I Copied Some Files to/from My USB Stick, but When I Access It Later, the Files Are Not There

When you plug in your USB stick, Ubuntu automatically mounts it. When you copy files to or from the stick, the files are copied over in bursts. Due to the way the kernel in Ubuntu works, sometimes there can be a slight delay before your files copy. If you remove the USB stick before copying has finished, some or all of the files may not have copied over successfully.

To ensure that everything you do with the USB stick is complete before you remove it, you should unmount it. To do this, right-click the drive icon on your desktop or in Places > Computer, and select Unmount. Give it a few seconds, and when the light on the drive has stopped flashing, you can safely remove the USB stick from your computer.

My CD-ROM/DVD Drive Is Not Working

If you are having problems accessing your CD-ROM/DVD drive, it is most likely because it is not mounted. Click Places > Computer, and look at the CD-ROM/DVD drive icon in the window. If the CD drive is not mounted, the icon looks like a drive; otherwise, it looks like a disc. If the drive isn't mounted, right-click it, and click Mount Volume.

My CD-ROM/DVD Drive Won't Eject

If you press the eject button on your CD-ROM drive and it won't eject a disc, click Places > Computer, right-click the CD-ROM/DVD drive, and select Eject. If this doesn't work, load up a terminal by clicking Applications > Accessories > Terminal, and type:

```
foo@bar:~$ eject
```

I Bought a Device, but It Doesn't Work in Ubuntu

When you buy a hardware device such as a graphics card, sound card, DVD drive, or Webcam, the device needs to have a driver installed for it to work.

Sometimes you need to go looking for a driver, or even find out whether Ubuntu supports it at all. To do this, search the Ubuntu forums or help wiki, or you can do a general search on the Internet for your device and the keyword Linux. After a bit of hunting around, you will probably find a driver that is available but obviously was not included with Ubuntu. Your first job should be to submit a bug report to say that the driver is not included in Ubuntu (see the subsection It Was Suggested I File a Bug

Report, but I Don't Know How, later in this chapter). Include in your bug report the location of where you found the driver.

My Computer Says It Is Out of Memory

If you get memory errors and have a reasonable amount of memory (256MB or more) and a swap partition, your memory may be faulty. To check whether your memory is working, restart your computer, and when you see GRUB loading, press Escape to display the boot menu. Select the memtest option, and a small tool will check your memory for errors.

The memtest utility tries its best to find problems with your memory, but there may be cases where memtest passes but the memory still has problems. To test this, try swapping the memory with some that is known to work and see if the problems go away. If they do, the memory is certainly faulty.

How Can I Copy Photos from My Mobile Phone to My Ubuntu Computer with Bluetooth?

Ubuntu has built-in Bluetooth support. If, when you attempt to pair the device with your computer, a popup doesn't automatically appear, go to System > Preferences > Bluetooth and change to "Always display icon." A small Bluetooth icon will appear in the notification area in the upper right. Clicking on that icon will bring up a dialog. Choose Setup New Device, and then follow the wizard.

NOTE   Some devices have fixed pins, which the graphical utilities cannot currently handle. See https://bugs.launchpad.net/ubuntu/+source/bluez-gnome/+bug/284994 for more information.

I Can Read My USB Storage Device, but I Can't Write to It

If you are having trouble writing to a USB key or external USB hard drive, there are a number of possible causes of the problem.

The first and most simple to diagnose is that you may not have permission to write to the device. When you plug in the drive, right-click the icon that appears on your desktop, and select Properties. In the window that appears, click the Permissions tab and ensure that the Others line has the

Write checkbox selected. If it is not selected, you don't have permission to access the drive.

QUICK TIP If you do have sufficient permissions but still can't write to the drive, jump to the next subsection, I Still Can't Write to My Drive!

To change these permissions, fire up a terminal, and move to the /media folder:

```
foo@bar:~$ cd /media
```

Now take a look at which drives are in there:

```
foo@bar:~$ ls -al
```

In the output that appears, you should see usbdisk as one of the entries. Now change the permissions so everyone can access it:

```
foo@bar:~$ sudo chmod a+w usbdisk
```

You should now be able to access the disk.

I Still Can't Write to My Drive!

If you have permissions to access the drive but still can't write to it, the problem is likely to be a filesystem issue. On a storage device such as a floppy disk, USB key, or hard drive, a specific type of filesystem is used to manage how the files are written to the physical disk. Ordinarily, you don't need to worry about this. But when things go wrong, it's time to figure out the details.

There are a number of different filesystems. The default Linux filesystem is ext3. In the Windows world, a few other filesystems are available, such as FAT16, FAT32, and the NTFS system used by Windows NT.

Although FAT16 and FAT32 are fully supported in Ubuntu, an NTFS filesystem cannot yet be written to reliably on a Linux computer. However, recent new code has gone into the Linux kernel to write to NTFS with FUSE or a kernel module. This code is still rather experimental and not included in a stock Ubuntu system, so be careful when playing with it.

To find out which filesystem the device uses, run the following command:

```
foo@bar:~$ sudo mount
```

In the output, look for the /dev/sda1 or /dev/sdb1 line. USB devices are usually located at either of these locations. You can see the filesystem next to where it says type, as in this example:

```
/dev/sda1 on /media/usbdisk type ext3 (rw,noexec,nosuid,nodev)
```

In this example, the filesystem is ext3. You can also add the umask=0000 option if you want to allow any user to read the disk.

If the filesystem is supported (ext3, VFAT, FAT16, FAT32) but you still can't access the disk, the filesystem may be corrupted. In cases such as this, it makes sense to format the disk with a new filesystem.

Before you format your disk, make *absolutely sure* that you are happy to remove the entire contents of the disk. If you need the files on the disk, have a look around the Internet and post to the Ubuntu forums to see if anyone else can help you before you format the disk. *Formatting really is the last option you have available!*

How Do I Format a Disk?

When most people think of formatting a disk, they think it is the process of deleting everything on the disk. Formatting a disk actually involves a little bit more, and it completely replaces the filesystem on the disk.

A side benefit to formatting a disk is making the disk work on different computers. Only certain types of filesystems are supported by each OS, and formatting a disk with a common filesystem can ensure that it works with these different operating systems. As an example, if you format a USB key with the ext3 filesystem, it won't work in Windows. If you use the VFAT filesystem, it will work in both Windows and Linux.

Formatting is fairly simple, and you just need to know the location of the device. USB storage devices (such as USB keyring drives and key fobs) tend to be located at /dev/sda1 or /dev/sdb1. Make sure that you have the right device, and then use one of the many mkfs commands to create the relevant filesystem. As an example, to create an ext3 filesystem, use the following command:

```
foo@bar:~$ sudo mkfs.ext3 /dev/sda1
```

A range of other mkfs commands can be used to create other filesystems:

- mkfs
- mkfs.cramfs
- mkfs.ext2
- mkfs.ext3
- mkfs.jfs
- mkfs.minix
- mkfs.msdos
- mkfs.reiser4
- mkfs.reiserfs
- mkfs.vfat
- mkfs.xfs

Each of these commands is used in the same way.

The Keys on My Keyboard Spit Out the Wrong Letters/Symbols

Every keyboard on a computer has a particular keyboard layout and locale attached to it. The keyboard layout specifies how many keyboard keys you have, in what order, and the locale specifies what each key does.

The locale is particularly important as letters and symbols vary dramatically in different locales. Aside from different types of letters, common symbols are often placed in different areas. As an example, on some keyboards the double quote (") is on the key above the right Shift key. On some keyboards, it is Shift-2. Having the wrong keyboard settings can be incredibly frustrating, and if the symbols printed on your keys don't match up to the symbols spat out when you press the keys, your keyboard settings are incorrect.

To fix this, click System > Preferences > Keyboard. Click the Layouts tab, and next to the Keyboard model box click the Choose button to select your keyboard model if you know it. If you don't know it, use the default setting. Now click the Add button, and resize the window so you can see the keyboard layout diagram more easily. Choose a different locale that matches your keyboard, and then click OK.

Now click on the Keyboard tab, and use the Type to Test Settings box to test whether your keyboard settings are correct.

My Remote Control Doesn't Work

If you want to use a remote control with your Ubuntu computer, you need to install the Linux Infrared Control (LIRC) package in Synaptic. LIRC is the library, and it supports a wide range of remote control units.

The first step is to determine which LIRC driver is required for your particular remote control. Take a look at the list of remotes on the LIRC site at www.lirc.org, or use your favorite search engine if your remote is not listed on the site.

LIRC includes a number of built-in drivers. You can see which ones are included by running the following command:

```
foo@bar:~$ lircd –driver=help
```

When you know which driver is required and you know your installed LIRC supports your hardware, you can edit the hardware.conf file in the /etc/lirc file to configure which one is used. Simply set the DRIVER line to the driver you selected. With this complete, restart LIRC:

```
foo@bar:~$ /etc/init.d/lirc restart
```

With LIRC ready and running, you can test it by running the following command:

```
foo@bar:~$ /etc/init.d/lirc restart
```

When you press the buttons on your remote control, a code should appear. This code can be mapped to a button on your remote by editing the lircd.conf file in /etc/lirc. For more information, see http://help.ubuntu.com/community/InstallLirc.

How Do I Find Out Which Hardware Works in Ubuntu Before I Purchase It?

Currently, there is no centralized device database to search for hardware that works with Ubuntu.

A good place to start is to look at https://wiki.ubuntu.com/HardwareSupport. You should then search the discussion forums and use Google to find out whether anyone else has used the hardware you're considering. Although not ideal ways to dig out your answer, the forums and Google are likely to give you the information you need until the full device database is complete.

System Administration

Traditionally, Linux has been very popular with system administrators. This has been due to not only Linux's incredible flexibility and power but also to the UNIX philosophy that drives much of the Linux platform. System administrators spend much of their day in the command line crafting strings of commands that hook together to do something interesting. With this powerful underlying command-line platform, so much is possible.

System administration is sometimes fraught with its own fair share of problems, though. This section lines up some of the problems and attempts to resolve them.

How Do I Schedule Things to Happen?

Built right into Ubuntu is a very powerful system for scheduling things to happen at specific times or at regular intervals. This system, called cron, allows you to specify the timing details and the command to run in a special file called a crontab.

The crontab is a simple text file that holds a list of commands to be run at specified times. These commands, and their related run times, are controlled by the cron daemon and are executed in the system's background. More information can be found by viewing the crontab's man page, and we will run through a simple crontab example soon to demonstrate how it is used.

The system maintains a crontab for each user on the system. The easiest way to edit your own crontab is via the gnome-schedule tool, which, once installed, can be launched from Applications > System Tools > Scheduled Tasks.

If you want to edit another user's crontab or the root crontab, you can also use a text editor. This text editor is opened when you use the -e option on the crontab command. To create a crontab, open a terminal and run the following command:

```
foo@bar:~$ crontab -e
```

The default nano text editor will open an empty crontab file. When adding crontab instructions, each line represents a separate crontab entry, also known as a cron job.

Crontab Sections   A typical line in a crontab looks like this:

```
00 01 3 5 6  ps ax
```

Each of the sections is separated by a space, with the final section having one or more spaces in it. No spaces are allowed within sections 1–5, only between them. Sections 1–5 are used to indicate when and how often you want the task to be executed. This is how a cron job is laid out from left to right:

- **Minute:** (00–59)
- **Hour:** (00–23; 0 = midnight)
- **Day:** (1–31)
- **Month:** (1–12)
- **Weekday:** (0–6; 0 = Sunday)
- **Command:** code

If you read each line in the crontab from the left and use these column descriptions, you can see how the instruction is built up. Here's an example:

```
01 04 1 1 1 /usr/bin/somedirectory/somecommand
```

This example runs /usr/bin/somedirectory/somecommand at 4:01 A.M. on any Monday that falls on January 1. An asterisk (*) indicates that every instance (every hour, every weekday, every month, and so on) of a time period should be used:

```
01 04 * * * /usr/bin/somedirectory/somecommand
```

This example will run /usr/bin/somedirectory/somecommand at 4:01 A.M. on every day of every month.

Comma-separated values can be used to run more than one instance of a particular command within a time period. Dash-separated values can be used to run a command continuously:

```
01,31 04,05 1-15 1,6 * /usr/bin/somedirectory/somecommand
```

This example will run /usr/bin/somedirectory/somecommand at 1 and 31 minutes past the hours of 4:00 A.M. and 5:00 A.M. on the 1st through the 15th days of every January and June.

The /usr/bin/somedirectory/somecommand text in these examples indicates the task that will be run at the specified times. It is recommended that you use the full path to the desired commands as shown here. The crontab will begin running as soon as it is properly edited and saved.

Crontab Command Options   There are a number of options you can pass to the crontab command to make it do different things. Here are some common options:

- The -l option causes the current crontab to be displayed on standard output.
- The -r option causes the current crontab to be removed.
- The -e option is used to edit the current crontab using the editor specified by the VISUAL or EDITOR environment variables.

When you edit a crontab file, the modified crontab is checked for accuracy and, if there are no errors, installed automatically.

An Example   Following is an example of how to set up a crontab to run updatedb, which updates the slocate database. Open a terminal application, type `crontab -e`, and press Enter. Then type the following line into the editor, substituting the full path for the one shown here:

```
45 04 * * * /usr/bin/updatedb
```

Save your changes, and exit the editor. The `crontab` command will let you know if you made any mistakes. The crontab will be installed and begin running if there are no errors. That's it. You now have a cron job set up to run `updatedb`, which updates the slocate database every morning at 4:45.

Note that a semicolon (`;`) or double ampersand (`&&`) can also be used in the command section to run multiple commands consecutively:

```
45 04 * * * /usr/sbin/chkrootkit && /usr/bin/updatedb
```

The semicolon will cause both commands to be executed. The double ampersand will cause the second command to execute only if the first command does not fail. This example will run `chkrootkit` and `updatedb` at 4:45 A.M. daily, provided that you have all the listed applications installed.

How Can I Copy a File from One Computer to Another?

The easiest way to copy files between machines is to use the Places > Connect to Server dialog box to make a connection using the graphical file manager. If you would prefer to do this on the command line, use the following command:

```
foo@bar:~$ scp file.txt jimmy@chin.com:/home/jimmy
```

The `scp` command works the same as the normal `cp` command, but it copies the file (here, file.txt) to another server (chin.com) using a specific user account (jimmy) and into a particular directory on the remote computer (/home/jimmy).

I Know an Application Is Available in Ubuntu, but Synaptic Can't Find It

If you are browsing through Synaptic and can't find a package that you know is available for Ubuntu, it is likely that you have not enabled the additional repositories.

To fix this, load Synaptic and select Settings > Repositories. Select the Community Maintained and Software Restricted by Copyright or Legal Issues checkboxes. Click Close to accept the settings and then click the Reload button to refresh the package list. Your package should now be listed.

I Am Running Ubuntu on an Older Computer, and I Would Like a Faster Desktop

Unlike other operating systems, Linux has the flexibility to scale incredibly well across different computers with different levels of horsepower. With the huge range of open source available, you can tweak your system so that it can be optimized in lots of different areas. This is particularly useful for recycling PCs. Some large organizations throw out older hardware that cannot run the latest OS from Microsoft. In many cases, these computers are actually perfectly usable if the software is optimized a little. Some open source groups have been set up to take these old machines, install Linux, and provide them to their local communities.

The first aspect to optimize is the GUI. Make certain you turn off any Desktop Effects. This can be done in the System > Preferences > Appearance tool under the Desktop Effects. After you have done that, you can change the way windows look when dragged. Open the terminal and type the following:

```
gconftool-2 --type bool --set
/apps/metacity/general/reduced_resources
true
```

Another option is to use another desktop environment, such as Xfce in Xubuntu (Figure 6-8).

You may also want to explore applications that are more lightweight. As an example, instead of using OpenOffice.org for word processing, try Abiword, a lightweight word processor than includes several features. For other types of applications, try the following alternatives:

- **Web browser:** Instead of Firefox, use Galeon.
- **Terminal:** Use an xterm instead of the GNOME terminal.
- **Spreadsheet:** An alternative to OpenOffice.org for spreadsheets is Gnumeric.

Figure 6-8 Also look at the Xubuntu distribution, which includes the lightweight Xfce 4.4 instead of GNOME.

I Reinstalled Windows, and Now Ubuntu Won't Start!

The first thing your computer does when you turn it on is read a special place on your hard disk called the master boot record (MBR). The information written there tells the computer what to do next. When you installed Ubuntu, it placed a boot menu on the MBR that lets you choose from which system to boot.

Unfortunately, when you reinstall Windows, it will recreate the MBR, not taking into consideration that any other OS may exist and replacing it with an MBR that only boots Windows. This is no good, and you naturally want to be able to replace it with the menu that lets you choose which system to boot.

Grab the CD you used to install Ubuntu on your computer. If you don't have it anymore, download a CD image from www.ubuntu.com/download, and burn it on a blank CD. If you used the live CD to install, you will need to use the alternative installation CD with the traditional text mode installer.

Insert the CD in the drive, and restart your computer. It will boot on the CD instead of using the hard disk. After Ubuntu starts, open gnome-terminal. You need to find the main hard drive with the /boot menu on it, likely hda1 or sda1. Mount this drive:

```
foo@bar:~# mount  /dev/hda1 /mnt
```

You now need to "chroot" into the mounted hard drive with:

```
foo@bar:~# chroot  /mnt
```

You now need to launch GRUB, which will take you to the GRUB prompt, and then type:

```
grub>find  /boot/grub/stage1
```

This will output a number like hd0,3.

NOTE   GRUB numbers the hard drives from 0 and mounts from a, with partitions in GRUB from 0 and mount from 1. This means that hda1 is hd0,0

Now you need to set the root partition with:

```
grub> root (hd0,3)
```

And then set up GRUB and exit with:

```
grub> setup (hd0)
grub> exit
```

Then restart your computer, and you should boot into GRUB and then back into Ubuntu.

How Do I Fix My Disk After a Power Failure?

Although the Ubuntu development team takes every care to ensure every possible situation is catered for, power cuts are one of the most difficult problems to resolve. Computers rely on power, and when it is dramatically removed from the system, the whole Ubuntu world in your computer shuts down immediately. The problem with this is that sudden power failure causes your Ubuntu machine to shut down improperly. When you next start the computer, you may then be prompted with a confusing fsck message. What is this, and how do you fix it?

The fsck program is a little tool to fix hard disks that don't have consistent filesystems, that is, filesystems typically made inconsistent by power failures. When the disk is inconsistent, Ubuntu automatically runs fsck to fix it. It asks you a bunch of questions that only a filesystem developer really understands, and you feel obliged to say Yes to each of them. As such, you sit there hammering the Y key over and over answering the questions.

There is a quick and simple fix to this problem. Instead of wearing out your Y key, you can simply edit one file and have any errors automatically fixed for you.

If your system is already running the desktop, open a terminal. Enter the following command:

```
foo@bar:~$ sudo gedit /etc/default/rcS
```

Now change the FSCKFIX line to the following:

```
FSCKFIX=yes
```

Save the file, and the next time you reboot, fsck will fix any detected disk problems without you having to intervene.

If you are using the character-based login, use the following command:

```
foo@bar:~$ sudo nano /etc/default/rcS
```

Change the FSCKFIX line as above, and then press Ctrl-O and Ctrl-X to save and exit.

Ubuntu Takes Up Too Much Disk Space on My Old Computer

If you are running Ubuntu on an older computer with a limited amount of disk space, you may want to choose software with more limited space requirements. Luckily, Ubuntu gives you incredibly flexible options when you're choosing which software you want to install. There is a variant of Ubuntu specifically for older computers, called Xubuntu. Xubuntu is based on Xfce, which is a lighter desktop than KDE or GNOME. To install Xubuntu on an existing Ubuntu system, install the xubuntu-desktop package. You can also download an .iso file of Xubuntu at www.xubuntu.org.

My Computer Is Running Quite Slowly—How Can I Find Out What Is Going On?

If you are having performance problems, there may be a particular process on your computer gobbling up all of the memory. Launch the System Monitor under the System > Administration menu and go the Processes tab. You will see which applications are using more CPU and RAM. You can also use top on the command line:

```
foo@bar:~$ top
```

The top command shows the current processes on your computer that are using the most system resources. If you see a particular program taking up an unusual amount of resources, that may be the culprit.

Some processes (such as the Apache Web server) fork and replicate themselves when used. Another useful technique is to see how many of these processes are running:

```
foo@bar:~$ ps ax | grep theprogram | wc -l
```

This command takes a listing of the processes running on the system, uses grep to search for a specific process, and then counts the number of lines returned, thus indicating how many processes are running.

How Can I Learn the Different Options for Commands?

Every command in Ubuntu has a small reference card included called a man page. This page displays the range of available options. Access it by typing man, and then enter the command:

```
foo@bar:~$ man grep
```

Another method of listing the options is to use the -h or –help options:

```
foo@bar:~$ grep --help
```

How Do I Get My Root Account Back?

In a default Ubuntu installation, the root account is disabled. Instead, the user account created during the installation process is used with sudo to access administer facilities. The sudo command is used extensively to temporarily take on root privileges when needed.

If you want to get the root account back, run the following command:

```
foo@bar:~$ sudo passwd root
```

Enter your user account's password, and then enter a new root password. You will be asked to verify the new root password.

TIP   **Tired of Typing sudo?**

If you want to type in a number of root commands and don't want to constantly prefix every command with sudo, run the following command:

```
foo@bar:~$ su -
```

This will upgrade your terminal to the root user. You can also use the -i switch in sudo:

```
foo@bar:~$ sudo -i
```

Everything you type in now is as the root user. To go back to your original user, use the following command:

```
foo@bar:~# exit
```

When using this command, note that when you are a normal user, the prompt ends with a $ symbol, but when you are working as the root user, it ends with a # symbol.

To disable the root account at a later date, run the following command:

```
foo@bar:~$ sudo passwd -l root
```

This will lock the root account.

I Forgot My System Password—What Can I Do?

Although passwords are indefinably essential and useful, they are also prone to being forgotten. With an increasing number of nasties out there on the Internet wanting to suck away your passwords, you need to think of more complex passwords, which are in turn harder to remember and easier to forget.

If you forget the system password, you need to jump through a few more hoops to reset your password. Restart your computer, and when you see the word GRUB appear on the screen, press Escape to see the boot menu. Select the recovery mode option from the menu. When the computer boots, it will present you with a root shell. At the prompt type:

```
foo@bar:~# passwd username
```

Follow the prompts to set a new password. Finally, reboot the computer with the following command:

```
foo@bar:~# reboot
```

How Do I Access My Windows Partitions?

If you are running Ubuntu on a computer with a Windows disk, you may want to read and write to the disk. Look on your Desktop for an icon labeled sda1 or hda1. This is your Windows partition.

QUICK TIP　　Be wary of deleting files on a Windows partition from Ubuntu. Doing this indiscriminately can accidentally render your Windows install unusable.

How Do I Add Users?

To add a new user to your computer, select System > Administration > Users and Groups. When the window loads, click the Add User button, and then just fill in the details. To do this in the command line, use the adduser command:

```
foo@bar:~$ sudo adduser jimmy
```

This adds a user called jimmy.

Other

Now, we'll finish this chapter with a collection of other common problems and quirks that don't fit neatly into any of the other categories.

Running Another OS in Ubuntu

Some of you read the title of this recipe and wondered how on earth you can run another OS on an existing OS. Surely such a thing is not possible? Well, actually, it is.

In recent years, virtualization technology has been developed to simulate a computer in software. You can use this technology to boot a virtual computer in a window and run an entire operating system on it. There are a few options open to the Ubuntu user to enable this functionality: qemu, kvm, and VirtualBox.

Qemu and kvm have a similar core and are both command-line based, although various graphical front ends exist to simplify their use. The main differences are their speed and hardware support. Many modern CPUs have hardware features (often called VT, VMX, or SVM) that enable virtualization software to more closely interact with the hardware to improve performance. kvm supports VT where qemu does not. Qemu does have an optional extra kernel-level module called kqemu, which mitigates the lack of VT support and improves performance accordingly.

VirtualBox comes in two main incarnations: a free open source edition (OSE) and a binary-only version. The binary-only nonfree version is almost identical to the OSE but also currently features USB support.

In recent versions of Ubuntu, the OSE edition of VirtualBox is available in the universe repository. The nonfree version of VirtualBox can be obtained from virtualbox.org, where an additional Ubuntu-compatible repository can be used to simplify installation.

All of the above-mentioned virtualization options can run Windows, FreeBSD, Netware, and even other Ubuntu installations. We now describe how to get started with each of the three in turn.

To discover if your CPU has hardware virtualization support, issue the following command. If there is no output, then your CPU does not have VT support.

```
foo@bar:~$ egrep '^flags.* (vmx|svm)' /proc/cpuinfo
```

First, use Synaptic to install either qemu and kqemu or kvm (select kvm if you know your CPU has VT support). When it has installed, use the file manager to create a folder in your home directory called emu. Now load a terminal and run the following commands:

```
foo@bar:~$ cd qemu
foo@bar:~qemu$ qemu-img create hd.img 350M
```

The last parameter (350M) indicates the size of the virtual drive in megabytes. Feel free to adjust this to your liking.

NOTE   Whether you are using qemu or kvm, the command is still qemu-img, because kvm is largely based on qemu.

If you're using kvm, you will need to load the necessary kernel-level modules to enable VT support. They should be loaded automatically upon boot-up, but if they're not, then you can forcibly attempt to load them with the following command:

```
foo@bar:~emu$ sudo modprobe kvm
```

The next step is to boot an install CD in the virtual machine (replacing qemu with kvm, if necessary, in the following examples):

```
foo@bar:~emu$ qemu -boot d -cdrom /dev/cdrom -hda hd.img
```

When your installation has finished, reboot the virtual machine:

```
foo@bar:~emu$ qemu -boot c -fda /dev/fda -cdrom /dev/cdrom -hda hd.img
-user-net -pci -m 256 -k en
```

With the setup complete, you can add a link to the new OS on your panel. Right-click on the panel where you want to create the launcher, and choose Add to Panel > Custom Application Launcher. Enter the following details:

- **Name:** VirtualMachine
- **Command:** `qemu -boot c -fda /dev/fda -cdrom /dev/cdrom -hda ~/emu/hd.img -user-net -pci -m 256 -k en`

Choose an icon for your new OS.

Alternatively, if you choose to use VirtualBox (either OSE or nonfree edition), you can skip all the command-line fun above and instead use the graphical tools provided to manage your virtual machine.

Install VirtualBox either from the standard Ubuntu repository or from the virtualbox.org site. Once you do, you will find the icon for VirtualBox in the Applications > System Tools menu.

Click the New icon to start the Create New Virtual Machine Wizard. Give your virtual machine a description and select an OS and version you plan to run in the virtual machine from the drop-downs available. On the next panel, select the amount of your host computer's memory you wish to give to the virtual machine while it's running. Finally, use the Create New Virtual Disk wizard on the following pane to create an automatically expanding virtual disk image on your hard disk.

Once the image is created, use the Settings icon back in the main screen of VirtualBox to specify the boot device as either your local CD/DVD ROM drive or a previously downloaded ISO image of the OS you plan to install. If your CPU supports VT, then you will be able to select Enable VT-x/AMD-V from the General > Advanced tab. Modern versions of VirtualBox support an easily configurable host networking option that enables any virtual machine you create to appear as if it were a host on your network. The alternative (NAT) will prevent the virtual machine from accessing your network, as if it were using a firewall.

Once the virtual machine has been configured, it can be started from the VirtualBox main screen. Additionally, from the menus, it's possible to suspend and power off a running virtual machine.

It Was Suggested I File a Bug Report, but I Don't Know How

Ubuntu is a collaboratively developed system in which hundreds of developers from around the world work together to build a simple yet powerful distribution. With so much software involved in Ubuntu, bugs and problems can naturally creep into the system. If you believe that the problem you have is not a configuration or hardware error, it may well be a bug. Anyone can submit a bug, and it is encouraged that regular users of Ubuntu contribute bug reports where possible.

Bug reports are handled on a special Web site called Launchpad, which resides at http://launchpad.net/ (Figure 6-9).

Launchpad provides a complete environment in which bugs can be tracked and future features are merged into Ubuntu. Launchpad is designed not only to make bugs for Ubuntu easy to report but also to support bug reports for other systems, too. This means that developers can work together to resolve problems.

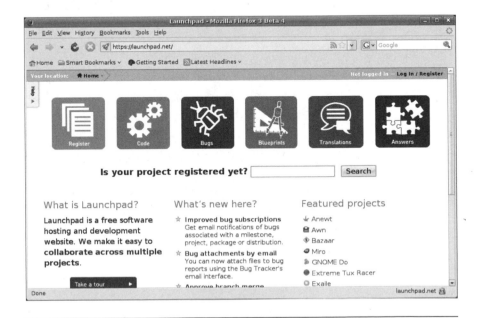

Figure 6-9 Launchpad is where the bug reports live.

To report a bug, click on the Help menu in the application for which you want to report the bug. Select Get Online Help. Firefox will now load and take you to the Launchpad site. To use Launchpad, you need a user account, so click the Register link to register your account. Enter your e-mail address, and you will be e-mailed registration details. When you have completed the registration, log in to Launchpad. You can always access your application in Launchpad by using the Get Online Help menu item.

TIP   **Another Way into the Bug-Tracking System**
You can also access the bug-tracking system by going to Launchpad, clicking the Bugs link in the right sidebar, and then entering the name of the application in the text box farther down the page. If possible, it is generally recommended that you use the Help menu approach as it will automatically pick the right application for you.

The first step is to check whether the bug has already been reported. In the right sidebar of Launchpad are a series of menu options. Each bug added to the system is automatically given a unique ID for the bug, and you can search for this number if needed. You can alternatively search for something related to the problem. As an example, search for "crash" or "hang." If you find your bug has already been reported, you can stay updated with changes related to the bug by clicking the Subscribe link in the right sidebar.

If no bug exists, you should report it yourself. To do this, click the Report a Bug in *<application name>* in Ubuntu link. Simply fill in the Summary box with a single-line description of the bug, and then use the Description box to fill in the details. You should be as detailed as possible and include your computer's specifications, any special steps you went through to trigger the bug, the effects of the bug, and how you expected the software to work. Try to be detailed, but keep everything you say relevant to the bug. If you would prefer to keep your bug report confidential, select the checkbox for that, but it is highly recommended that you keep your bug reports public if possible. This means that as many people as possible can see the report and possibly act on it.

With the bug submitted, you will receive e-mail updates about the progress the developers are making to fix the bug. In some cases the developers may ask you to run commands or try different things to help nail down the bug so they can fix it.

Bug reporting is an essential process in which everyday users of Ubuntu can really help keep the software as bug-free and stable as possible. It is a truly valid contribution to the open source community.

TIP   **Need a Hand?**
If you need help reporting a bug, ask for support on the Ubuntu-users list, IRC, or the forums. The community will be more than happy to help.

How Can I Monitor the Weather?

Besides looking out the window, you can add a weather applet to a panel that shows the current temperature along with an icon that indicates sunshine or rain. Right-click a panel, and select Add to Panel. Drag the weather applet (under Accessories) to an empty spot on the panel, and click Close. Now right-click the weather applet, select Preferences, and select the Location tab. From here you can select your city or a city in the vicinity. Click Close when you are done. If you want more detailed information, just click the applet.

How Do I Make Ubuntu Bread?

With so many recipes in this chapter to solve common problems or perform small tweaks and optimizations, it seems unfair not to include an actual recipe. This recipe was posted to the popular Ubuntu forums to create some special Ukrainian egg bread called kalach, which is much like challah or any other egg bread. The twist, of course, is that it is shaped like our favorite distribution's logo (Figure 6-10).

To create this bread, you will need the following ingredients:

1 teaspoon of yeast

3/4 cup warm water (100°F/40°C)

3 eggs

3 to 5 cups flour

1/4 cup sugar

1/4 cup oil

pinch of salt

Figure 6-10 The Ubuntu loaf

First, put the yeast in the warm water while you gather the other ingredients.

Beat the three eggs in a bowl and save a teaspoon of the egg mixture for later. Add three cups of flour to a big bowl along with the egg, sugar, oil, and salt. When the yeast is bubbly, add it in too. Knead. If the mixture is crumbly, add water. If it is too sticky, add more flour. The dough should be firmer than your average bread dough to keep its shape.

Cover the bowl with a damp towel, and let the dough rise in a warm place. When it has doubled in size, punch it down, and roll it out into three ropes.

Make the ropes less than one inch (2.5 cm) thick so that the loaf will bake evenly. Do this on a large surface. You need a lot of room. Use a bit of oil if things are sticky. Your dough should be somewhat stiff, so this should not be a problem.

You should end up with three ropes that are a little less than three feet (75 cm) long. Pinch them together on one end, and set them horizontally on your work surface.

Now braid the ropes. Take the lowermost rope and place it between the other two. The middle rope is now the lowest rope. Move it into position by bringing it down to where the other rope (lowermost) used to be. Take the topmost rope and place it between the other two. Take the rope that is now highest and pull it up to its position as topmost rope. Place the lowermost rope between the two others. You get the picture. . . .

When you have a long braid, snip off the ends, and join the ends to form a circle. Join the individual ropes together as well as you can. Place the loaf on an oiled cookie sheet. Take the snipped-off bits and form two long strands. Intertwine them by putting them side by side and holding one end while rolling the other end with the palm of your hand. Stretch this out around the bottom of the big braid and join the ends together.

Cover the kalach with a damp towel and let it double in size (about an hour, maybe less on a hot day). Brush it with the egg mixture. You should have enough to cover the loaf completely. Bake at 350°F/180°C until it becomes dark brown. Let it cool.

Be very careful. One of our dogs jumps up on the table to eat this bread. It is embarrassing when guests find the dog with the half of the bread that she could not finish under the table.

How Can I Prevent the Pain I Get in My Fingers When I Type?

If you feel pain or numbness in your fingers, you are likely suffering from repetitive strain injury (RSI). This common complaint typically afflicts those who work with computers for long periods every day. The constant movement of the fingers in such a repetitive fashion can cause swelling and pain in the fingers and wrists. RSI can also affect your neck, back, legs, and other areas.

If you suspect you have RSI, you should first consult your doctor. RSI is a condition that requires treatment. This treatment can come in the form of physiotherapy, regular breaks, workspace adjustments, and in some extreme cases, medication or surgery.

One of the most common methods of reducing RSI is to take regular rest breaks. It is a good idea to break about once an hour. Your desktop can help with this. Click on System > Preferences > Keyboard, and select the Typing Break tab. You can use the settings in the tab to enforce a break once an hour.

Another type of break is a micropause. These breaks usually occur every couple of minutes, and the break lasts for only a few seconds. These breaks are intended to be less intrusive and give your hands a chance to regularly rest for a short period to allow the blood to flow. A useful little tool called Workrave has been developed to enforce regular micropauses. Use the Synaptic package manager to install Workrave.

TIP   **Remember!**
Always consult a doctor about any health problems you might have. RSI in many cases is a treatable problem, but your doctor can best advise you on the recommended treatment.

Summary

Software by its very nature is subject to inaccuracies, bugs, and usability problems—and users by their very nature are subject to errors, mistakes, and misjudgments. Although every release of Ubuntu makes Linux and computing far easier to use and more flexible than the previous release, there are always going to be occasions when something just doesn't work.

Hopefully, this chapter has provided some useful solutions to some of the typical problems you may face when using Ubuntu. If this chapter does not answer all your questions, though, head over to the incredible Ubuntu forums at www.ubuntuforums.org to tap into a huge community of people who can help.

CHAPTER 7

The Ubuntu Community

- Venues
- Teams, Processes, and Community Governance
- Getting Involved
- Summary

COMMUNITY IS A WORD OFTEN used in discussions of Ubuntu. Early articles about Ubuntu bore subtitles asking, "Would you like some community with that?" The earliest press releases and communiqués from the project emphasized a "community-driven approach" to operating system development and distribution. Also, the highest-level governance board in Ubuntu is called the Community Council. Canonical, Ltd. employs a full-time community manager (Jono Bacon, one of the authors of this book). And we made a very conscious decision to spend an entire chapter of this book describing the Ubuntu community. In fact, all three editions are dedicated to the Ubuntu community!

Still, while the Ubuntu community is important, it is not always easy to succinctly describe it. Ubuntu is, in large part, developed and funded by Canonical, Ltd. The community, almost by definition, extends far beyond Canonical, Ltd. The Ubuntu project has members and self-declared activists (Ubunteros), but the Ubuntu community is more than even those with such explicitly declared relationships. The project contains a wide variety of different venues for participation. But while the community is active in each of these areas, its scope is even wider.

The Ubuntu community is the collection of individuals who build, promote, distribute, support, document, translate, and advocate Ubuntu—in myriad ways and in myriad venues. Most people in the Ubuntu community have never met, talked with, or heard of each other. Members of the community are linked by their contributions, both technical and nontechnical, and by Ubuntu itself. These contributions have built Ubuntu as a distribution, as a social movement, as a set of support infrastructures, and as a project. In short, they have built Ubuntu *as a community*. While any active software development project has a number of people making contributions, not every project has a community.

Community is also a term that represents a promise by the Ubuntu project to remain inclusive. The focus on community means that volunteers are not only welcome but also essential. It means that Ubuntu is a "place" where individuals can come together to create something greater than the sum of its parts. The word *community* gives a nod to the fact that while much development work is paid for by Canonical, Ltd., and while some people contribute more hours, more effort, more code, more translations, more documentation, or more advocacy work to Ubuntu than others, no individual or subgroup can take credit for everything that Ubuntu has become. In Ubuntu, no contribution is expendable. Having a community also reflects Ubuntu's goal to provide a low barrier for entry for these contributions. Anyone who cares about Ubuntu can contribute to the project and can, in whatever ways are most appropriate, become a participant in the Ubuntu community.

This chapter provides a bird's-eye view of the venues and processes in which the Ubuntu community is active. First, it takes a tour through the venues through which the Ubuntu community communicates. It continues by looking at the way the community is organized and the processes by which that organization works. Finally, it walks you through the ways *you* can participate in the Ubuntu community and contribute to its success.

Venues

As we described in Chapter 1, transparent and public communication was an early goal of the Ubuntu project. Technical and community decisions are made publicly and are accessible to all interested parties. When this is impossible (e.g., when there is a face-to-face meeting and it's simply not possible for *everyone* interested to attend), the community attempts to publish summaries and minutes and to provide avenues for feedback. Ubuntu contains no "member only," "developer only," or "decision maker only" back channels except to preserve individual privacy or security—and the Ubuntu community refuses to create them. All work in Ubuntu occurs in places where *everyone* can view the work, and anyone who agrees to engage constructively and respectfully can participate.

Of course, this activity is public only to those who know where to find it. This section tries to document the venues for communication in Ubuntu as completely as possible. It describes the places where discussions of development, support, and advocacy take place. While nobody can engage in communication in *all* of the venues described, knowledge of what exists allows participants to be more informed when they need to choose the right place to ask a question or to make a suggestion.

Mailing Lists

The single most important venue for communication in Ubuntu is the Ubuntu mailing lists. These lists provide the space where all important announcements are made and where development discussions take place. There are, at the time of this writing, 280 public e-mail lists. This number is constantly growing—there were less than half as many when we wrote the third edition of this book a year ago and half that many a year before that!

An up-to-date, full page of mailing lists for Ubuntu can be found at http://lists.ubuntu.com, where users can see a list of available mailing lists, view archived discussions, and subscribe to lists through a Web interface.

Lists are one of the oldest forms of communication by e-mail. A mailing list provides a single e-mail address that, when mailed to, will then relay the received message to a large number of people. In Ubuntu, lists are topical, and individuals can subscribe to a mailing list if they want to receive information on the list's topic. All mailing lists at Ubuntu are hosted at lists.ubuntu.com. If you would like to send a message to a list, simply e-mail *<mailing list name>*@lists.ubuntu.com, replacing *<mailing list name>* with the name of the list you are trying to mail.

With a few exceptions (e.g., the e-mail lists for the Technical Board or Community Council), *anybody* can subscribe to any Ubuntu list. In most cases, the capability to send e-mail to lists is restricted to list members (membership in lists is, of course, open to anyone). This means that all e-mail sent to a list from someone who is not a member of that list is put into a queue to be reviewed by a human moderator before it is broadcast to list members. This is done as an antispam measure. Users can subscribe to lists and then configure the system to never send e-mail. For several e-mail lists, *all* messages are moderated. This is largely to ensure that lists remain "low volume" or "announcement only."

Ubuntu's mailing lists are run by the popular Mailman software, which may be familiar to some users. Mailman makes it simple to subscribe to lists, to unsubscribe, and to configure any number of options about mail delivery. One popular option is to receive a daily digest of messages rather than a separate e-mail each time a new message is sent. This is all available through a Web interface at http://lists.ubuntu.com. Users can also subscribe to lists by sending an e-mail with "subscribe" in the subject line to *<mailing list name>*-REQUEST@lists.ubuntu.com.

While each list plays an important role in the Ubuntu community, the following central lists warrant a little more detail. You might find it a good idea to subscribe to them.

ubuntu-announce This fully moderated list relays all important announcements for the Ubuntu project and usually contains less than one e-mail per week. It is the first place where new releases are announced and where other important information can be found first. If you use Ubuntu, you may want to consider subscribing to this list. If you subscribe to only one list, this should be it.

ubuntu-devel-announce This fully moderated list contains announcements related to the development of Ubuntu. It is low volume and contains one to three e-mails per week. If you work with code in Ubuntu, use a development release, or contribute on any technical level, you should be on this list. If you are at all involved in development for Ubuntu, this (in addition to ubuntu-announce) is *the* list you must subscribe to.

ubuntu-users This is a primarily support-oriented list for questions and answers that Ubuntu users have. It is a *very* high-volume list, but it is an excellent place to ask questions and have them answered. It is a useful general-purpose list for discussion of any issue that pertains primarily to using Ubuntu.

ubuntu-devel-discuss This list is the primary open list for general-purpose discussion of Ubuntu development. If you are looking to contribute to Ubuntu in any technical way, you should subscribe to this list and begin to follow the discussion. The list has a relatively high volume of e-mails.

ubuntu-devel This list is a moderated list for discussion of Ubuntu. While subscribing remains free, posting to the list is restricted to those who are Ubuntu developers or chosen other developers. Others may post, but all posts are checked by a moderation team.

sounder   The sounder list is the unmoderated community chitchat list. *Sounder* is the collective noun used to describe a group of Warthogs and was initially the e-mail list that supported the small, invite-only group of users who tested the Ubuntu 4.10 Warty Warthog release before it was announced to the world. The list has been kept for historical reasons under the old name but now provides a venue for discussing anything that is off topic in the other venues. It frequently hosts discussion of Ubuntu news, events, advocacy, and activism and is an important list for any community member who is participating and contributing to Ubuntu in less technical ways. If you are interested in a peek into early Ubuntu history, you can also read the archives from the beginning days of the list.

Internet Relay Chat

While mailing lists provide the primary venue for asynchronous communication (i.e., not at the same time), there is still an important need for synchronous, or real-time, collaboration. Internet Relay Chat (IRC) fills this niche. While it was designed primarily for group (i.e., many-to-many) communication in channels, it is also equipped with private messaging capabilities that facilitate one-to-one communication—all instantaneously. It is very similar to instant messaging or chat room communication. While time zones and a round globe make it difficult for the global Ubuntu community to meet at the same time, many users and developers take advantage of IRC's capability to let anyone chat about an issue in real time or to ask a question and have it answered immediately.

Like mailing lists, IRC channels provide a venue for a variety of different types of communication in a variety of different subcommunities in Ubuntu. There are many different channels, including channels in a variety of languages.

All official Ubuntu IRC channels are located on the FreeNode IRC network, which also hosts a range of other free and open source software projects. Users can connect to IRC using several pieces of software in Ubuntu, including Pidgin, XChat-gnome (Figure 7-1), and IRSSI. Like the ubuntu-users e-mail list, #ubuntu is designed for help and support. When joining any channel, users should carefully read the topic as many fre-

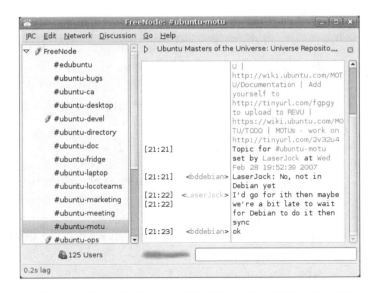

Figure 7-1 XChat-gnome is an IRC client that allows Ubuntu users to connect to the Ubuntu IRC channels.

quently asked questions are answered there, and moderators of the channel can be annoyed by users who ask questions the moderators have already taken the time to answer in the channel's topic.

Currently the #ubuntu channel is usually the biggest channel on the FreeNode network, with over 1,000 simultaneous users at most times—and it's continuing to grow—especially around releases. Another important channel is #ubuntu-devel, which is reserved for discussion of Ubuntu development. Similarly, Kubuntu users hang out in #kubuntu and developers in #kubuntu-devel. Edubuntu and Xubuntu have similarly named user and support channels. To keep #ubuntu focused on support, all general chatter has been moved to #ubuntu-offtopic, and there are similar channels for Kubuntu, Edubuntu, and Xubuntu. Support for development releases has moved to #ubuntu+1. Maintaining channels with specific purposes has allowed the support community to stay focused and help as many people as possible. A full list of channels can be found at http://help.ubuntu.com/community/InternetRelayChat.

Web Forums

The official Ubuntu forums are the most frequently used venues for communication in Ubuntu. For a number of reasons, many users prefer communication through a Web-based forum or bulletin board over mailing lists. The Ubuntu forums were created to satisfy this group and have done so with amazing success.

The forums are accessible online at ubuntuforums.org and have shown an impressive amount of usage. Statistics as of the time of writing show activity of more than 6,600,000 messages on more than 1,000,000 topics in nearly 100 different forums. The forums also boast more than 822,000 users with around 10,000 active at any given moment. The forums continue to grow explosively. The topics discussed in the forums run the gamut. These are roughly broken down into the following categories:

▪ Support discussion including spaces for questions about specific hardware (e.g., Dell computers with Ubuntu preinstalled, or networking and multimedia cards) and specific use cases (e.g., desktop or server users)

▪ Ubuntu community discussions, including spaces for talk of people working on art for Ubuntu, those working in science and education, and those developing new documentation and tutorials

▪ Forum-specific community discussion spaces, including several more social spaces and places for administrative and community governance discussions

Each category includes subforums, each containing many threads. Many of these forums provide important spaces dedicated to important community discussions, including:

▪ A forum to highlight community announcements and news

▪ A discussion area for support for a variety of third-party projects built on top of Ubuntu that are useful primarily to Ubuntu users or that otherwise serve the Ubuntu community

▪ Forums for discussion and planning for local community teams (discussed later in this chapter) from across the world

By covering such ground, the Ubuntu forums provide an impressive support resource. They offer an excellent venue for both asking questions and answering questions, both receiving support and making important contributions to the Ubuntu community. If you are interested in any of these, the forums are a good place to begin.

The only caveat regarding the forums worth mentioning is that they are not frequently used by those developing Ubuntu—although there are exceptions to that rule. If users want to send messages directly to the Ubuntu *developers*, the forums may not provide the most effective tool. If users want to get involved in technical contributions to the project, they will, in all likelihood, have to augment their forums' patronage with the use of mailing lists or Launchpad. To help mediate this issue, the forums staff has created several forums that act as two-way gateways between the forums and the mailing list. The ubuntu-users mailing list is one such list. This means that users can read and participate in the ubuntu-users mailing list using the Web by simply participating in the associated Web forum—software makes sure that messages go between the two venues. Similarly, there are one-way forums for the ubuntu-announce and ubuntu-devel-announce mailing lists. Another exciting endeavor, the forums/developer ambassador projects, is a group of volunteers who are specifically charged with monitoring the forums and the other resources and acting as a bridge for users and topics that, for whatever reason, deserve attention in both areas.

The forums were founded by and are moderated and maintained entirely by volunteers and are governed by the Forums Council, which currently contains no Canonical employees. You can find out more in Chapter 11, "Introducing the Ubuntu Forums," dedicated completely to this wonderful resource.

Wikis

Since nearly day one, a large chunk of Ubuntu documentation and support has taken place in the official Ubuntu wiki (Figure 7-2). In case you don't already know, a *wiki*—pronounced "wik-ee"—is a Web site where any viewer can add, remove, or edit content. The first wiki was created by Ward Cunningham in 1995, and wikis have shown themselves to be an extremely effective tool for collaborative writing in recent years. The term is shortened from *wiki wiki*—Hawaiian for "quick." Many wikis have been created. Most

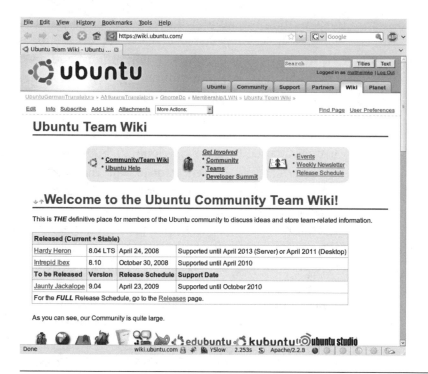

Figure 7-2 Front page of the Ubuntu wiki

famous among these wikis is the online encyclopedia Wikipedia, which now contains more than 2.3 million articles in the English version alone.

There are several Ubuntu wikis, but two are central to the community. The first is the community support and documentation wiki at http://help. ubuntu.com/community. It is edited and directed by the Ubuntu Documentation Team and focuses on issues of community-produced technical documentation for Ubuntu. The second wiki is at http://wiki.ubuntu.com and is meant to be used for everything else. The documentation wiki can be thought of as a project to build an expansive manual through community contributions and editing. The general-purpose wiki is used for specification writing and traffic, conference organization, meet-ups, pages for teams and individuals involved in Ubuntu, and absolutely anything else that is in written form and relevant to the Ubuntu community. Both wikis can be edited, added to, or reorganized by anyone in the community who creates an account, and edits are unrestricted. Since registration is required, each change can be traced to a particular user. There are more than 19,000 pages in the general-purpose wiki. The documentation wiki, created in 2006, has grown to almost 3,000 pages.

Unlike other documentation that ships with Ubuntu, anyone can fix an error, inaccuracy, or out-of-date fact in the wiki. As a result, there is no good way to determine whether information in the wiki is correct. It cannot be subjected to the same type of quality assurance workflow that a document such as this book might be. However, it is also *much* more likely to be up to date in the quickly changing world of Ubuntu development, where there is a new release every six months. The wiki provides a venue for this level of up-to-date information with a low barrier to entry and, as a result, acts as an invaluable resource for the community.

The two major wikis each run the Moin Moin wiki software, and the use and operation of the wikis is identical. To use the wikis, you can either search or browse them. Searching is the most common way to get information from the wiki, and users can easily search either titles or the full text of the wiki. To achieve the best results, it is usually best to search titles and then the text to ensure that you look for more relevant information first.

For people who prefer to browse, the general-purpose wiki is explicitly divided into a number of categories that include the following:

- Resources
- Community
- Events
- Releases

The documentation is browsable in sections that try to serve users at different stages of familiarity with Ubuntu or with particular types of problems. The major divisions in the community documentation wiki include these:

- General help and information for new users
- Help for those switching from Mac OS X, Windows, or another Linux distribution who want a quick guide using analogies they are familiar with

- A large variety of information for people to read after they have installed Ubuntu and have questions about applications or types of use

- Information on maintaining and troubleshooting Ubuntu installs

- Help on connecting and configuring hardware

Most of these categories are relatively self-explanatory. Additionally, the general wiki provides a prominent link to information and support resources in languages other than English. The comprehensive list at www.ubuntu.com/support/local provides both links to pages within the wiki that include documentation and information in languages other than English and links to more than a dozen other wikis that are in another language entirely. Users looking for wiki pages in a language other than English are advised to visit this page.

The Fridge

The Fridge (http://fridge.ubuntu.com) is the quirky community portal for Ubuntu. In many Western cultures, refrigerators provide a central sort of "bulletin board" in a family's home. Because refrigerators are magnetic, children and parents can use magnets to hang pieces of paper that they want to share with the community of people who come in contact with that fridge. For children, this often includes good grades, news reports, or other information that someone is proud of or wants to share. The Fridge, bearing the tag line, "It's cool . . . It's fresh . . . Stick it on The Fridge!" tries to create such a shared resource within the Ubuntu community. The Fridge home page is shown in Figure 7-3.

The Fridge is perhaps best described as the community portal for Ubuntu. It is part news site, part grassroots marketing and advocacy site. It hosts developer interviews, news, a picture gallery, a calendar with a list of upcoming events, polls, a list of Ubuntu-in-the-press citations, and much more. The core content on the site is arranged as a Web log. Users frequently set The Fridge as their home page or subscribe to the site via its RSS feed. The Fridge is unique in the community in that it appeals to a wide variety of Ubuntu participants—developers, advocates, translators,

Figure 7-3 The Fridge home page

users—and provides a venue where each group can share information with others. There is a story every two to three days on The Fridge, although this may increase to up to several stories a day with time. Users can comment and discuss each story on The Fridge in an associated forum in the Ubuntu forums.

Anyone can contribute content to The Fridge. If you would like to contribute, you can do so by sending your suggestions for features, articles, or even a piece of original work (such as an article, photo, or event review) to The Fridge editors at fridge-devel@lists.ubuntu.com.

Developer Summits and Sprints

While the vast majority of the work of the Ubuntu community takes place online, Ubuntu developers do, from time to time, meet face to face. Since

Ubuntu was first released, there have been several public developer summits and sprints organized and funded by Canonical, Ltd. Highlights include:

- The Mataró Sessions in Mataró, Catalonia, Spain, in December 2004—the first Ubuntu development summit

- Ubuntu Down Under in Sydney, Australia, in April 2005

- Ubuntu Below Zero in Montreal, Canada, in November 2005

- Ubuntu Developer Summit Paris, in Paris, France, in June 2006

- Ubuntu Developer Summit Mountain View at Google Headquarters in Mountain View, California, in November 2006

- Ubuntu Developer Summit Boston in Boston, Massachusetts—in November 2007, the most recent developer summit at the time of writing

With Canonical, Ltd., Ubuntu tries to organize these meetings so that they occur once per release, usually toward the very beginning of a release cycle, so that the specifications and goals for the forthcoming release can be discussed, thrashed out, and decided upon. These meetings move around the globe geographically so that, over a several-year period, a large percentage of the Ubuntu community will be able to attend at least one summit and meet with other developers.

While the format changes slightly each time, these meetings have been between one and two weeks in length. Frequently, a given attendee stays for only one week. At Ubuntu Below Zero, the second week was devoted almost entirely to discussing, implementing, and developing infrastructure related to Launchpad (see Chapter 10). The format of these summits has changed as the attendees have experimented with different methods for structuring the events and maximizing the efficiency of these short periods. One common theme, though, is a process of writing specifications.

At developer summits, attendees describe features that they would like to see in the next Ubuntu release. At an arranged time or in a series of meetings, a small set of interested users and developers works to draft a written specification. This process of drafting involves brainstorming and ends up with a formal, approved spec that describes a problem or need and provides a detailed description of how it will be fixed or implemented. While these specifications are often technical in nature, they are also used to describe goals that may pertain to localization, documentation, or community building. For example, both The Fridge and the planning of each summit began as a specification. With time, these specifications are categorized in terms of priority for the upcoming release. Later, individuals will claim or be assigned some set of these specs. Paid developers at Canonical, Ltd. frequently take responsibility for the highest-priority technical specs. Each specification is written up and improved on the wiki so that Ubuntu hackers who cannot attend the summit are still able to participate.

These conferences have, so far, occurred in hotels with conference centers and have been attended by up to several hundred people. The exception was a recent summit, which was graciously hosted by Google. The meetings have been wholly organized and funded by Canonical, Ltd., which ensures that its employees attend and also distributes funds for other active volunteers to travel. This funding tends to be divided up based on the contributions of volunteers over the last release cycle and their geographic proximity to the summit location. This is done to minimize travel expenditures and to ensure that users around the world get a chance to attend a conference when it comes near them.

In addition to the biannual summits, Canonical, Ltd. organizes a number of sprints each year. These sprints tend to be one- to three-week intense collocated work sessions that involve a team or subteam tasked with a well-defined goal. They provide a time when team members can write code, write documentation, make plans, or do whatever else is necessary to fulfill that goal. The sprints attempt to squeeze large amounts of work into a short period of time and have earned a reputation for being exhausting, fulfilling, amazingly productive, fun experiences. These sprints are work sessions and are often limited to a small group of Canonical, Ltd. employees. In many situations, they also include volunteer attendees as well.

User Conferences

Developer summits and sprints are effective but are primarily of interest to technically minded people or individuals who are already very actively involved in the Ubuntu community. Their goal is to accomplish work through high-bandwidth face-to-face interaction among existing teams. User conferences try to provide an alternative space for users who are not yet actively involved in the community. These conferences attempt to bring people up to speed on Ubuntu and to provide a space for community building, support, and networking.

While many local community teams have regular meetings and their own Ubuntu events, there have been several larger-scale Ubuntu user conferences to date, and several more are currently being planned. These conferences fall into two major classes. The first class is a set of laid-back, lightly organized, day-long "unconferences" called Ubucons (short for Ubuntu Conferences). Ubucons have been held many times, the first two at Google headquarters, in Mountain View and in New York City, and others are designed to coincide with the much larger Linux World conferences that many other Ubuntu users attend. The unconference format means that much of the schedule is left up in the air until the morning of the meeting and that many of the attendees are encouraged to come prepared with their own demonstrations, talks, and workshops and with a list of things they would like to learn. Attended by a group of about a hundred users and a handful of developers, Ubucons have provided a simple way for users to connect with each other. Additionally, Ubucons have, to date, also provided space for "installfests" where users can bring computers and have Ubuntu installed on their machines by other Ubuntu users, developers, and aficionados.

Any active group of Ubuntu users can plan a Ubucon, and there are several Ubucons currently being planned for a variety of locations around the world.

The second major class of conferences is Ubuntu Live. The first Ubuntu Live was held in 2007, and a second occurred during the summer of 2008. Ubuntu Live is designed to be a larger, more traditional conference for users and businesses interested in Ubuntu and has occurred alongside the popular Open Source Conference (OSCON) in both 2007 and 2008. The first Ubuntu Live was held in 2007 and was organized by Canonical and O'Reilly, the latter of which organizes several of the most well-attended and professionally produced conferences in the free and open source software world.

While conferences and summits act as a site for major technical advances in brainstorming and development, they are also fun and enjoyable experiences. They provide a venue for users to put faces to names, IRC nicks, and e-mail addresses, and they provide for enjoyable, humorous, and productive interaction. In addition to work, there are frequent card-playing, eating, drinking, and athletic activities. Many Ubuntu users from the local area who've attended because they were curious have gone on to become some of the community's most important contributors. Attending a conference is like taking a drink from an Ubuntu fire hose. It is frequently overwhelming but can ultimately be a useful, productive, and rewarding experience as well.

Planet Ubuntu

It is hardly surprising that most of the Ubuntu community is highly geared toward gathering and distributing information and communication about Ubuntu. Of course, before the Ubuntu community is a group of people working on the project of building, supporting, and spreading a GNU/Linux distribution, it is first *a group of people*. For the Ubuntu community to really feel like a community, its members should have some idea of what other members are up to—both in their Ubuntu work and in their lives that extend beyond Ubuntu.

Planet Ubuntu (http://planet.ubuntu.com) tries to capture this element of the Ubuntu community (Figure 7-4). Planet is a Web log aggregator and can be thought of as a blog of blogs. Planet retrieves the latest journal or blog entries from Ubuntu members who have chosen to add their content to the system and then publishes a single blog that includes, in reverse chronological order, all of the latest entries. Much of the content in Planet Ubuntu is about Ubuntu. Sometimes this is because members choose to include only those entries that directly pertain to Ubuntu. Others publish everything from their lives, including things that may not directly pertain to the project. Often, the content also includes information from the personal lives of community members so that the community knows what its members are up to. In this way, Planet provides a good way for participants to put their stamp on the Ubuntu community—both technically and nontechnically.

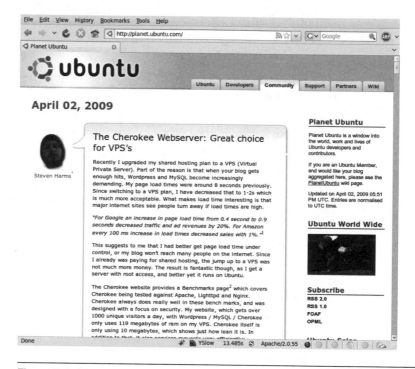

Figure 7-4 Planet Ubuntu

Teams, Processes, and Community Governance

Ubuntu operates under the famous hacker mantra of "rough consensus and running code." The project attempts to forge consensus, to make good technical decisions, and to move forward. It attempts to minimize politicization wherever possible and to distribute power to those who are best at getting good work done. Mark Shuttleworth explains, "This is not a democracy, it's a meritocracy. We try to operate more on consensus than on votes, seeking agreement from the people who will have to do the work."

The project attempts to keep disagreements from spiraling out of control by enforcing mutual respect at all times with its Code of Conduct described in Chapter 1. Disagreements, of course, are inevitable and can be technical or nontechnical in nature. The community needs to be able to deal with these and, toward that end, has created a lightweight governance system that aims to ensure that disagreements are resolved carefully and that the project always has a strong, fair, and responsive direction.

The Ubuntu Web site describes the goals of its community governance system as threefold.

1. Ensure that a process is defined that allows people to contribute to decisions regarding the Ubuntu community and distribution.
2. Ensure that decisions regarding the Ubuntu distribution and community are made in a fair and transparent fashion.
3. Ensure that necessary decisions are actually made, even when there is no clear consensus amongst the community.

With these goals in mind, Ubuntu's system is based on the delegation of decision-making power to small and medium-sized teams. When disagreements arise, they are handled within a relevant team. In the cases of some larger teams, team councils handle a variety of dispute resolutions in a very structured fashion. When teams cannot resolve their own disagreements or when there are disagreements between teams, issues are forwarded to either the Community Council or the Technical Board—depending on whether the issue is technical in nature. As the financier and the project's progenitor, Shuttleworth sits on both boards and occupies a special position as the self-appointed benevolent dictator for life (SABDFL). Users can participate in the Ubuntu governance structure by serving on teams and by approving members of both the Community Council and the Technical Board as Ubuntu members and maintainers.

Teams

Most work in Ubuntu is delegated to a set of teams, each responsible for a particular area of work in Ubuntu. A sample of important teams (which is by no means complete) might include the forums, marketing, art, documentation, kernel, server, laptop, and translation teams. Anyone with an interest in a particular aspect of the Ubuntu project can join a team's discussion and contribute to its decisions.

When participants feel that a particular area is underserved, they can go ahead and build a new team by beginning work and writing up a proposal for consideration by the Community Council, which approves the creation of all new teams. Rather than catalyzing work with the creation of a team, the Community Council likes to recognize existing work with official team

within the Ubuntu project. The Community Council is charged with supervising the social structures, venues, and processes of the project.

The Community Council's day-to-day work involves five major areas in Ubuntu. The first, and the most straightforward, is the maintenance of the Ubuntu Code of Conduct. The Community Council is the only body that can approve revisions to the code. Because the Community Council does not ask each member to "reagree" to the code when it is changed, each of these revisions must be fully within the spirit of the previous drafts.

The second charge of the Community Council is the arbitration of disputes that cannot be handled within a particular team or that arise between teams. Very frequently, these are disputes about the Code of Conduct that may require clarification of a part of the Code of Conduct or a description of whether any of the code was in fact violated by a particular action or behavior. However, the Community Council's purview is not limited to Code of Conduct violations, and the Community Council is available to handle disputes in any nontechnical situation. In most situations, the Community Council does not take action against individuals but, rather, helps group members come to agreement or consensus among themselves. If this fails, the Community Council can ask a maintainer or other member of the community to apologize and refrain from particular behavior or to leave the community. The Council promises that nobody will be asked to leave without a substantial review and an opportunity to defend him- or herself.

A third area of council work is the creation and dissolution of teams and the appointment of team leaders. New teams are proposed to the Community Council in the manner described earlier in the section on teams, and the Community Council either approves the request or asks the proposer to wait. Defunct or inactive teams can similarly be dissolved by the Community Council. In cases where team leadership is requested, the Community Council can appoint leaders of teams or shift leadership to different team members. In most situations, the appointment of team leaders is an internal team matter but, when requested, the Community Council is available to intervene.

Fourth, the Community Council is responsible for approving and welcoming new members to the project. This will be described in more depth in the upcoming subsection on membership.

Finally, the Community Council is responsible for all community-related structures and processes. New types of teams, requirements for membership, and core philosophical documents should first be approved by the Community Council. Community members who wish to suggest new structures or processes can submit their proposal to the Community Council for discussion and approval.

The Community Council meets every two weeks on IRC. Any community participant can submit an item or proposal for discussion by the Community Council. Meetings are open to the community, but the Council seeks only consensus or votes from Council members—although it consults representatives from the team that submitted the proposal and other community members. If an open meeting becomes too noisy, the Council reserves the right to move to a private channel for the duration of the meeting. To date, this has never happened. In all situations, full transcripts of meetings are published immediately following a Community Council meeting. The Community Council at the time of this writing consists of Benjamin Mako Hill, Mark Shuttleworth, James Troup, Daniel Holbach, Corey Burger, Matthew East, and Mike Basinger. Notably, only Shuttleworth and Troup are Canonical employees. Appointments to the board are made by Shuttleworth and subject to confirmation by a vote among all members. Appointments are for a period of two years.

The Technical Board

The Ubuntu Technical Board is responsible for the Ubuntu project's technical direction. By handling all technical matters, the Technical Board complements the Community Council as Ubuntu's highest rung of project governance. In particular, the Technical Board is responsible for three major areas of Ubuntu policy: package policy, release feature goals, and package selection. Also, the Technical Board is available to arbitrate any technical disagreements or issues within or between teams in a manner similar to the one described earlier in relation to the Community Council.

The Technical Board's first responsibility is Ubuntu's package policy. The Technical Board maintains the policy document, which describes the processes and standards to which all Ubuntu packages are held. Since the policy is constantly evolving, each Ubuntu release is associated with a specific version of the Ubuntu package policy as determined by the Technical

Board. Any suggestions or proposals about policy are suggested to and considered by the Technical Board.

Also, the Technical Board is responsible for maintaining Ubuntu's feature goals for each release. During each release cycle, there is a date defined as Feature Freeze, after which no new features are added. The Technical Board sets these dates and decides when and if the rules can be bent for a particular feature or piece of software.

Finally, the Technical Board is responsible for maintaining the *list* of pieces of software (i.e., packages) in Ubuntu. In this capacity, the Technical Board determines which software is installed in the default desktop installation and which packages qualify for full support as part of the main component of Ubuntu. Users and developers can propose a particular piece of software for inclusion in main, the base install, or a desktop install. In all cases, the ultimate decision will be made by the Technical Board.

Like the Community Council, the Technical Board meets at least every two weeks on IRC. Also like the Community Council, any user can submit an item or proposal for discussion by the Technical Board ahead of the meeting. Meetings are open to all interested parties, although decision making and voting is restricted to Technical Board members. Full transcripts and rules about noise, as they pertain to the Community Council, also apply to the Technical Board. The Technical Board at the time of this writing comprises Matt Zimmerman as board chair, Scott James Remnant, and Mark Shuttleworth. Nominations for the Technical Board are considered at the beginning of each release cycle. Like the Community Council, appointments are made by Shuttleworth but are subject to confirmation by a vote among the maintainers instead of all members. Appointments are made for a period of one year.

The SABDFL

Mark Shuttleworth jokingly refers to himself as Ubuntu's SABDFL—self-appointed benevolent dictator for life. He plays an admittedly undemocratic role as the sponsor of the Ubuntu project and the sole owner of Canonical, Ltd. Shuttleworth has the ability, with regard to Canonical, Ltd. employees, to ask people to work on specific projects, feature goals, and bugs. He does exactly this.

Shuttleworth also maintains a tie-breaking vote on the Technical Board and Community Council but has never used this power and has publicly said that he will not use it lightly. In situations where the boards are split and there is no one "right" answer, the SABDFL will provide a decision instead of more debate. The SABDFL exists to provide clear leadership on difficult issues and to set the pace and direction for the project. In exchange for this power, he has the responsibility to listen to the community and to understand that the use of his SABDFL authority can weaken the project.

Ubunteros and Ubuntu Members

Membership in the Ubuntu project is one official way that the project recognizes sustained and significant contributions. The first level of membership in Ubuntu is as an Ubuntero (formerly, the name was Ubuntite). Ubunteros are Ubuntu activists and can be any person in the Ubuntu community who has explicitly committed to observing the Ubuntu Code of Conduct. Ubunteros are self-nominated and self-confirmed. Using Launchpad, participants can generate a GPG encryption key and "sign" the Code of Conduct as a way of pledging to uphold it within the Ubuntu community. By doing so, that participant automatically gains status as an Ubuntero.

The next, more significant, step is official membership. Official membership is available to any Ubuntero who has demonstrated a significant and sustained set of contributions to the Ubuntu community. These contributions can be of any kind—technical or nontechnical—but need to be of a form that can be represented to the Community Council, which will consider each application individually. A list of types of contributions that qualify appears in the following section on getting involved. The Community Council tries to be flexible in the variety of different types of contributions that it accepts in consideration of membership.

Members are responsible for confirming, by voting, all nominations to the Ubuntu Community Council. They also may be asked by the Community Council to vote on resolutions put to the general membership. In exchange, members gain the right to an @ubuntu.com e-mail address and the right to carry Ubuntu business cards. Membership lasts for two years and is renewable. Members who fail to renew their membership will be marked as inactive but, with renewed activity and a simple procedure that involves approval of the Community Council, can be easily reactivated.

The process to become a member is relatively straightforward and is documented in depth on the Ubuntu Web site. Most important, it requires that users document their contributions on a wiki page that includes links to code, mailing list messages, documentation, or other relevant material. Membership applications should also include testimonials on work and involvement in Ubuntu from current Ubuntu members.

Getting Involved

Users can participate in the Ubuntu community on a variety of levels and in a multitude of ways. The following subsections, adapted largely from a page with links to relevant resources online on the Ubuntu Web site (www.ubuntu.com/community/participate), provides a good list of ways in which people can get a running start in the Ubuntu community. An expanded but unofficial list appears at http://wiki.ubuntu.com/ContributeToUbuntu. Both lists are broken down into the major ways to get involved.

Advocacy

The easiest way for someone to contribute to the Ubuntu community is simply by telling others about Ubuntu. Advocacy frequently occurs in a variety of ways. One good method involves joining or starting a LoCo team. LoCos, described earlier in this chapter, provide a method through which you can get involved in Ubuntu activities. If users do not have a LoCo and do not have the critical mass of users to start one, they might help build support by giving a talk about Ubuntu to a local Linux User Group or other technical group. Advocates can also order CDs at no cost and can distribute them. Through these and other means, advocacy provides a great way to spread the word about Ubuntu and offers a low-barrier opportunity to make contributions to the community.

Support

One of the most meaningful ways that users can contribute to Ubuntu is by helping others use the software. Users can do this by joining the support-oriented mailing lists, IRC channels, or forums, as described in detail earlier in this chapter. By responding to requests for help in each of these venues, users can help other users get up and running on Ubuntu. Even if users are themselves beginners, the knowledge they gain in solving even simple problems enables them to help users who run into the same issues.

Ideas and Feedback

Another way to contribute to Ubuntu is by helping steer the direction of the project by describing a vision or providing ideas. This can be done by participating in discussion and brainstorming sessions at conferences and on the Ubuntu wiki. By monitoring specifications as they are written and creating feedback, especially at early stages, users can make meaningful contributions. However, users contributing ideas should remember that talk is cheap. Users are wise to work with others to help turn their visions into reality.

Documentation

When a user is stumped by a problem, chances are good that other users will also be frustrated by it. If users are not in a position to write code to change the situation, they may be able to help others by writing up their experiences and documenting the solution. Ubuntu has a vibrant documentation team and community, and writing documentation is a great low-barrier way to make meaningful contributions to the Ubuntu community.

Users aiming to contribute to Ubuntu's documentation would be advised to take notes as they puzzle through problems and to document solutions when they find them. Before writing, users should also check to see whether documentation for a particular problem already exists. When it does, users would be wise to choose to improve or augment existing documentation rather than write a new document. Similarly, users can also make meaningful contributions by reading through existing documentation and fixing factual, technical, stylistic, spelling, and grammar errors. Users who spend a large amount of time working on documentation may, with time, also want to join the Ubuntu Documentation Team, which can help organize and coordinate this work in terms of Ubuntu documentation goals.

Artwork

For those users who feel that their strengths are primarily artistic, there are many ways to improve the style and feel of the Ubuntu desktop through wholly artistic contributions. For example, Ubuntu is always in need of new ideas for wallpapers, icons, and graphical themes. Inkscape, similar in many respects to Adobe Illustrator, is a great piece of free software in Ubuntu that proves useful for this type of work. As with documentation, there is an Ubuntu Art Team that helps coordinate artistic work within the Ubuntu community.

Translation and Localization

The discussion of LoCos should have already made it clear that translation is a great way that anyone with a firm understanding of English and another language can contribute to the Ubuntu community. Translation through Rosetta (described in Chapter 10) allows users to translate as little as a single string or as much as an entire application. Through its easy interface and Web-based nature, it provides a low-barrier road to contribution. Serious translators should join a local community team and the ubuntu-translators mailing list so that they can stay in touch with other Ubuntu localizers.

Quality Assurance and Bugs

Quality assurance (QA) is something for which many companies hire special engineers. In Ubuntu, the Development Team relies on itself and the community to test software before it is released to let developers know about problems so that the bugs can be squashed before the vast majority of users ever see it. To test software, users merely need to upgrade to the latest development version of Ubuntu and to upgrade regularly. When users helping out with QA find bugs, they should report them in the Ubuntu bug-tracking system, Malone (see Chapter 10). They can also help by "triaging" bugs, closing or merging duplicates, or verifying bugs and adding information to a bug's description. If you intend to become involved in QA, you should subscribe to the ubuntu-devel-announce mailing list, and you should consider monitoring ubuntu-devel as well.

Programming and Packaging

The final way that users can contribute to the Ubuntu community is through the production of code. Because Ubuntu is free and open source software, users can get access to every piece of software that Ubuntu supports. This allows users to package additional software for inclusion in Ubuntu, to fix bugs, and to add features. Developers, like people testing software, should subscribe to the ubuntu-devel-announce mailing list and should consider monitoring ubuntu-devel, too. The best way to begin making contributions is then through the MOTU team as a MOTU hopeful, as described earlier. Users can also look through a list of specifications to find a project that they find personally interesting. In some situations, there are even bounties available—small amounts of money offered to those who fulfill a small feature goal that has remained unfilled for some period of time.

Summary

Ubuntu is a vibrant and diverse community that is active around the world and in many languages. Its activities happen primarily online in a variety of virtual venues, including mailing lists, IRC, Web forums, wikis, and two special Web-based community portals known as The Fridge and Planet Ubuntu. Ubuntu complements this virtual activity with real-life meetings and conferences. The Ubuntu community is broken down into a variety of teams and processes. At the top of this government structure is the Ubuntu Community Council, the Technical Board, and SABDFL Mark Shuttleworth. Through a variety of ways, this community is designed to facilitate contributions easily. Ultimately, these contributions are recognized through a process culminating in official project membership and enfranchisement.

CHAPTER 8

Using Kubuntu

- **Introduction to Kubuntu**
- **Installing Kubuntu**
- **Navigating in Kubuntu**
- **Customizing Kubuntu**
- **System Administration**
- **Managing Files with Kubuntu**
- **Common Applications**
- **Finding Help and Giving Back to the Community**
- **Summary**

THE KUBUNTU PROJECT STRIVES to take the best of Ubuntu and the best of the K Desktop Environment (KDE) to produce a great Linux distribution. This chapter covers information ranging from what exactly Kubuntu is to how to manage and keep your Kubuntu system up to date with the latest applications and fixes. The goal of Kubuntu is to provide a graphically beautiful and easy-to-use Linux operating system, an OS that is simple to customize to your desire.

Introduction to Kubuntu

Kubuntu is an official product of Ubuntu—a complete implementation of the Ubuntu OS led by Jonathan Riddell (an employee of Canonical, Ltd.) and an army of developers. However, Kubuntu uses KDE as the graphical user interface instead of GNOME, as in Ubuntu. The main goal of Kubuntu is to be an integrated Linux distribution with all of the great features of Ubuntu, but based on KDE. Since Kubuntu is an official part of the Ubuntu community, it adheres to the same Ubuntu manifesto: Great software should be available free of charge and should be usable by people in their own language and regardless of disability. Also, people should be able to customize and alter their software in ways they deem fit.

Like Ubuntu, Kubuntu makes the following commitments: Kubuntu will provide the very best translations and accessibility infrastructure that the free software community has to offer; Kubuntu will always be free of charge, and there is no extra cost for an "enterprise" version; and Kubuntu will always provide the latest and best software from the KDE community.

Looking for a certain piece of software? Kubuntu has it, with more than 1,000 pieces of software in its repositories, including the latest kernel version and, of course, the latest KDE. The standard desktop applications (Web browsing, e-mail, word processing, and spreadsheet applications) allow Kubuntu to replace any current desktop OS. If you are running servers—whether they're Web servers, e-mail servers, or database servers—Kubuntu can do that as well.

A History of KDE

In 1996, Matthias Etrich posted a now famous newsgroup post that described some of the problems he had with the UNIX desktop.

UNIX popularity grows thanks to the free variants, mostly Linux. But still a consistent, nice looking, free desktop environment is missing. There are several nice either free or low-priced applications available, so that Linux/X11 would almost fit everybody's needs if we could offer a real GUI....

IMHO a GUI should offer a complete graphical environment. It should allow a user to do his everyday tasks with it, like starting applications, reading mail, configuring his desktop.... All parts must fit together....

The goal is NOT to create a GUI for the complete UNIX-system or the System-Administrator.... The idea is to create a GUI for an ENDUSER.

With that post, he started building the KDE Project. KDE originally stood for the Kool Desktop Environment but was adapted to be K Desktop Environment. The mascot for KDE is a green dragon named Konqi, who can be found in various applications.

Matthias chose to develop KDE around the Qt toolkit, and by 1997, the first large, complex applications were being released. However, there was much debate because Qt was not licensed with a free software license. Two projects came about from this debate, one named Harmony, which would use only free libraries, and another project called GNOME. In 1998, the Qt toolkit was licensed under a new open source license called the Q Public License (QPL), and in 2000, Qt was released under the GNU General Public License.

KDE is primarily a volunteer effort. However, many companies employ developers to work on this project. Some of these companies include Novell (through the purchase of SUSE Linux) and Trolltech (the company that produces the Qt toolkit).

KDE 4.0 came with a great number of changes to the desktop environment, including the introduction of Plasma, Solid, Krunner, and many other infrastructure changes, most of which are discussed throughout this chapter.

KDE 4.2 is the current version of KDE that ships with Kubuntu 9.04. Significant improvements have been made over the first release of KDE, and most of the KDE 3 applications have been ported over to KDE 4.

For more information on KDE, visit the project's Web site at www.kde.org. The project's home page also provides information on how you can help with the project and contribute to the KDE community.

A History of Kubuntu

When Ubuntu was first being discussed, there were rumors that it would be based only on GNOME and that KDE would be left out. Jonathan Riddell, a KDE developer, posted an article on his blog that soon became the Number 1 hit on Google for Ubuntu Linux. The article states:

> The signs are there that this could be something big, more so than the likes of Linspire, Xandros or Lycrosis. Unlike those companies, they [Canonical, Ltd.] understand Free Software and open development. It is likely to be a GNOME-based job, but maybe there is a KDE developer out there who is working for them without letting on. If not I'm always available.

This post started a flurry of activity for both Riddell and the others who wanted to participate.

A lot of changes needed to be made to get Kubuntu working correctly. A hardware abstraction layer (HAL) had be changed; programs and packages, along with a clean Kmenu, changed to fit the philosophy of Ubuntu, had be created; and more people needed to join the project. It was a conscious decision to keep the default KDE colors and icons in order to remain as close to KDE as possible.

Kubuntu 9.04 is a unique and important release. It was released in two versions and includes KDE 3.5.9 and Kubuntu 9.04 (KDE4 Remix). This chapter focuses on Kubuntu 9.04 (KDE4 Remix). Also, Kubuntu 9.04 differs from Ubuntu 8.04 in that Kubuntu is not a long-term support version; 9.04 is supported for 18 months.

Kubuntu 8.10 was released in October 2008 and was the first version to include KDE 4 as the default version of KDE. This change upset quite a few members of the community who felt KDE 4 was not ready for prime time. Kubuntu 8.10 included both KDE 4 and KDE 3 apps in order to make it feature complete. A big change in 8.10 was the ability for you to select the language settings right from the boot up. This feature allows for more localization and sets the system in the language you understand the best.

Kubuntu 9.04 will have only KDE 4 applications installed, which necessitated some changes in the default applications. The big changes include switching the package manager to KPackageKit instead of Adept and using Quassel as the default IRC client instead of Konversation, which was dropped because it was not ported over to KDE 4. The current version of KDE shipping in 9.04 is 4.2.

Kubuntu is quickly building a sizable community of its own. There are not only more and more package maintainers and a growing, dedicated documentation team but also many community and fan sites to help provide support and the most current information, including forums located at www.kubuntuforums.net. Kubuntu has grown tremendously from just one developer to a large group as it continues to improve the quality of the distribution.

Installing Kubuntu

Installing Kubuntu is just like installing Ubuntu. It is pretty much a snap. Let's start with where you can find it.

Where to Find Kubuntu

Kubuntu is available at www.kubuntu.org/download.php. An image file can be downloaded and then burned onto either a DVD or a CD-ROM. Two different types of Kubuntu images can be downloaded and used. The first is the desktop CD, which allows the user to test and run Kubuntu without changing any settings. The second is the alternate install CD, which provides for a more advanced installation.

The desktop CD of Kubuntu 9.04 is the primary way to install Kubuntu on your system. This CD is a great way to demonstrate the power of Kubuntu to your friends before they install it on their systems. The desktop CD acts as a live CD and allows Kubuntu to run on your system without erasing anything already installed.

Can I Switch to Kubuntu If I Have Ubuntu Installed Already?

If you have installed Ubuntu on your system already, it is extremely easy to install and configure Kubuntu. In Synaptic, find the package kubuntu-desktop, which provides all the necessary programs to have your system look and act like Kubuntu. Don't worry—you can still switch between Ubuntu with GNOME and Kubuntu with KDE. Once Kubuntu is installed, you can choose which desktop environment to use, either GNOME or KDE. Also, if you have Kubuntu installed already and wish to install Ubuntu, it is just as simple to switch: Just install ubuntu-desktop through Software Management, and you will be using the GNOME desktop.

Once you have installed the kubuntu-desktop package, end your GNOME session and choose Session from the menu. Select KDE instead of GNOME as your window manager, and then select Make Default. From now on, KDE will start for you when you sign on.

Installing from the Desktop CD

Kubuntu has the ability to install directly from the desktop CD, so there is no need to download separate CDs; simply download the desktop CD and show off to your friends how great Kubuntu is, or give it a test run for the first time. Kubuntu's live installer program is called Ubiquity.

After you start up the desktop CD, an icon called Install appears on your desktop. Choose to install Kubuntu, and Ubiquity guides you through the installation phase (Figure 8-1).

Ubiquity guides you in setting up the correct country and time zone (Figure 8-2).

Once you have answered these questions, Ubiquity prompts you to select the correct keyboard layout (Figure 8-3), create a username and password, configure your disk and its partitions (Figure 8-4), and create your username and assign a name to the computer (Figure 8-5).

When everything is all set, click Install to finish the installation (Figure 8-6).

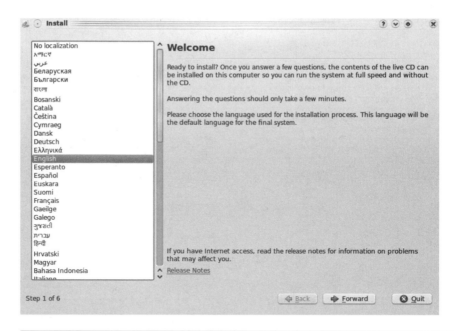

Figure 8-1 Welcome screen of Ubiquity

Figure 8-2 Selecting the correct time zone

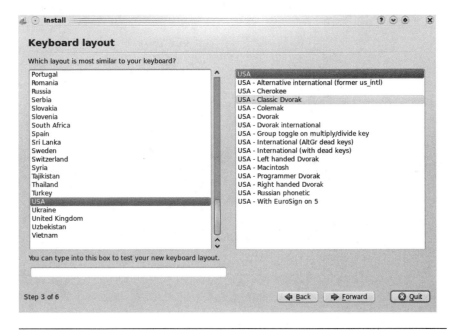

Figure 8-3 Selecting the keyboard layout

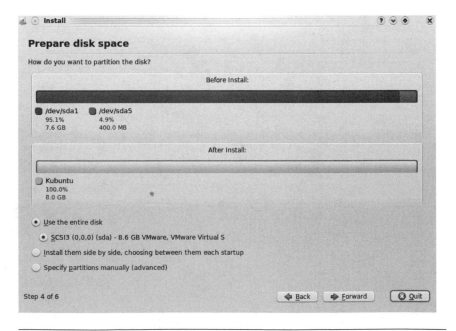

Figure 8-4 Configuring the disk partitions

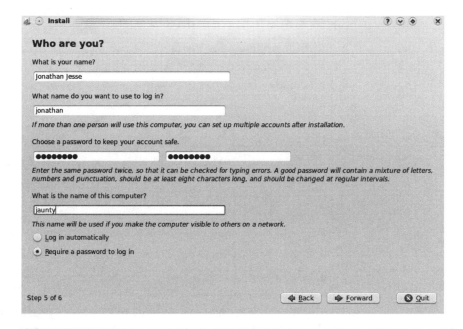

Figure 8-5 Configuring the username and computer name

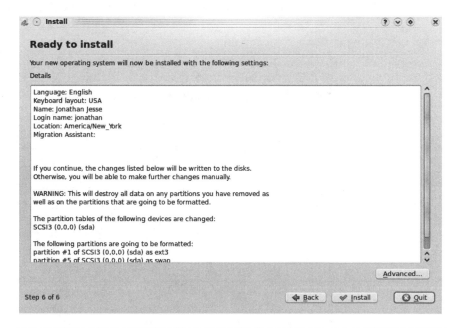

Figure 8-6 Finishing the installation

Navigating in Kubuntu

All of the applications in Kubuntu can be accessed through the Application Launcher (Figure 8-7), which is located in the bottom left corner of the Task Manager.

An additional change in KDE4 to the Application Launcher is how applications are named. Instead of program names (familiar to those who have previously used some version of KDE) such as Konqueror, Akregator, and Kontact, the applications are named after their purpose. For example, Akregator shows up as RSS Feed Reader, and Konqueror shows up as Web Browser.

Once you click on the Application Launcher, you are presented first with Favorites, which is a list designed for applications that are used regularly. You can add any application to the Favorites at any time. Kubuntu 9.04 ships with Web Browser, Systems, and File Manager already listed in the Favorites section. To remove an application from the Favorites portion of the Application Launcher, right-click on the application and select Remove From Favorites. Likewise, to add an application to the Favorites section, right-click on the application you would like to add and select Add to Favorites.

Figure 8-7 KDE4 Application Launcher

After the Favorites tab is the Applications portion of the Application Launcher. These applications are organized according to type of program. For example, Instant Messenger (Kopete) is located under the Internet section, while CD & DVD Burning (K3B) is located under the Multimedia section.

The third tab is the Computer tab. This tab provides quick access to different folders within the file system, including the home directory network folders and the CD-ROM drive. The Computer section is divided into Applications (System Settings), Places (Home, Network, Root, Trash), and Removable Storage (Floppy Drive, CD-ROM, and any USB drives).

The fourth tab is the Recently Used section, which is populated by both applications and documents that have recently been used.

One of the best features of the new Application Launcher is the Search Bar at the top of the page (Figure 8-8). The search program searches both menus in the Application Launcher and the Web for information.

Figure 8-8 Using the Search portion of the Application Launcher

Shutting Down Your Computer and Logging Out

To shut down your computer, log out, or switch users, go to the Application Launcher, and under the tab labeled Leave, select the option you would like. This section is divided into two subsections: Session and System. Since Kubuntu is a multiuser system (many users per system), you can easily switch to a parallel session as a different user under the Session subsection. Also under Session, you can Lock the Screen or Logout (ending the current session). Under the System subsection, you can either shut down (Turn off the computer) or restart (Restart the computer). Figure 8-9 shows these options. Also, you can lock the session or Logout by right-clicking on the desktop and selecting the correct option.

Using sudo Instead of a Root Account

A large change for many seasoned users of other Linux distributions is the lack of a root account. Upon installation, you are not prompted to create a root password. The password created with the first user, your password, will allow you to access the administrative functions. You will need the sudo password often when configuring the system or making global changes.

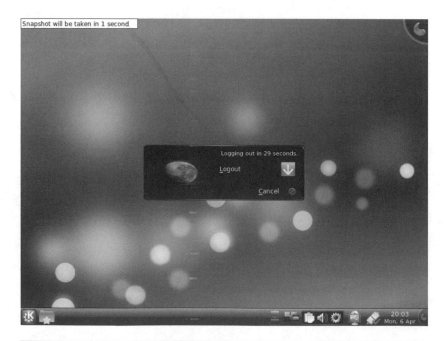

Figure 8-9 Logging out of Kubuntu

Customizing Kubuntu

A major feature of Kubuntu is the ability to customize almost everything and anything in the system. If you don't like the desktop background, change it. Would you like to remove the new Application Launcher and go back to the old Kmenu style?

Customizing Plasma

Continued improvements in KDE 4 have been made to Plasma, the replacement for Kdesktop. A great amount of customization can be done with Plasma, including the addition or subtraction of widgets. From the Plasma Web page (http://plasma.kde. org), Plasma is defined as "the component that is 'in charge' of the desktop interface; the desktop, panel (often referred to simply as the task bar), and related elements."

Widgets allow you to add and remove items from your desktop. A widget can be something from the Application Launcher, for example, or a clock showing a different time zone. Widgets can be added to the desktop only if the desktop is unlocked. To add widgets, either right-click on the desktop and select Add Widgets or click on the Plasma Toolbox located in the top right-hand corner of the desktop (Figure 8-10).

Additional widgets are available through the extragears package (installed via Software Management) and also on kde-look.org under the Widgets section. In fact, in KDE4, the Application Launcher and Task Manager are both widgets that can be added or removed for complete customization. If the old Kmenu is more your style, remove the Application Launcher widget and replace it with the Application Launcher Menu.

To change the background on the desktop, right-click on the desktop and select Configure Desktop. This opens up the Configure Desktop – Plasma Workspace where you can change the picture, positioning, color, and preferences for managing icons. New wallpaper can be added through Get Hot New Stuff.

Choosing how the desktop looks can help give a personalized feel to Kubuntu. If the appearance seems lacking, you can make further changes by choosing System Settings > Appearance. You can further customize things, such as color, icons, and style. Kubuntu is all about customization,

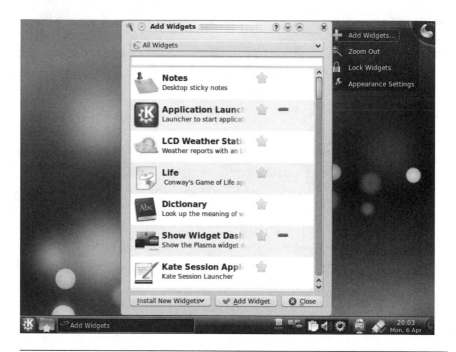

Figure 8-10 Adding Widgets via the Plasma toolkit

something you may be sick of hearing about, and there are many ways to change the desktop's appearance, which almost guarantees that no two users will have identical desktops.

Get Hot New Stuff

Looking for the latest screen saver, desktop background, or other cool things for your Kubuntu installation? Kubuntu fully supports the Get Hot New Stuff (GHNS) framework of KDE. GHNS allows people to upload templates to a server and have other users download and use that template. In an interview posted on KDE News (http://dot.kde.org/1110652641), Josef Spillner describes exactly how the process works.

> [U]ser A is using a spreadsheet application and modifies a template that comes with it. This template can then be uploaded to a server and eventually be downloaded by user B by checking the contents of the "Get Hot New Stuff" download dialogue.

The GHNS framework (Figure 8-11) shows up in several places throughout Kubuntu.

Figure 8-11 The GHNS framework at work

Different applications have the ability to download information from the Internet and from KDE sites. Throughout applications in Kubuntu, you will find references to Get More, which uses the GHNS framework.

System Administration

Like any computer application or system, Kubuntu occasionally needs administrative support. Do not be afraid of personally administrating your Kubuntu system. While system administration is not completely foolproof, a lot of changes have been made to help make administration easier. Knowledge of command line will go a long way, but the developers have made sure to provide graphical interfaces wherever it makes sense to do so. Everything from changing the IP address (e.g., from DHCP to a static address) to installing packages can be done without having to drop down to the command line. This section focuses exclusively on system administration performed through the graphical interface.

Installing New Packages

As mentioned earlier, Kubuntu is built around some of the same applications and systems as Ubuntu. All applications are installed through packages. Like Ubuntu, Kubuntu uses the Advanced Package Tool (APT), and also like Ubuntu, Kubuntu has a wonderful graphical interface. Kubuntu's graphical installer is called KPackageKit.

In previous versions of Kubuntu, Adept software was used to install and update packages; however, this application was no longer being developed and also was not updated for KDE 4. The developers of Kubuntu switched to KPackageKit, and many improvements to the application were made during the release cycle. The developers of KPackageKit and the Kubuntu developers worked together to make sure this application was up to the quality that Kubuntu users expect.

KPackageKit is found in the Application Launcher under Applications > System as Software Management and can also be launched through Krunner as Software Management.

Upon launching Software Management, you are presented with the KPackageKit application (Figure 8-12).

Three options are available in Software Management: Add and Remove Software (through the Software Management section), Software Updates, and Settings.

In order to add a new piece of software, type the name of the application in the search bar. The screenshots in Figures 8-13 and 8-14 show searching for a chess game and then selecting it for installation.

Figure 8-12 KPackageKit

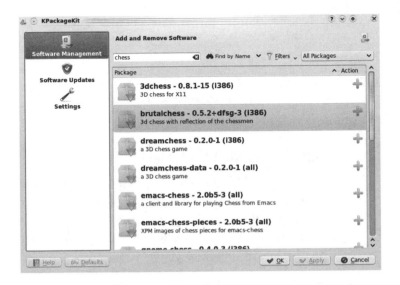

Figure 8-13 Searching for a chess game

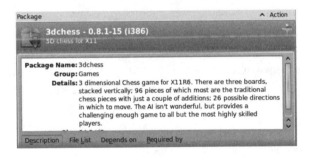

Figure 8-14 Selecting 3dchess for installation

Once you click on the application to install, more details about the package are displayed, including the description of the package, the file list, other packages that depend on this package, and other packages required by this package. This information allows you to understand what files are being installed and to make sure the correct packages are being downloaded and installed so the application works properly.

To install the application, click on the "+" (plus sign).

This will queue the package to be installed; click on Apply to set up the application on the system. Unlike Microsoft Windows, Kubuntu is great about not forcing a system restart in order for the new application to work correctly.

NOTE: A restart could be required if the version of KDE or the kernel is changed, but it is not necessary for the more typical and common update.

Managing Repositories

The Software Management application has the ability to manage the repositories you would like to use. To change which repositories are being used, open Software Management and select settings and the select "Edit Software Sources." After you provide the correct password, a new window will open up (see Figure 8-15).

Software Sources is divided into five sections: Kubuntu Software, Third-Party Software, Updates, Authentication, and Statistics.

Packages are organized into four groups or repositories: main, restricted, universe, and multiverse. The main repository contains applications that are free software, programs that allow for complete distribution and are supported by the Kubuntu team. When you install something from the

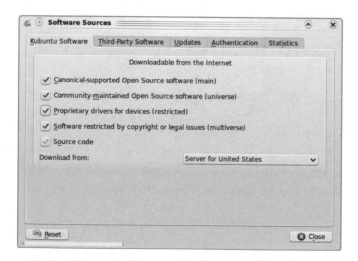

Figure 8-15 Software Source lists

main repository, you are guaranteed to receive security updates and support through the various venues.

Anything from the multiverse repository contains software that is not free, which is defined by the Kubuntu Main Component License Policy. Software here is used at the user's own risk.

Third-party software is not supported by Kubuntu.

Upgrading Kubuntu

If you are currently using Kubuntu 8.10 and would like to upgrade to Kubuntu 9.04, you can use the update manager to install the new version. There is no need to purchase new software or reload your system; just update from the current version to the latest stable release. From the console, type `sudo do-release-upgrade` and watch your system upgrade from Kubuntu 8.10 to Kubuntu 9.04.

How to Keep the System Up to Date

Kubuntu will check to see if your system is up to date. Software Management will notify you in the task bar and prompt you to update your system.

In the Settings portion of Software Management, you can change how often the system checks for updates (by default, it is every week). Another setting that can change is whether or not the system will automatically install the updates or prompt you for your updates.

System Settings

System Settings allows users to make changes to the system, including settings for sound, user accounts, mouse behavior, and network configuration. If you are familiar with KDE, you may recognize that System Settings replaces the K Control Center. Figure 8-16 shows System Settings.

System Settings can be found in the Application Launcher, or type System Settings in the search bar of the launcher, or in KRunner. (KRunner is accessed by either right-clicking on the desktop and selecting Run Application or by hitting ALT-F2.) When making changes in System Settings,

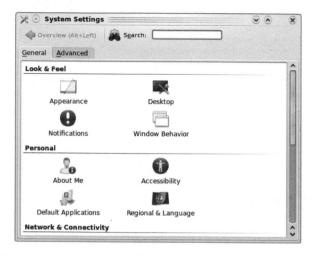

Figure 8-16 System Settings

you will be prompted at times to enter your password. Changes made that require a password are systemwide and will affect all users of the Kubuntu system.

System Settings is divided into two tabs, General and Advanced, and each tab is further divided into sections based on tasks. Under the General tab are the following sections: Look & Feel, Network & Connectivity, and Computer Administration. The Advanced tab contains two sections: Advanced User Settings and System.

When moving through the different options, be sure to select Overview to return to the main screen of System Settings instead of clicking on the X. Doing so may take some getting used to.

Look and Feel

The Look & Feel section allows further customization of your Kubuntu system. Sections here include Appearance, Desktop, Notifications, and Window Behavior. One of the options in this section is to customize the splash screen, known as the ksplash (Figure 8-17), displayed after you log in.

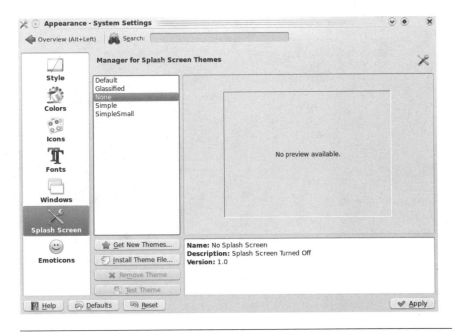

Figure 8-17 Customizing the splash screen

Personal

In the Personal section, you can change information about yourself, including your password, settings for your region and language, default applications, and accessibility options.

Computer Administration

The Computer Administration section allows you to add or remove software and to change items such as the date and time, display, fonts, input actions, keyboard and mouse settings, and multimedia.

The Display section allows you to change the screen resolution and orientation. If you are using an external monitor or a projector, this is where you would customize those settings. The Power Control Section deals with whether or not the monitor should turn off or go into standby to help conserve power. Figure 8-18 shows the display section of System Settings.

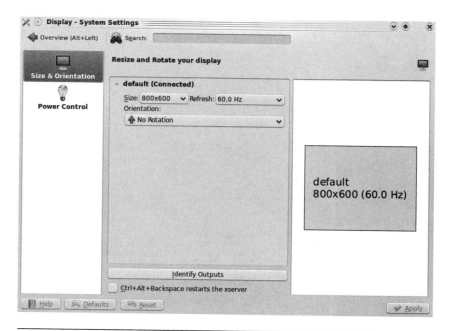

Figure 8-18 Display section of System Settings

Add or Remove Software

New to Kubuntu 9.04 is the addition of Add or Remove Software to System Settings. By opening this portion of System Settings, you open up KPackageKit to install new software. This functions the same way as described under the section Installing New Software.

Advanced Tab

The Advanced tab of System Settings allows for further customization of user settings. This section is divided into Advanced User Settings and System.

Advanced User Settings

The advanced user settings portion of the Advanced Tab allows you to customize things such as how Kubuntu handles audio CDs, digital camera settings, file associations, and so on.

One section, the Service Manager, shown in Figure 8-19, allows you to configure what services start during boot up of the computer. In order to

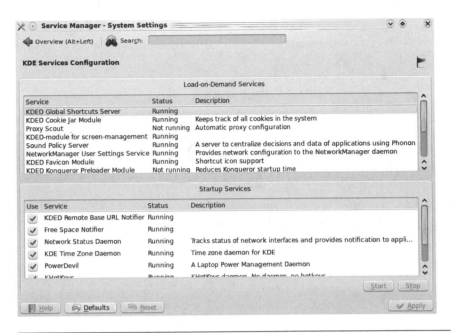

Figure 8-19 Service Manager

make changes, first put in your password and then you can start and stop services that are running.

Also in Advanced User Settings is the ability to configure how Akonadi (Akonadi configuration) and Nepomuk (Desktop Search) work. These two utilities are new to KDE4.

"Akonadi is a cross-desktop storage service for Personal Information Manager data (calendars, contacts, email, etc.) and also for the metadata" (http://pim.kde.or/akonadi for more information). Nepomuk can work together with Akonadi and helps you organize the information and metadata on your machine. (For more information, see http://nepomuk.semanticdesktop.org.) Another portion of Nepomuk is Desktop Search, which provides the ability to search for files and applications on your system. These two applications can be configured through System Settings.

System

Changes made to the entire system are made in this section.

Changes include Printer Configuration, Login Manager, Network Management, PolicyKit Authorization, and Power Management.

Printer Configuration

Major changes have been made in the Printer Configuration section to integrate setting up and managing printers in System Settings instead of in a different application. To add a new printer, click on the New Local Printer button and then follow the steps as shown in Figures 8-20 and 8-21.

Network Management

Another addition in System Settings for Kubuntu 9.04 is for Network Management. This section differs from the Network Settings under Network & Connectivity on the General tab, which deals with how your system connects to the network. The Network Management section allows you to configure different wireless or wired connection settings and helps you set up a VPN (virtual private network) connection. See Figure 8-22.

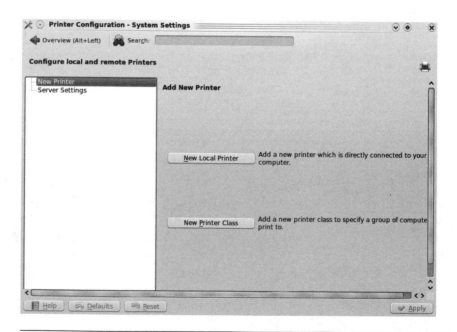

Figure 8-20 Adding a new printer

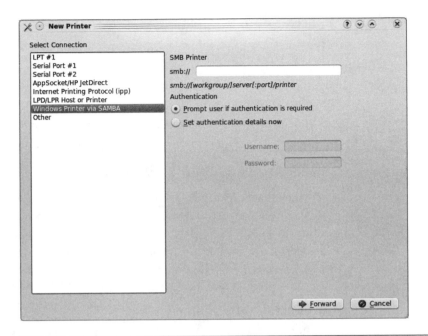

Figure 8-21 Add a Windows printer via SAMBA

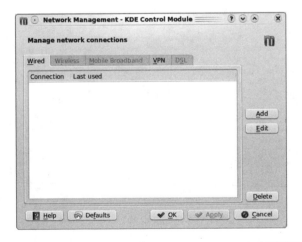

Figure 8-22 Network Management

PolicyKit Authorizations

Another new addition to System Settings is PolicyKit Authorizations (Figure 8-23). PolicyKit itself is an application that controls systemwide privileges. It allows nonprivileged users and processes to work with privileged processes. PolicyKit provides a fine level of control, and this part of System Settings allows you to customize how PolicyKit is enabled in Kubuntu.

Managing Files with Kubuntu

Now that you have your system installed and set up the way you would like, it is time to learn how to navigate the different files and access information in Kubuntu. This starts with the default file manager, Dolphin. Konqueror, another application that can be used both as a Web browser and a file manager, is discussed later in the chapter.

Introduction to Dolphin

Dolphin was first introduced during the 7.10 release schedule as d3lphin. The KDE4 version, Dolphin, is now included as the default file manager (see Figure 8-24).

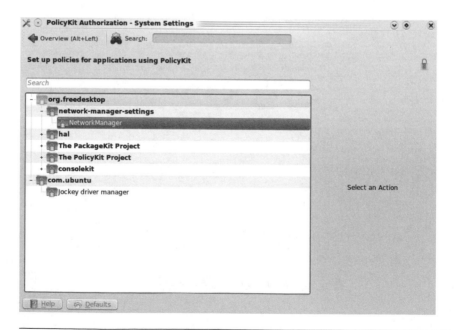

Figure 8-23 PolicyKit Authorizations

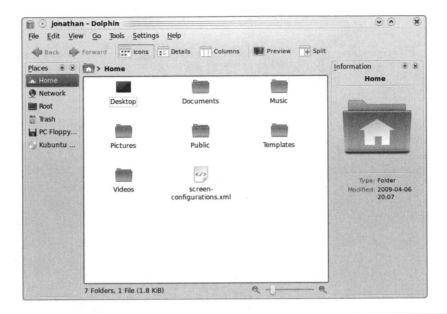

Figure 8-24 Viewing the Home Directory in Dolphin

Konqueror, which is also the KDE Web browser, was the previous default file manager. Over time, Konqueror development focused increasingly on the Web browser, while ignoring its file manager functionality. Dolphin focuses only on local files, is built on the Konqueror back end, and should be familiar to many KDE users.

Another key feature of Dolphin is the ability to use a split view to have multiple directories open in the same window, without having to switch tabs. An example of the split view of Dolphin is shown in Figure 8-25.

Dolphin is a very powerful file manager that nicely complements Konqueror. The two programs are often used in tandem.

Changes to the File Structure

Kubuntu 9.04 release utilizes the XDG Base Directory Specification of the freedesktop.org standards.

XDG directories specify a default set of folders within a user's home directory. Some of these folders are Desktop, Downloads, Templates, Music,

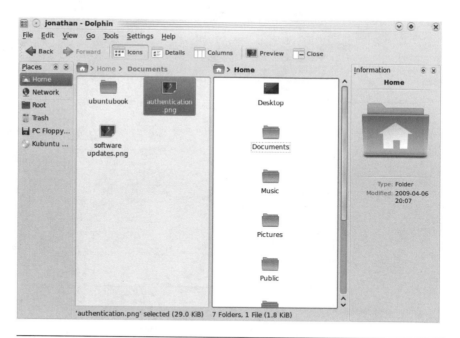

Figure 8-25 Dolphin Split View

and Video. The goal is to help create a standard location for files to be stored in a variety of different desktop environments (see Figure 8-26).

Introduction to Konqueror

Konqueror may be the old default file manager in Kubuntu, but it still has a lot to offer. As a file manager, Konqueror can do nearly everything you need (Figure 8-27). You can browse files through either an icon view or a tree view. Copying, pasting, moving, and deleting files are all simple tasks with Konqueror. A nice feature of Konqueror is that directories are automatically updated. This means that if a file is created in a directory currently being viewed, you do not need to refresh the directory to see the changes.

One of the great things about Konqueror is how much you can do within it. Need access to media files? Simply type media:/ and browse your media files. All kinds of other shortcuts, called kioslaves, exist in Konqueror, including ones for searching the Web with Google (gg:/*KEYWORD*) and even browsing files via ssh through sftp://. Need help finding a file on your system? Simply use locate:/ to have Konqueror find it for you. You can visit

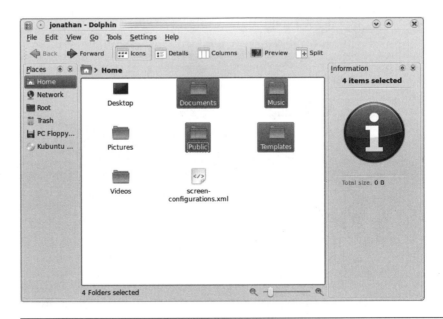

Figure 8-26 Viewing XDG directories in Dolphin

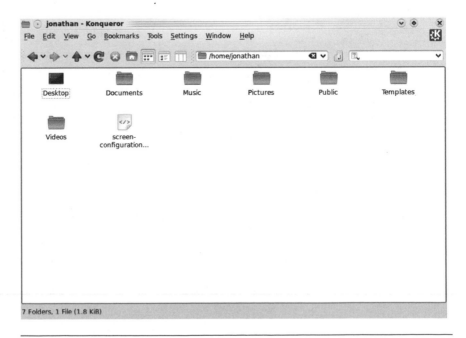

Figure 8-27 Konqueror

the different system folders through system:/. Many shortcuts and key-words like this are built into Konqueror, including Google Suggest in the search bar.

Accessing Windows Partitions

A lot of people still have Windows partitions on their hard drives and would like to access the information stored there. Kubuntu can browse these files in read-only mode. By default, Kubuntu mounts the Windows partition in the /media directory. See Figure 8-28 for an example of access-ing the Windows drive in Dolphin.

Accessing USB Drives

USB drives are everywhere these days, and Kubuntu handles them quite eas-ily. Simply connect your USB drive, and it will mount automatically. It will then be available under Dolphin through the media folder. Before removing the drive, make sure you unmount it by right-clicking on the device and selecting Eject. The device can then be safely removed.

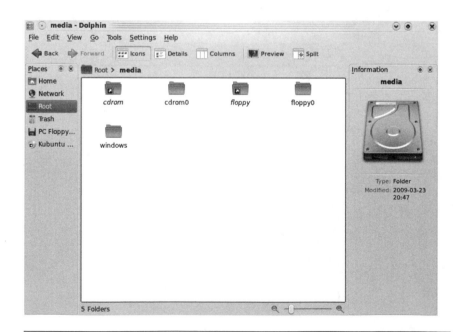

Figure 8-28 Accessing the Windows partition in Dolphin

Managing Music

Amarok is the default application for browsing and managing your music collection. Kubuntu 9.04 includes Amarok 2, which is a large rewrite of Amarok. Amarok is a powerful program that can track your podcasts and music and even provides access to an open music store (Magnatune). Magnatune is a music store that is completely free of DRM (Digital Rights Management) restrictions. Looking for Online Radio stations? Amarok provides access to multiple online radio stations through Cool Streams and also Shoutcast Streams. Amarok can also manage your portable music player (Figure 8-29). Once you have connected your music player, it will show up in the device section. Then feel free to manage your files and playlists.

The first time Amarok is launched, it recommends installing additional multimedia packages from the restricted repository. Depending on where you live, you may encounter some legal restrictions for installing these pieces. The recommended packages are for MP3 Tag Reading and Encoding, Flash, Video Codecs, MPEG Plugins, and DVD Reading. A notification from Update Notifier will load in the Taskbar, and after double clicking, you will be prompted to select which components to install. To install these packages, you need the administrative password.

Common Applications

Kubuntu comes with a large number of applications preinstalled and configured, including Web browsers, office applications, and e-mail programs. Remember, since choice is a huge feature of Kubuntu, if you do not like the default applications, you can always change them. All of these applications are available through the Application Launcher.

Figure 8-29 Managing your music player in Amarok

OpenOffice.org

The default office application for Kubuntu 9.04 is OpenOffice.org 3.0.1. This version is an update of the second major release of the suite that includes Writer, Calc, Impress, Draw, and Math; the first three can be launched from the Application Launcher. (Draw and Math are not available from the menu and are launched from within one of the other applications.) Note that the developers of Kubuntu have renamed the applications in the Application Launcher to better reflect what each does. For example, Writer is renamed Word Processor.

Each of these programs is easy to use and can help you switch from the Microsoft Office product line. In fact, the OpenOffice.org suite is included in the desktop CD and can be installed on a Windows system to help you get comfortable and ready for a switch to Kubuntu. Each application corresponds to a similar application in the Microsoft product line. Calc is very similar to Excel, Writer works like Word, and Impress replaces Power-Point. OpenOffice.org can handle all but Microsoft Access files without problems, and the whole suite is ready to be used in a corporate environment as well as for personal use.

To demonstrate the power of OpenOffice.org, let's create a new document. To start OpenOffice.org Writer, open the Application Launcher and navigate to Office and then Word Processor. You can also launch KRunner (Alt-F2), type Word processor, and hit Enter.

Writer resembles any other word processing software you have used. Simply start typing your letter or paper as you normally would, and use the toolbar for formatting options, including changing alignment, setting boldface or italic type, and other needs.

When you are done working on a document, save it by selecting File > Save or by typing Ctrl-S. OpenOffice.org saves documents in the Open Document format. This file format is a standard across the world. You can also save documents in other formats, including Microsoft Office and Adobe PDF. To save as a PDF file, just click the PDF button on the main toolbar (located next to the print icon) and enter a filename.

Web Browsing with Konqueror

As mentioned earlier, Konqueror can function as a Web browser as well as a file manager. To launch Konqueror, open the Application Launcher and navigate to Internet, then Web Browser. Alternately, you can launch KRunner (Alt-F2) and type in Konqueror. Like other modern Web browsers, Konqueror provides tabbed browsing, the ability to have multiple Web pages open in the same window. To do this, select File > New Tab or press Ctrl-T. A new tab will be created in your open Konqueror window. A cool feature is that you can be browsing the Web in one tab, browsing your home directory in another tab, and also browsing network folders in a third tab. All of these functions can help manage your taskbar and keep your desktop looking clean and sharp.

As a Web browser, Konqueror enables you to set bookmarks, change your home page, and use all the other features you would expect from a Web browser.

Navigating around the Internet is no different in Konqueror than in any other Web browser, including Firefox, Opera, Netscape, and Internet Explorer. Just type the Web address into the address bar and hit Enter. For example, type in www.kubuntu.com to visit the home page for Kubuntu.

To search using Google, simply move to the search bar, and directly to the right of the address bar type in what you are looking for. Konqueror will use Google to find it for you.

TIP   If you are using Konqueror in the file manager mode, the Google search bar defaults to locate, which will search your hard drive instead of using Google's search to search the Internet.

Often when browsing the Web, you will see an orange icon at the bottom of Konqueror. This means there is an RSS feed available. To track this feed, simply click on it, and Konqueror will add it to your subscribed feeds in Akregator. We'll talk more about Akregator later in this chapter.

Using Firefox for Browsing the Web

Allowing choice is a key feature of Ubuntu distributions. Kubuntu can use the latest version of Firefox (3.0 as of this writing), which needs to be installed through KPackageKit. Firefox has taken the Web browser world by storm and is as good as or even better than Internet Explorer. Firefox not only provides better features and a better browsing experience but also adheres better to Web standards. Like Konqueror, Firefox includes tab browsing (File > New Tab or Ctrl-T), bookmarks, and everything you would expect of a modern Web browser.

Firefox has many different extensions that can be plugged in to allow greater flexibility for your Web browser. The most common plug-ins are for using Macromedia Flash and Java, which some Web pages require.

Installing a plug-in is as simple as visiting a Web site that requires it. A yellow bar will indicate that you are missing a plug-in. Click on the Install Missing Plug-ins button to install the required plug-in.

Burning CDs—Audio and Data

Another common task is creating or burning audio and data CDs. Kubuntu's default CD creation program, K3b (installed through KPackage-Kit), is a very easy-to-use utility that can help you create backup CDs or even new music CDs. K3b provides a very familiar interface for burning and copying CDs (Figure 8-30).

Simply click on one of the icons from the main Kreator screen that describes the project you would like to create, for example, a new audio CD, a new data CD, or a new data DVD project. You can even copy a CD. After the new project has been started, simply drag the files you want from the top section to the lower section (Figure 8-31).

Once you have moved the files, select Burn, and sit back while your new CD is created.

Instant Messaging

Instant messaging is another feature that we almost cannot live without these days. Kopete, Kubuntu's default instant messaging client, handles

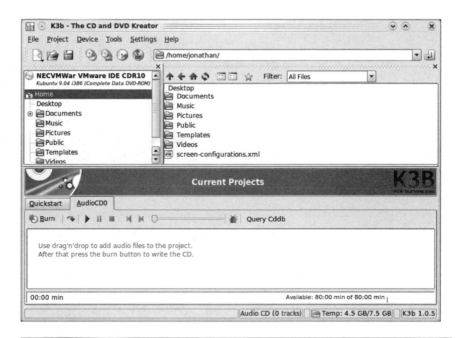

Figure 8-30 K3b

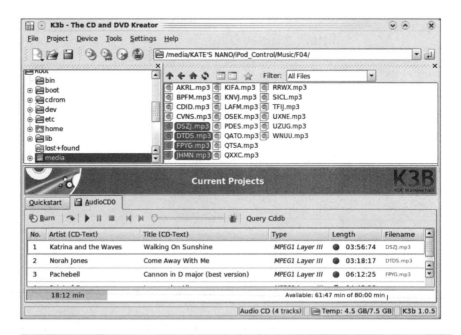

Figure 8-31 Just drag and drop the files.

this task very well. You can find it under the Internet section in the Application Launcher. You can also launch Kopete from KRunner or the Search bar of the Application Launcher by typing Kopete. The beauty of Kopete is that it can connect to all of the major service providers, so you do not have to have multiple programs open. Kopete can handle ICQ, MSN Messenger, Yahoo! Messenger, and AOL Instant Messenger (AIM), and because Google Talk (Google's instant messenger program) is built around the Jabber protocol, Kopete can handle that as well. Kopete also can work with MSN Webcams.

In order to use Kopete, you need to configure accounts. Select Settings > Accounts, and then configure the different accounts you would like Kopete to use. Kopete can save your passwords to these accounts and even automatically connect upon start-up.

Once the accounts are configured correctly, you can change Kopete's behavior to fit your preferences. Many options can be selected, including away settings, what happens when a new message arrives, and even how the system starts up.

Internet Relay Chat

A great place to find support for Kubuntu is Internet Relay Chat (IRC), which can be accessed by using Quassel and the different IRC channels. Join irc.ubuntu.org and then come over to #kubuntu to get many of your support questions answered. Quassel by default is set up to access #kubuntu (Figure 8-32), but more channels can be added. The people in #kubuntu are full of great knowledge and can probably solve any issues that you have.

To launch Quassel, type either Quassel or IRC in the Application Launcher and click on the application.

Kontact

These days almost everyone uses e-mail, and almost everyone uses some form of calendar program to keep track of appointments and schedules. Kontact, Kubuntu's default PIM (Personal Information Manager), takes care of all these tasks plus more.

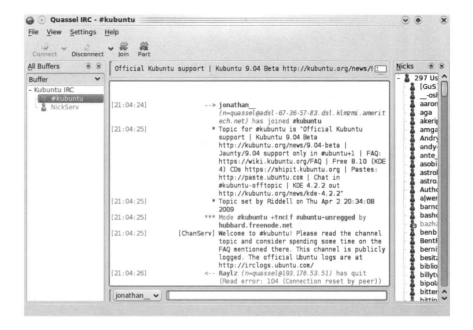

Figure 8-32 Quassel connected to #kubuntu

To start Kontact, go to the Application Launcher and then to the Internet section. You can also start it from KRunner or by typing Kontact in the Search Bar of the Application Launcher. Figure 8-33 shows an example of the Kontact window.

Looking at the figure, you can see that Kontact has a lot of different features. We cover several of the program's options in the following subsections.

KMail is the program that handles e-mail. It can be run separately from Kontact if you choose. The first step in configuring Kontact is to set up KMail to send and receive e-mail.

Setting Up Your E-Mail Account You will need several pieces of information to set up KMail. Your ISP or system administrator should be able to provide these details.

- Type of e-mail server (such as POP or IMAP)
- Mail server name (such as mail.domainname.com)

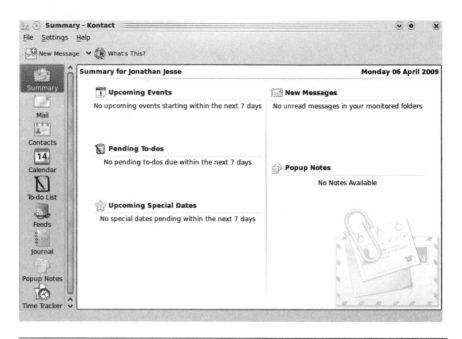

Figure 8-33 Kontact

- Mail account's username and password
- Authentication type (typically password)
- Outgoing mail server name

Configuring Kontact is easier than it may look. Once Kontact is open, select Settings and then Configuring Kontact. From the Configure Kontact panel, select Mail followed by Accounts. Under the tab labeled Receiving, add the information provided from your ISP as the incoming mail information. Once that account has been created, add a new account under the Sending tab that matches the outgoing mail information provided by your ISP.

Using KOrganizer   KOrganizer is included with Kontact. It will track your schedule and provide reminders of your appointments. Upon switching Kontact to calendar mode, you will see a month view on the left and individual days on the right, as Figure 8-34 shows.

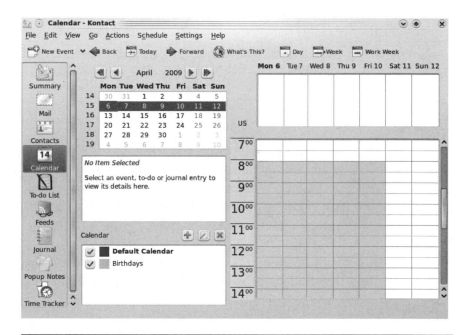

Figure 8-34 KOrganizer, Kontact's calendar mode

You can set up two different types of events in Kontact:

- **Meetings:** events scheduled with different people
- **Appointments:** general events

It is easy to add a new meeting or appointment. Find the date for the event in the month view, right-click, and select New Event. In the new window that opens, fill out the Summary, Location, Time, and Description boxes. You can also set up Kontact to remind you when it is time for the appointment.

Using Akregator   Another great application that is part of Kontact (or can be used separately) is Akregator, an RSS program that can track your favorite Web feeds. Due to the integration of Akregator and Konqueror, any Web page that has an RSS feed will have an orange icon in the corner of the program (Figure 8-35) that helps you add it to your list.

RSS

Figure 8-35 RSS icon to use to add a feed to Akregator

Simply click on the icon and select Add to Akregator. Akregator will keep your feeds up to date by automatically checking for new content. Another bonus of the integration between Konqueror and Akregator is that Web pages can be opened within Akregator to post comments and view more information than what is provided by the Web feed.

As you can see, Kontact is a great program that helps you organize your life, track your favorite Web sites through RSS, and handle your e-mail.

Kiosk Mode

Kiosk mode allows an administrator to configure KDE and all aspects of the desktop and prevent the end user from changing the settings.

KDE stores all of its configuration information in text files. These files control everything from the default background to whether or not a person can add bookmarks. To see the locations of the configuration files, simply type kde-config -path confi from the Konsole. Note that the order applied is the reverse order of what is displayed. By simply changing one of the files in the highest priority, the last listed in the kde-config statement, you can affect what all users see.

To change the background for all users, simply edit the Wallpaper section found in kdesktoprc, located in /usr/share/kubuntu-default-settings/kde-profile/default/share/config.

As previously discussed, each user can change the desktop to meet his or her own needs. However, an administrator can make it so some things cannot be changed. Simply insert [$i] at the top of the file for each application you would like to make immutable.

Along with enabling or setting changes, an administrator can remove user access to certain items by simply editing the kde globals file and adding a [KDE Action Restrictions] [$1] section.

There are plenty of additional items that can be limited and changed in Kubuntu.

Exploring the Kubuntu Landscape

Unlike many other operating systems, Kubuntu includes a large number of applications installed by default. These tools have been selected to allow you to install Kubuntu and then just get your work done. Some of the applications installed by default have been covered already. Unfortunately (or fortunately, depending on how you look at it), there are too many applications to discuss in this book due to space restrictions.

To partially solve that problem, here is a quick summary of many programs that are available from the Application Launcher, including how to find them and brief descriptions.

- **Kate:** Application Launcher > Utilities > Kate
  This simple and powerful text editor is great for editing documents, making quick notes, and programming. There is a vast range of plugins for items such as spell checking, statistics, and syntax highlighting.

- **Calculator (Speedcrunch):** Application Launcher > Utilities > Calculator
  Speedcrunch is an extremely powerful calculator that can help you solve both basic and advanced math problems.

- **Konsole:** Application Launcher > Utilities > Konsole
  Beneath the desktop is a very powerful command-line core. Konsole allows you to access this command line by putting a nice window frame around it. Konsole is great for command-line junkies, those who prefer to do things with a graphical interface. Konsole can be completely customized to meet your command-line needs.

- **Performance Monitor (KSysGuard):** Application Launcher > System >
  Performance Monitor
  The Performance Monitor provides information about how your
  Kubuntu system is functioning. Having problems with an application
  taking too much memory? How would you know? KSysGuard
  provides this information.

- **System Logs Viewer (KSystemLog):** Application Launcher > System >
  System Logs Viewer
  Interested in what is going on with your system? Kubuntu keeps track
  of files and access logs that can be viewed through this program.

- **Internet Dial-Up Tool (KPPP):** Application Launcher > Internet >
  Internet Dial-Up Tool
  Need help connecting to your ISP through a modem? KPPP will help
  take care of this. KPPP can help set up your modem and even set up
  your dial-up connection.

- **Remote Desktop Connection (KRDC):** Application Launcher >
  Internet > Remote Desktop Connection
  KRDC can help you connect to remote systems either through the
  remote desktop protocol (RDP) or through virtual network
  connection (VNC). Simply type in the address and click on Connect.
  KRDC can save the settings for each computer you connect to.

- **PDF Viewer (Okular):** Application Launcher > Graphics > PDF Viewer
  KPDF provides you with the ability to open and view files saved in the
  Adobe PDF format.

- **Screen Capture Program (KSnapShot):** Application Launcher >
  Graphics > Screen Capture Program
  KSnapShot allows you to take screenshots and save them in different
  formats. The great thing about KSnapShot is that you specify the
  exact amount of the screen that will be captured. This program was
  used to take all of the screenshots for this chapter.

- **Image Viewer (Gwenview):** Application Launcher > Graphics >
  Image Viewer
  Gwenview is the default application for viewing images in Kubuntu.
  All different types of images can be opened, including .png, .jpeg, and
  .bmp.

- **KDevelop:** Application Launcher > Development > KDevelop
  While not installed by default, KDevelop is a wonderful integrated

development environment (IDE) that can help you with your coding projects. This application must be installed via KPackageKit.

■ **Marble:** Application Launcher > Education > Misc > Marble
Marble is a 3D mapping and globe application. Additional map information is available through GHNS.

■ **KRandRtray:** Application Launcher > System > Screen Size and Rotate
This application is used to rotate and resize the monitor. It also detects and configures external monitors.

Tips and Tricks

The more you use Kubuntu, the more tips and tricks you will learn to help make your computer experience better and easier. Kubuntu can be configured to do almost anything you would like.

Run Programs Automatically When Kubuntu Starts   You might like to start some programs automatically every time you log in to your system. For example, to help you with your Kubuntu work, you might want to access various channels of IRC every day via Konversation. There are four easy steps to set this up using the session management feature of KDE.

1. Launch all the applications you would like to open automatically.
2. Open up System Settings from the Application Launcher, and click on the User Management section.
3. Click on the Session Manager button on the left, and make sure that the Restore Manually Saved Session checkbox is enabled.
4. Log out, saving your sessions.

Log In Automatically to Kubuntu When the Computer Starts   It is possible to set up Kubuntu so that a user is logged in automatically when the computer boots. This change is not recommended for most computers because it is insecure and may allow others to access your information.

1. Open up System Settings from the Application Launcher, and click on the Advanced Tab.
2. Click on Login Manager.
3. Click on Administrator Mode, and enter your password.

4. Select the Convenience tab, and Enable Autologin.

5. Select the user to autologin from the drop-down menu, and select an appropriate time delay.

Automatically Turn On Numlock When Kubuntu Starts   If you are sick of always having to turn on numlock, the change is very simple to make.

1. Open up System Settings from the Application Launcher, and select Keyboard & Mouse.

2. Under the Numlock on KDE Startup, enable the Turn On checkbox.

3. Click on Apply to save your settings.

Finding Help and Giving Back to the Community
Finding Help

Kubuntu provides a lot of ways to find the information you need to solve a problem. A great place to start is on the IRC channel #kubuntu, which, as we noted earlier, can be accessed through Konversation. There are always wonderful and knowledgeable people in this channel who can answer almost any question. If you prefer to use the Web for answers, the Kubuntu wiki, found at http://wiki.kubuntu.org, has a large amount of information loosely organized with a great search function built in. A third place to find information is the Kubuntu forums at www.kubuntuforums.com. Google is also a great resource. Chances are that someone else has come across your problem before and has written a solution to the issue.

Giving Back to the Community

Kubuntu is built around a great community of people who give back what they learn. There are many ways to get involved and share your love of Kubuntu. A great place to find out how you can make a difference is at www.ubuntu.com/community/participate. Not everyone involved has to know how to create packages, understand how the kernel works, or be a great programmer. Kubuntu also has a place for people to write wiki pages or help with documentation needs.

Summary

Kubuntu is a great part of the Ubuntu project and is quickly maturing. From its start as the idea of a single developer to many people working together, Kubuntu is becoming the KDE distribution of choice. However, there is still room for improvement and additions to the setup. A large community of people discusses every day, either through IRC or e-mail, ways to make these improvements. Bugs and other issues are quickly resolved without the additional cost of new programs.

Kubuntu is going to be around for the long haul, and each new release delivers a better, cleaner, and more polished OS. Help spread the word about the project, and get involved by helping out.

CHAPTER 9

Using Edubuntu

- Introduction to Edubuntu
- Installing Edubuntu as an Add-on
- Applications
- Using Edubuntu in LTSP Mode
- Managing Your LTSP Server
- Managing Your Edubuntu Clients
- Controlling and Managing the Users' Desktops
- Troubleshooting LTSP
- Finding Help and Giving Back to the Community
- Summary

Introduction to Edubuntu

Several Ubuntu advocates have leveled the counterintuitive suggestion that the groups of users who have the most problems switching to Ubuntu are those with the most computer experience. For the technically competent, learning Ubuntu often involves *unlearning* something else. But while for most of those reading this book, Ubuntu is an alternative operating system, for many others in an extraordinarily exciting generation of users, Ubuntu is a *first* operating system. No team or project within Ubuntu has done more to target, support, and grow this group of users than the Edubuntu project.

The community-driven Edubuntu project aims to create an add-on for Ubuntu specially tailored for use in primary and secondary education. Edubuntu exists as a platform for tools for teachers and administrators. But the real thrust, of course, and the real purpose, is to put free and open source software into the hands of children. In doing so, Edubuntu provides children with a flexible and powerful technological environment for learning and experimenting. Based on free software, it offers educational technologies that are hackable and that can ultimately be used by students and teachers on *their own terms*. Distributed freely, its gratis nature serves an important need for schools where technology programs are always understaffed and underfunded. Fluent in Ubuntu and in free software, the children who, right now, are growing up using Edubuntu are offering the Ubuntu community a glimpse of where it might go and the generation of Ubunteros that may take us there.

While the Ubuntu, Kubuntu, and Xubuntu desktops highlight the products of the GNOME, KDE, and Xfce communities respectively, the Edubuntu project aims to provide the best of everything in Ubuntu—properly tailored for use in schools and as easy to use as possible. One thing that made Edubuntu popular was its amazing ability to integrate thin clients, allowing the use of one powerful machine (the server) to provide many very low-powered, often diskless machines (the clients), with their entire OS. (See the section What Is LTSP? for more information.) This model, while uninteresting for most workstation and laptop use by home or business users, is a major feature in classroom settings where it can mitigate configuration and maintenance headaches and reduce the cost of classroom deployments substantially.

A History of Edubuntu

Edubuntu started life as two specifications written in the Ubuntu Down Under developer summit by Eric Harrison, Jeff Elkner, and the LTSP developer team to implement an educational version of Ubuntu based on a thin client architecture. The rest of the Ubuntu team valued the goals of their specifications and saw Ubuntu's use in education as both appropriate and important. As a result, the specifications' priority was set too high— they *had* to be implemented.

Enter Oliver Grawert, an important community contributor to Ubuntu who was new to Canonical and did not yet have specific duties and responsibilities within the project. Grawert wanted to work on one of the Edubuntu specifications and, prompted by Ubuntu lead developer Matt Zimmerman, took both. Over the process of the next release, Edubuntu turned into a full-time job for Grawert and a full-fledged offering for Ubuntu and Canonical.

Shortly after being given the specifications, Grawert attended an education summit and met with several educators, administrators, and developers, as well as the core of Skolelinux in Bergen, Norway, to get a deeper insight into the matter. In turn, Canonical sponsored an event in London where the core of the Norwegian Skolelinux team, joined by educators from South America, Spain, Great Britain, and other areas of the world, attended to discuss the future of the educational OS. Together they decided on the core application list and that LTSP would be required by default.

Edubuntu's goals were simple but expansive and provided a map for the project.

1. Conquer the classroom.
2. Grow to school size.
3. Expand to fit even into municipalities.

Shortly after this, in October 2005, the first edition of Edubuntu based on Ubuntu 5.10 (Breezy Badger) was born. Since then, the community has grown massively, and Edubuntu is now worked on by many developers from around the world with a small but growing list of deployments.

In 2008, it was decided that the developers of Edubuntu should focus more on bringing the best educational applications to the desktop rather than trying to maintain an entire distribution of their own. As a result, Edubuntu is no longer a distribution like Ubuntu, Kubuntu, or Xubuntu, but rather an "add-on" for users. What this means is that you can easily either use an add-on CD image or install the Edubuntu suite of tools using the Synaptic Package Manager to any existing installation of Ubuntu, Kubuntu, or Xubuntu. Along with this change came an additional name as well: Ubuntu Educational CD.

Where to Find Edubuntu

Edubuntu is found in the same place as the Kubuntu and Ubuntu distributions. If you visit www.edubuntu.org, you can download a disc image and then burn it to a CD.

Installing Edubuntu as an Add-on

This section covers installing the Edubuntu add-on in a non-LTSP environment. This type of installation is not only the easiest, but is recommended for typical usage. Later in this chapter, installing the Edubuntu add-on in an LTSP environment is covered.

To utilize the Edubuntu add-on CD for installation, you must have previously installed Ubuntu 9.04. Currently, the add-on CD only works with the Ubuntu desktop. Once Ubuntu has been installed, simply insert the add-on CD into your CD-ROM drive. You will be prompted with a pop-up dialog, letting you know that the add-on volume has been detected and asking if you would like to view or install the content. To view the content, press the Start package manager button, or to install, press the Start add-on installer.

After you press the button for installation, the Add/Remove Applications window will open, allowing you to select what you would like to install. You can install separate applications or the entire Edubuntu desktop. Select the applications you would like to install by placing a check mark inside the boxes for each application, and then press the Apply Changes button.

If you have the Kubuntu or Xubuntu desktop, you can still install the Edubuntu desktop and applications. However, you cannot do so at this time from the add-on CD. The following instructions for installing via the Internet also apply to those of you with the Ubuntu desktop. All you need to do is open your desktop's package management application (Kubuntu uses KPackageKit, whereas Ubuntu and Xubuntu use Synaptic) and install the available educational packages. Alternatively, you can install the edubuntu-desktop package, which provides the entire Edubuntu experience for the GNOME desktop, or the edubuntu-desktop-kde package, which provides the same as the edubuntu-desktop package but with full KDE support. It is highly recommended to have a broadband Internet connection for doing this type of install.

Applications

There are many applications available for your Ubuntu, Kubuntu, and Edubuntu desktop in addition to those specified in the following two sections. For further information on installing extra applications, please refer to Chapter 4. If you are using Kubuntu, then it is best to refer to Chapter 8.

Standard Applications

The standard applications are now provided by the Ubuntu, Kubuntu, or Xubuntu desktop, with the ability to install the educational packages from Edubuntu either by the add-on CD or via the Synaptic Package Manager. Let's take a few moments to discuss some of the prominent packages installed with Ubuntu. To get a breakdown of the standard applications available in the other projects, please review their respective chapters.

Educational Applications

Let's take a walk through the Edubuntu Educational menu, found at Applications > Education. You will find a brief summary for all applications here, as well as more detailed explanations and screenshots of some of the more advanced packages.

GCompris Administration   This is the administration tool for the GCompris set of tools, which is described a little later. Using this tool, you can create separate profiles for different users of GCompris and enable or disable the list of available activities.

Kalzium   Kalzium presents the pinnacle of periodic table exploration for users of any ages. In its simplest form, it provides a quick and easy reference to the periodic table. Kalzium includes 105 of the naturally occurring elements, many of which are accompanied by sample pictures. If the user hovers the mouse pointer over an element symbol in the periodic table, a balloon appears showing the selected element's name, atomic number, and mass (Figure 9-1).

For more advanced users, Kalzium provides a fascinating way to explore the periodic table. Using the left-hand panel, users have access to the timeline, boiling point, and melting point sliders. When users move these sliders, the elements on the periodic table change color according to their dates of discovery, boiling points, or melting points, respectively. Users can then start to see patterns emerging in the periodic table right in front of their eyes.

As well as presenting the basic information, Kalzium provides very advanced statistics on each of the 105 elements present.

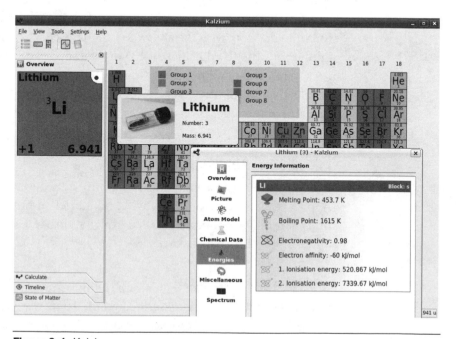

Figure 9-1 Kalzium

Kanagram Kanagram is a simple package that messes up the letters of a word to create an anagram that children must then unscramble. The package comes with hints, a cheat feature that reveals the word, and built-in word lists, which can be extended.

KBruch KBruch is a math program to help students practice the use of fractions. It comes with four distinct modes of play.

- **Fraction Task:** In this exercise, the user is given a fraction sum that must be solved by adding the numerator and denominator. The difficulty of the sum can be changed by the user, who has control over the number of fractions to use, the maximum size of the main denominator, and the mathematical operations to use, such as addition, subtraction, multiplication, and division.

- **Comparison:** This exercise is designed to test the user's understanding of fraction sizes by making him or her compare two given fractions.

- **Conversion:** The Conversion mode tests the user's skills at taking a given number and converting it into a fraction.

- **Factorization:** Factorization tests the user in calculating the factors of a given number. Factorization is a key skill in using and manipulating fractions.

KHangman This modern version of a classic game helps children learn to spell and recognize letter patterns in words. KHangman shows a blank base to start; as the user chooses letters, they are entered into the word if correct or placed on the tries list if incorrect, in which case the hangman begins to grow. KHangman comes with three built-in word lists, but these can be extended easily.

Kig For people wishing to learn about geometrical construction in mathematics, Kig is a must. It is an extremely powerful package but very simple to use. Kig allows users to create complex geometrical abstractions from over thirty simple tools, such as points, parallel and perpendicular lines, arcs, bisectors, circles, and hyperbola (Figure 9-2). When creating abstractions, Kig uses other lines and points already on the diagram to lock onto, making it easy to achieve high precision.

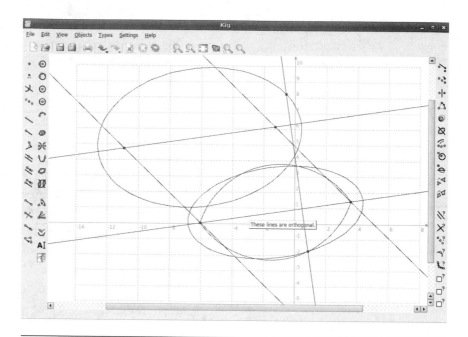

Figure 9-2 Kig

Kig also has some testing tools included. Once a geometrical diagram has been drawn, it is often required to prove a concept by showing that two lines are indeed parallel or perpendicular. Kig offers these tools and more in an easy-to-use manner. Just clicking on the tool prompts the user to choose the item to test against. Then, each time the user hovers over another item while moving the cursor around, Kig will pop up with a message to tell whether or not it satisfies the test case.

KmPlot KmPlot is a mathematical function–graphing program for Edubuntu. The package has a powerful expression parser built in and can plot different functions simultaneously and combine their function terms to build more complex mathematical functions. KmPlot also supports functions with parameters and functions in polar coordinates. KmPlot can create graphs to a very high precision, making it excellent for teaching purposes.

KStars With information on over 130,000 stars and 13,000 deep sky objects, KStars is one powerful package when it comes to space exploration. The main view in KStars follows the time and date to provide the user with a constantly updating view of the night sky. Constellations are highlighted and star clusters marked for clarity (Figure 9-3).

KStars has a simplistic user interface, which makes it ideal for amateurs all the way up to astronomy experts. Celestial objects can be right-clicked for more information and can then be tracked and examined in even more detail.

In addition to the huge celestial object database, there are some other fantastic features in KStars. The Calculator, for example, allows the user to compute coordinates and other figures for a variety of objects and scenarios. KStars can even be hooked up to a telescope to allow real-time tracking of what the screen shows.

The What's Up Tonight? tool provides an overview of what objects will be visible in the sky on that particular night, with the ability to then center on an object and track it in real time. The Altitude vs. Time feature allows users to see how the altitude of a celestial object varies with time during

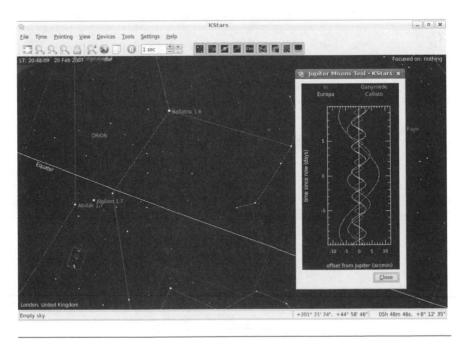

Figure 9-3 KStars

the day. With a built-in scripting language, KStars is the most comprehensive astronomical observation application in the open source community.

KTouch   In this day and age, typing is an everyday occurrence for most people. KTouch is a tutor that gives help and support to those wishing to learn the art of touch typing. With fifteen levels and automatic level progression, KTouch is a fairly advanced tutor program, offering statistics and alternative language options, too.

KTurtle   KTurtle is a Logo programming language interpreter for Edubuntu. The Logo programming language is very easy to learn, and thus young children can use it. A unique quality of Logo is that the commands or instructions can be translated, so the user can program in his or her native language. This makes Logo ideal for teaching children the basics of programming, mathematics, and geometry. One of the reasons many children warm to Logo is that the programmable icon is a small turtle, which can be moved around the screen with simple commands and can be programmed to draw objects (Figure 9-4).

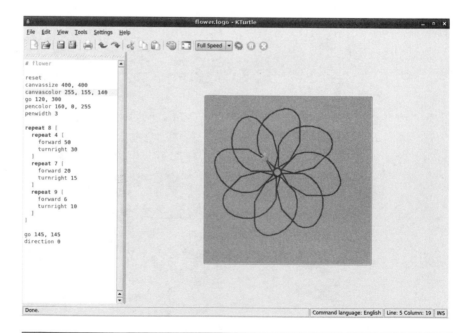

Figure 9-4 KTurtle

By typing in commands such as `turnleft 90`, `forward 4`, children are using a language native to themselves while also learning procedural logic. KTurtle can even handle simple subroutines, so it's easy to extend the programming onward and upward.

With the introduction of KDE 4, Edubuntu includes a group of brand new educational packages. Following is a brief summary of each new application.

Marble   Marble, the desktop globe, is a virtual globe and world atlas, which can be utilized to learn more about the Earth. With the ability to pan and zoom, click on a label to open a corresponding Wikipedia article, and view the globe and maps with various projections, Marble is a welcome addition to Edubuntu's educational packages.

Parley   Parley, the digital flash card, allows you to easily remember things utilizing the spaced repetition learning method, otherwise known as flash cards. Features include different testing types, fast and easy setup, multiple languages, the ability to share and download flash cards, and much more.

Step   Step is an interactive physics simulator that allows you not only to learn but to feel how physics works. By placing bodies on the scene and adding some forces such as gravity or springs, you can simulate the law of physics, and Step will show you how your scene evolves.

Blinken   Blinken takes you back, back to the 1970s, as a digital version of the famous Simon Says game. Watch the lights, listen to the sounds, and then try to complete the sequence in order. Blinken provides hours of fun with the added benefit of learning.

Others Not on the Education Menu   Some educational applications are not located in the Education menu. Here are brief descriptions of two of them.

- **Tux Paint:** Applications > Graphics > Tux Paint
  Tux Paint is a drawing package for younger children. Although geared toward a younger audience, Tux Paint still packs in some of the more advanced features of drawing packages and can draw shapes, paint with different brushes, use a stamp, and add text to the image. The

Magic feature allows many of the more advanced tools normally found in full-fledged photo editors to be used, such as smudge, blur, negative, tint, and many more. There is also the facility to save as well as print.

■ **GCompris:** Applications > Games > GCompris
GCompris is a set of small educational activities aimed at children between two and ten years old and is translated into over forty languages. Some of the activities are game oriented and at the same time educational. Among the activities, there are tasks to educate children in computer use, algebra, science, geography, reading, and more. More than eighty activities are available in the latest release. GCompris won a Free Software Award that took place in France in 2004.

Using Edubuntu in LTSP Mode
What Is LTSP?

Perhaps one of the most useful features within Ubuntu is the LTSP environment. It's worth spending a few minutes reading this section to understand exactly what the LTSP system is and what it can do for you. You'll soon realize its applications are not limited just to education.

LTSP stands for Linux Terminal Server Project. It aims to give the same functionality to current client/server models that were present in the mainframe/dumb terminal setups prevalent many years ago.

How Does LTSP Work?

The LTSP model centers around one powerful machine that acts as a server and several often much lower-powered machines that act as clients. The machines are all connected on a local area network.

This network allows all data required for booting the client's computer, which is normally held on the client's hard drive, to be served to the client over the network. If all the data required for booting the computer is provided over the network, the client machine requires no storage media at all, which leads to the term *diskless clients*.

TIP　　Clients require a network card, which can boot either via PXE or via Etherboot to allow initial booting for local media before piggyback booting from the network. More information on this can be found at http://rom-o-matic.net, where you can create bootable images for your network hardware. In essence, Etherboot is essentially a convenient way to emulate the PXE system on older hardware. Most newer motherboards and network cards come with PXE software on the chip.

Technical Details of the LTSP Boot Process

A client machine is switched on. After the hardware is initialized, the network card looks for an IP address via the DHCP protocol. The LTSP server in most cases acts as the DHCP server to the local network and sends the client machine its IP address. Figure 9-5 shows a diagram of the LTSP booting process.

Once the network card has bound the IP address to itself, it then makes a connection to the LTSP server and asks for the PXE configuration file. The LTSP server sends this file back to the client machine, which then makes a request for the kernel image. This is the base of the OS,

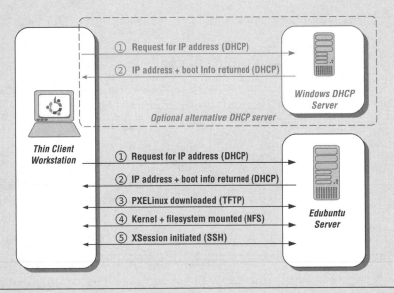

Figure 9-5 LTSP booting process　　　　　　　　　　　　　　　　*(continues)*

which provides the client with all the hardware drivers required to communicate with the server.

After this, an NFS connection is set up with the server. This is almost like a standard network share. The NFS share holds a very cut-down installation of Ubuntu, which consists almost entirely of an X server and an SSH-based login manager to connect to the server. Once the client machine has finished booting this small version of Ubuntu, the login screen is displayed to the user.

When a user logs in, an SSH tunnel is opened to the server, and an X session is initiated through this tunnel. All programs are run on the server, and it is only really the graphical interface that is piped back to the client machine. This allows the user to interact with the session and use a computer as normal.

The whole process is totally transparent to the user, but it is important to have a basic understanding of the underlying technologies present in LTSP to assist in the troubleshooting process and to be able to evaluate LTSP for a given task.

The Benefits of LTSP

Booting computers in this way does have some distinct advantages over the current preferred model of many powerful desktops, particularly where only a low budget is available.

- **Singular point of administration:** Working with this model means that only one computer needs to have new software installed on it. By using the Add/Remove tools as demonstrated later in this chapter, you can make applications automatically available to all clients as they are essentially all using the same machine.

- **Low-cost hardware:** Thin client machines are not required to be incredibly powerful since all processing is done by the server. This allows people to use much older hardware for their client machines, often reusing machines that were taken out of service for being sluggish several years ago.

- **Diskless clients:** Anyone who has spent time administrating a network knows that often a computer used regularly suffers from corrupt files on the hard disk and needs reinstalling. If a client has no disk, there is no chance of a user corrupting data on the client's hard drive.

- **Easy replacement:** If one of your thin client machines breaks down, you still have all your data stored on the server. Just replace the client hardware and carry on working. It really is as easy as changing a light bulb.

TIP   Thin clients can run on incredibly low-specification machines. People are running thin clients on recycled computers that are as low-powered as 133MHz Pentiums with 64MB of RAM. While performance becomes an issue on hardware this slow, simple tweaks to avoid encryption over SSH can mitigate these. Generally, a machine running at least a 400MHz processor with 128MB of RAM will make an excellent thin client.

Other Uses

The LTSP system has its uses in many other applications too. Imagine you are running an Internet cafe, where many people use the computers in exactly the same way. Each workstation would need the same set of applications installed. The tasks they are performing are not hugely CPU intensive, so a thin client system is perfectly suited to this type of application. You will also find LTSP solutions very commonly used in information systems (e.g., in airports) and in point-of-sale systems.

LTSP Availability in Ubuntu

The ability to install and configure the LTSP system automatically is available to the user with the Ubuntu alternate CD. Since Edubuntu is no longer available as a live or alternate CD, the LTSP server installation has been moved to the Ubuntu alternate CD. If installation of LTSP is required to an already installed Ubuntu, Kubuntu, or Xubuntu desktop or Ubuntu server, you should follow the instructions provided in the next section.

Installing an LTSP Server

Starting with Ubuntu 9.04, the LTSP installation process has one minor step prior to reading on. The first thing you need to do is acquire the Ubuntu alternate CD. LTSP server installation is no longer provided via an Edubuntu CD because the status of Edubuntu has changed from a distribution to an add-on. Once you have your LTSP server installed and configured, installation of Edubuntu and its applications is the same as previously presented in the "Installing Edubuntu as an Add-on" section of this chapter.

LTSP Server Configurations   The LTSP server install allows a great deal of flexibility and is designed to allow it to fit into any current network configuration. Essentially these fall into two categories: those that use the LTSP server as a primary gateway for all their LTSP clients and those that do not. Let's take a few minutes to discuss the relative merits of each system.

Using the recommended configuration requires the LTSP server machine to have two network interface cards (NICs). One of these cards is connected to the rest of the network, that is, to the Internet or to other servers on the internal network. The other card is usually connected to a private subnet of the network where only Edubuntu LTSP clients reside. Figure 9-6 shows this two-NIC setup. No network data is routed from the second network card to the first, so client machines must be authenticated on the LTSP server before having access to the Internet or the rest of the network. This makes for a secure network setup.

The benefit to this setup is that client computers cannot connect to the network unless the LTSP server permits them to. This also reduces network traffic on the rest of the network because while the LTSP clients are booting from the LTSP server, data is being transferred only on the private subnet and not on the rest of the network. Also, the clients receive their network addresses from the LTSP server, which frees up addresses on the rest of the network.

Using LTSP as simply another server on a network allows for a more flexible atmosphere. For a start, you require only one network interface card in the server to run using this configuration. The LTSP clients are connected to the normal network and could, assuming they had the capabilities to boot, access the network without the help of the LTSP server. Figure 9-7 shows this one-NIC setup.

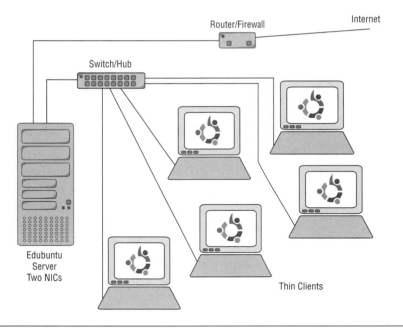

Figure 9-6 Two-NIC setup

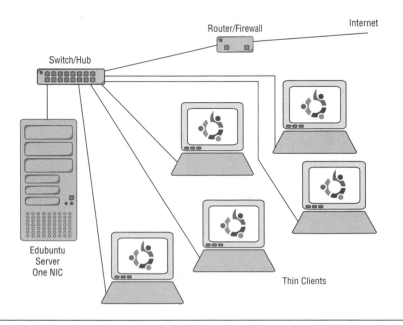

Figure 9-7 One-NIC setup

The benefits of this setup are that thin clients can be used with more than one OS. One establishment, for example, runs dual-booting Microsoft Windows and Edubuntu clients. This setup also allows users to have their LTSP thin clients receiving their DHCP network addresses from a single network server.

Essentially the choice of network design layout will impact the number of network cards installed in your server. It is primarily this that affects the difference between the standard Ubuntu install and the LTSP install.

The Installation Procedure   The installation procedure from the Ubuntu alternate CD looks very different from that of the desktop CD, but the questions asked are largely the same. The alternate CD is all text based, which can be a little daunting at first, but you will find installing Ubuntu in this way quicker because it doesn't require the entire desktop session to be loaded.

TIP   Remember that the server CD sets up LTSP for you. If you are planning to run an LTSP server, the easiest installation method is to use the Ubuntu alternate CD.

After the CD has booted, press F4 and select Install an LTSP server, and then select the Install to the Hard Disk option. Confirm by pressing Enter to begin the installation. Notice also the workstation and command-line options at this point.

The first question you are asked simply sets up the language used for the install procedure, as well as the language for the final system. You are then asked to choose your location.

Now you must choose your keyboard layout. The text-based installer has an auto-detection routine that will ask you to press a series of keys on the keyboard. From these keys, the installer can work out which keyboard layout will best suit you. If there are any keyboard variations, these are now presented for you to choose from.

The installer will now load various components. If you have more than one NIC in your computer, you will be asked to choose the primary card for the installation (Figure 9-8). By this, the installer wishes to know which network card is connected to the outside network or the Internet.

If your network has DHCP enabled, this card will be set up with an IP address from the network. You will then be prompted to choose a hostname for the LTSP server. If your network doesn't have DHCP enabled, you will have to set up the IP address manually.

The next step is to set up the hard disk ready for installation. By far the easiest method here is to select the default option of Guided Partitioning. If you wish to use LVM, please refer to the section on LVM in Chapters 2 and 5. If you require more in-depth partitioning or already have data on the hard drive that you do not want to lose, you will have to plan how you are going to proceed. If you are installing onto a computer that has partitions Ubuntu can resize, it will offer you that option. Doing this will allow you to have two operating systems installed on one computer and to switch between them at bootup. Whichever method you select, you will then be asked to confirm your partitioning choices.

TIP While the resizing utilities in Ubuntu are excellent, you should always back up your data before performing an operation such as this.

After this, you must choose whether or not your clock is set to Coordinated Universal Time (UTC). Your system clock should be set to UTC. Your OS is then responsible for converting the system time into local time.

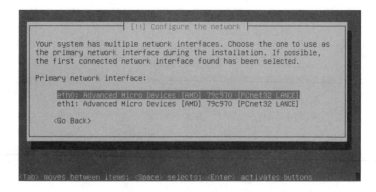

Figure 9-8 Selecting the primary network interface

Unless you have another OS that expects the system time to be the local time, you should answer "yes" here.

Now it's time to set up the first user on the system. Remember that this user will have full administrative rights. First, enter the user's full name, then the desired username, followed by the password twice. After this, the base system is installed.

After plowing through several steps, you are presented with a question about screen resolutions. For the type of system you are installing, a very high screen resolution could result in a slow connection between the server and the client. The default options are fine.

When this is completed, the installer begins building the LTSP client root filesystem (Figure 9-9). This is the very small version of Ubuntu mentioned earlier in this chapter. Essentially it consists of just a kernel and an X server.

TIP   This step appears to take a long time, and the progress bar isn't updated often. Be patient, have a snack—it will finish eventually.

Once the installation is complete, a prompt will ask you to remove the CD and press Enter to reboot the system into your new Edubuntu server.

Initial LTSP Server Setup   The DHCP server installed on your Ubuntu machine should start up automatically, so all that is left to do is to make your thin clients bootable from the network. If you are using the single network card setup described earlier and your network already has a DHCP

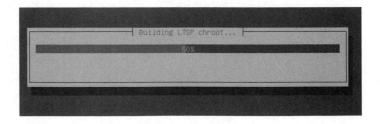

Figure 9-9 Building the LTSP filesystem

server running, *do not* start the Ubuntu DHCP server, as this will likely cause both DHCP services to be unavailable.

TIP   If you are still running the Dapper 6.06 LTS version of Edubuntu, there is a little bit more work to do. The latest versions of Ubuntu have an automatic DHCP configuration generator. This means that they do not require manual configuration in usual LTSP environments. The 6.06 LTS release needs manual configuration of the DHCP server; please visit https://www.edubuntu.org/GettingStarted for further instructions.

Initial LTSP Client Setup   Modifying a client computer to boot from the network is usually done by altering a setting in the machine's BIOS. It's a good idea to look at the manual for the computer's motherboard to find out how to alter these settings. For most machines it will simply be a case of entering the BIOS by pressing the Delete key at bootup and changing the boot device priority.

Once you've set up your client machines to boot from the network card, you should see a screen similar to the one Figure 9-10 shows on each of the clients. This means that the client machine has been issued with a DHCP address and that the PXELinux file has been loaded from the network.

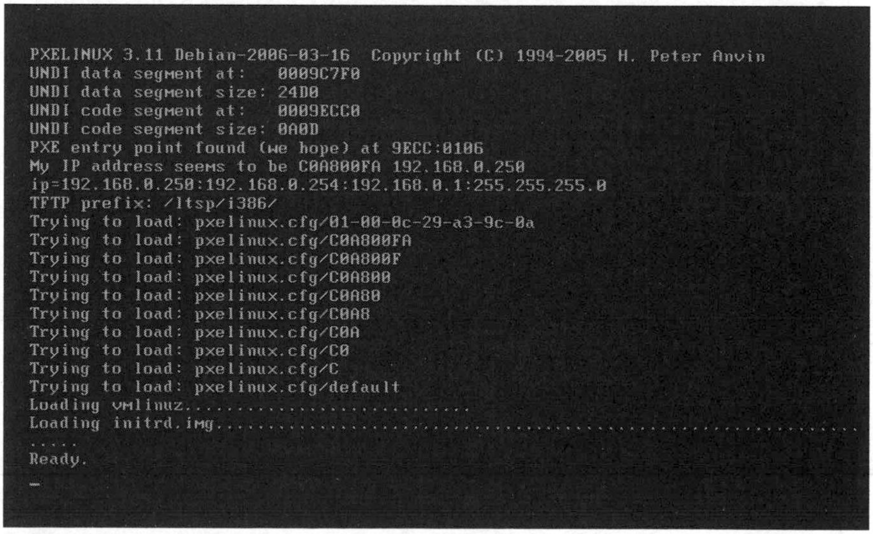

```
PXELINUX 3.11 Debian-2006-03-16  Copyright (C) 1994-2005 H. Peter Anvin
UNDI data segment at:    0009C7F0
UNDI data segment size: 24D0
UNDI code segment at:    0009ECC0
UNDI code segment size: 0A0D
PXE entry point found (we hope) at 9ECC:0106
My IP address seems to be C0A800FA 192.168.0.250
ip=192.168.0.250:192.168.0.254:192.168.0.1:255.255.255.0
TFTP prefix: /ltsp/i386/
Trying to load: pxelinux.cfg/01-00-0c-29-a3-9c-0a
Trying to load: pxelinux.cfg/C0A800FA
Trying to load: pxelinux.cfg/C0A800F
Trying to load: pxelinux.cfg/C0A800
Trying to load: pxelinux.cfg/C0A80
Trying to load: pxelinux.cfg/C0A8
Trying to load: pxelinux.cfg/C0A
Trying to load: pxelinux.cfg/C0
Trying to load: pxelinux.cfg/C
Trying to load: pxelinux.cfg/default
Loading vmlinuz.........................
Loading initrd.img...........................
.....
Ready.
```

Figure 9-10 DHCP boot

If your client boots up to the graphical login and the screen looks similar to the one shown in Figure 9-11, congratulations—you have successfully set up your LTSP thin client system. If not, refer to the Troubleshooting LTSP section near the end of this chapter.

Switching to Edubuntu If Ubuntu Is Already Installed   Just like Kubuntu, Edubuntu is simply a set of customized packages from the Ubuntu repository. In your chosen package manager, look for the package called edubuntu-desktop. This package will install both the Edubuntu desktop and all the other educational applications required. This step will also install the latest Edubuntu artwork package, which will customize your desktop with the latest educational wallpapers and themes. If you ever need to go back to the Ubuntu desktop for any reason, just install the ubuntu-desktop package and your system will be returned to its pre-Edubuntu-looking state. If you require an LTSP setup, you will have to do a fair amount of manual configuration.

Installing the LTSP Environment in Ubuntu or on a Desktop Installation

Perhaps you already have an Ubuntu machine and wish to make it available in an LTSP setup. To do this is a simple procedure and requires very

Figure 9-11 LDM login screen

little configuration. To begin, you must decide whether you require a DHCP server. If so, install the ltsp-server-standalone package. If you already have a DHCP server and are going to configure it to point to the LTSP server, by modifying the `filename`, `next-server`, and `root-path` options, you should install the ltsp-server package. Along with this, you will need the openssh-server package.

The easiest way to do this is to open a terminal window via the Applications > Accessories > Terminal link in the main menu. Once here, you should type the following commands to install the LTSP server and the SSH server. In our example, a DHCP server was not required.

```
sudo apt-get install ltsp-server openssh-server
```

TIP   If you require a DHCP server, modify the line above from `ltsp-server` to `ltsp-server-standalone`. You will also need to configure a second network device to an IP address of 192.168.0.1 before running the procedures described in this subsection.

All that is left to do now is to install the client chroot by running the following command:

```
sudo ltsp-build-client
```

After this, you should be able to boot your first thin client.

Special LTSP Cases

Setting Up LTSP to Coexist with an Existing DHCP Server   Sometimes you might not want your machines to be on a totally separate subnetwork. However, the problem then becomes that the current DHCP server will not be set up to serve the correct options to enable the clients to boot from the network. Modifying a Linux-based DHCP server is well documented; however, some establishments will require the modification of a Microsoft Windows DHCP server to allow network clients to boot from the network.

The following setup assumes that there are currently no thin client systems running on the Windows network. Opening up the Windows DHCP administration tool will allow you to create *reservations* for your machines. A reservation is an IP address tied to a specific MAC address. In this way, each time a machine requests an IP address from the DHCP server, it is always given the same IP address. This has its benefits as you can then set advanced options for the client as well.

For each client, you will need to create a reservation and then add the following options to each one (Figure 9-12).

- 017 Root Path: /opt/ltsp/i386

- 066 Boot Server Host Name: *<server ip>*

- 067 Bootfile Name: /ltsp/i386/pxelinux.0

It is recommended that you restart the DHCP server. After this, the clients should be able to correctly pick up their IP address from the server and then boot from the LTSP server via NFS.

TIP   You can also set these options as global parameters to be rolled out over the entire network. However, it is often advisable, at least in the beginning, to keep track of which machines are booting from the LTSP server.

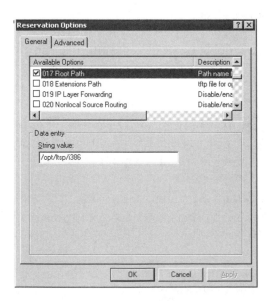

Figure 9-12 Windows DHCP Reservations

Dual-Booting with Another Operating System on the Hard Disk   Perhaps
you have a suite of computers that are already happily running another
OS, and you would prefer to keep both systems running for a while. Hopefully, after using Edubuntu for any length of time, you will eventually
make the switch permanent. In these situations, it is easy to set up the
server to allow the client to boot from either the network or the first hard
disk in the computer.

The bulk of the editing takes place in the pxelinux.cfg/default configuration file in the directory /var/lib/tftpboot/ltsp/<arch>/. The format of this
file is very similar to the old LILO configuration syntax (for those of you
familiar with that bootloader). The following sample configuration will
present a message to the client, which is explained later. The user can then
choose to either allow the system to boot its default configuration, which
in this example would be the local hard disk, or to type in the word linux
and press Enter, which would load the LTSP thin client.

```
DEFAULT localboot
TIMEOUT 50
PROMPT 1
DISPLAY display.msg

LABEL linux
   KERNEL vmlinuz
   APPEND ro initrd=initrd.img quiet splash

LABEL localboot
   LOCALBOOT 0
```

Let's take a look at the configuration file and break it down so that you can
create your own to suit your environment. (If this sample file fits the bill
for you, you can skip down to the part about creating the display.msg file.)

The DEFAULT keyword specifies which boot option will be chosen once the
timeout expires. The TIMEOUT option specifies how long to wait before
booting the default option. This timeout is measured in one-tenth of a
second; thus a value of 50 sets it for 5 seconds. The PROMPT option specifies
whether the PXE software displays the boot: prompt to enable users to
choose an operating system. The DISPLAY option displays a text file on the

screen as an introduction. In this case, the file is called display.msg and must be placed in the root LTSP directory, alongside the pxelinux.0 file. An example of this file is proposed a little later.

The three lines starting with *LABEL linux* define the *linux* option for booting. This is configured by the KERNEL and APPEND options, which you will notice are extracted from the original default file, as shown here:

```
DEFAULT vmlinuz ro initrd=initrd.img quiet splash
```

All that is needed now is the option for booting from the local hard drive, shown by the two lines starting LABEL localboot. These lines define the *localboot* option as used with the DEFAULT keyword earlier in the file. The only definition included in this option is the LOCALBOOT option, with a parameter of 0. This provides normal hard disk booting. Other parameters are available, as you can see by visiting the Syslinux home page, http://syslinux.zytor.com.

The display.msg file should contain some information that tells the user what to do to choose an operating system. Following is an example file that is suitable for the configuration above. When creating this file, it is suggested to use a number of blank lines before the text actually begins. This has the effect of clearing the screen so that users don't get confused by the PXELinux start-up text.

```
=================================================================

                 Welcome to the Multiboot System

               The system will start in 5 seconds...

      for Linux users type :  linux
      at the boot: prompt and press <enter>

=================================================================
```

After rebooting the client, you should now see the text from the display message file. It should look similar to that shown in Figure 9-13.

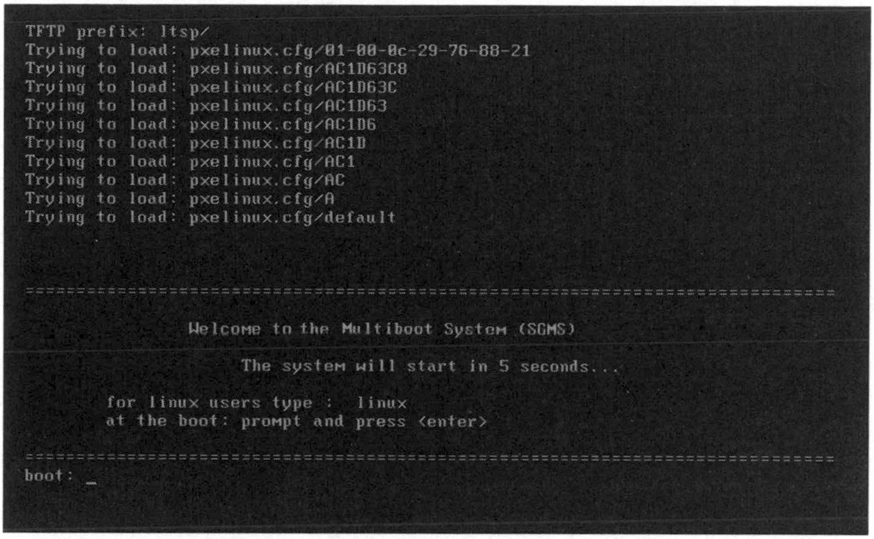

```
TFTP prefix: ltsp/
Trying to load: pxelinux.cfg/01-00-0c-29-76-88-21
Trying to load: pxelinux.cfg/AC1D63C8
Trying to load: pxelinux.cfg/AC1D63C
Trying to load: pxelinux.cfg/AC1D63
Trying to load: pxelinux.cfg/AC1D6
Trying to load: pxelinux.cfg/AC1D
Trying to load: pxelinux.cfg/AC1
Trying to load: pxelinux.cfg/AC
Trying to load: pxelinux.cfg/A
Trying to load: pxelinux.cfg/default




=========================================================================
             Welcome to the Multiboot System (SGMS)

                 The system will start in 5 seconds...

         for linux users type :   linux
         at the boot: prompt and press <enter>

=========================================================================
boot: _
```

Figure 9-13 Multiboot system in action

Managing Your LTSP Server
Updating the Server

Shortly after installation, you may notice a balloon message appear in the top right-hand corner of the screen informing you that updates are available for your system. It is advisable that you install updates because they help keep your system secure and bug free. To install these updates, simply click on the balloon or launch the update manager by going to the System > Administration > Update Manager link in the main menu.

You will be prompted for your password and then presented with a list of updates available for your system. If there are any updates that you do not want to install, simply untick them from the list at the top of the window. When you are satisfied, click on the Install Updates button. Downloading all the required packages from the Internet will take a while to complete, especially if this is the first time you have run the update manager since installation.

Installing Applications

By default, the operating system is configured to talk to all of the software repositories. These are explained in greater detail in Chapter 5. There are many more packages available in the universe and multiverse repositories; however, some may have different licensing. By using the Software Sources package, you can modify this list of repositories. Simply select System > Administration > Software Sources from the menu, and you will be presented with the Software Sources screen.

Whether you are running a thin client system or you installed Ubuntu or Edubuntu in a non-LTSP mode, you will at some point need to install extra applications onto the system. This is simple in either Ubuntu or Edubuntu and is achieved by selecting Applications > Add/Remove from the main menu at the top left of the screen. Enter your password when prompted, and you will see the Add/Remove Applications window appear.

In addition to being the central point for installing all extra software for your system, the Add/Remove Applications program has a special section just for education. Clicking on this will filter the available set of applications to show those that have a high relevance to educational establishments. At the time of writing there were over eighty applications available in this section, and the list keeps growing, as shown in Figure 9-14.

In the application list you will see some checkboxes next to the application names. If you want to install a particular application, simply tick the checkbox next to its name. You can select multiple applications before clicking the Apply button.

Once you have chosen your applications and clicked the Apply button, you will be guided through the rest of the procedure and asked to confirm your selections prior to installation. Edubuntu will now collect the packages from the Internet or the Edubuntu CDs and begin installing them on your machine.

If you have chosen a few packages, the installation step may take a while. Installing software in this way is easy because Add/Remove Applications will handle all the required dependencies and install those, too.

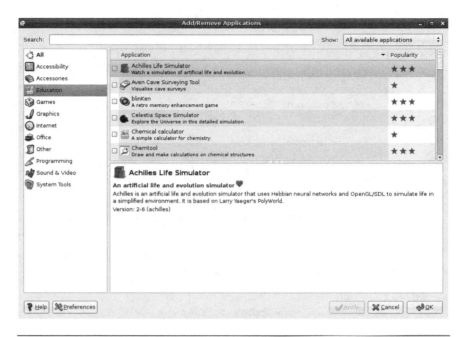

Figure 9-14 Educational applications available through Add/Remove Applications

Once the install has completed, the new applications should now be available on your Edubuntu machine. If you are running a thin client system, this now means that all the clients have the software available to them and can use it right away.

Removing Applications

Just as it was easy to install applications in Edubuntu, the same applies for removing them. The process is just the exact reverse of the install procedure. Load up the Add/Remove Applications utility and simply untick the applications that you no longer want to be installed.

Clicking on the Apply button will prompt you to confirm your decision before removing the packages you selected. The package will now no longer be available on the Edubuntu server or on any thin client machine that boots from the network.

Changing Your IP Address

At some point it may become necessary to change the IP address of the server. Changing the IP address of a normal machine would not usually have much consequence on the client machine. However, in an LTSP environment, changing the IP address will result in clients being unable to log in. This is because when the LTSP root is built, it is populated with SSH authorization keys, which allow authentication between the client and the server without a password.

The procedure for solving this issue is fairly simple. First, you must load a terminal window, using the Applications > Accessories > Terminal link in the main menu. Once this has loaded, you need to run the LTSP SSH key update script by typing the following command into the terminal and pressing Enter. You will be prompted for your password.

```
sudo ltsp-update-sshkeys
```

TIP   When entering your password, nothing is displayed on the screen, although your password is still being read by the computer. The password is not displayed for security reasons, but it is also not obfuscated. This prevents people who may be looking over your shoulder from seeing how many characters your password has.

TIP   It is possible here to update the SSH keys by simply restarting the network interface, using a command similar to the following one. You will need to replace *<iface>* with the interface identifier, usually something like eth0 or eth1.

```
sudo ifdown <iface> && sudo ifup <iface>
```

Once completed, your SSH keys will be updated, and after the clients reboot, they should be able to log in again.

Local Devices over LTSP

Since Ubuntu Edgy 6.10, Edubuntu has included the update to LTSP to allow what are called local devices. Plugging a USB storage device into a thin client machine, for example, will trigger the local devices mechanism, and the device will be correctly mounted and shown on the desktop of the client machine.

When using USB sticks with Ubuntu, you would normally have to unmount the device before removing it physically. This is so that Ubuntu has time to write all the data it needs to the USB stick and can safely unmount it. In the LTSP environment, using a USB stick is a little different. There is no unmount option because the data is written to the USB stick on a very regular basis. Hence you do not need to unmount it and can just remove it once the computer has finished writing information to it.

Local device support is set up by default in Edubuntu; however, to use it you must add to the fuse group the users who require access to such support. You can do this from the user manager. Start by going to System > Administration > Users and Groups option. From here, select the user to whom you wish to give local device access and click on the User Properties button. Click on the User Privileges tab, and from here tick the checkbox for allowing use of fuse filesystems, as shown in Figure 9-15.

Sound over LTSP

Since Ubuntu Dapper 6.06, Edubuntu has the ability to play sound through the speakers of the client machine. For versions of Edubuntu prior to 6.10

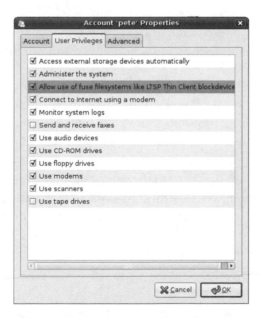

Figure 9-15 Setting fuse preferences

and LTSP setups installed on top of Ubuntu, you must add an entry to the /opt/ltsp/i386/etc/lts.conf file to enable sound for client machines.

The easiest way to edit this file is to hold down Alt-F2, which will bring up the run command dialog box. Type in the following command:

```
gksudo "gedit /opt/ltsp/i386/etc/lts.conf"
```

Clicking OK will bring up an editing window. Make sure to have at least a [default] section in the lts.conf file where you will add the following line:

```
SOUND=True
```

NOTE Dapper 6.06 LTS is very particular about the SOUND=True statement. You must type it exactly as shown, taking extreme care with capital letters and so on.

For all versions after 6.10 of Edubuntu, this is already done for you, and sound should work on client machines out of the box.

Printing over LTSP

There are two ways in which printing can be achieved in an LTSP environment. The first is for a printer to be connected directly to the server. In this instance, printing is set up in the usual way. You can find more details on this in Chapter 4.

The second way to allow printing is to make one of the workstation machines a print server. This feature was introduced in Ubuntu Edgy 6.10. Up to three printers can be attached to the workstation using the parallel and USB ports. LTSP uses the jetpipe program on the workstation to redirect printing from the server to the workstation. In order to attach a printer to the workstation, a change must be made to the /opt/ltsp/i386/etc/lts.conf file. The following is an example of some configuration options.

```
[00:4C:69:73:61:00]
    PRINTER_0_DEVICE = /dev/lp0
    PRINTER_1_DEVICE = /dev/usblp0
```

This will cause the jetpipe program to begin running as a background process and will open ports 9100 and 9101, where it will listen for a print stream from the server. This stream will then get redirected to the printer attached to the parallel port on the computer.

In this example, we use the client's MAC address to identify it on the network. Unless you know the MAC address of the client machine that the computer is connected to, you will need to run the following command to find it. When the client boots up, it will display its IP address in the bottom right of the login screen. Simply replace the *<IP>* in the following chunk of code with that IP address to find the MAC address of the client machine.

```
IP=<IP> ; ping -c1 $IP | grep "NULL"; arp -a | grep $IP
```

Here is an example:

```
pete@ubunt:~$ IP=192.168.16.5; ping -c1 $IP | grep "NULL"
pete@ubunt:~$ arp -a | grep $IP
? (192.168.16.5) at 00:12:50:30:5A:E5 [ether] on eth0
pete@ubunt:~$
```

All that is needed now is to create the print queue on the server, so that the client machines know the printer exists. This can be done in the usual way of adding a printer as shown in Chapter 4. The jetpipe program allows the workstation printer to be identified as an HP JetDirect system. To add the printer to the server, you will need to enter the IP address of the workstation and the port that the jetpipe service is listening on. The first printer you connect to a workstation will be on 9100, the second on 9101, and the third on 9102.

Using Other Window Managers with Edubuntu

Using other window managers with Edubuntu is easy. With versions from Edubuntu Edgy 6.10 forward, adding a window manager will result in a new option being present in the LDM login screen. This will allow you to choose which window manager to use when logging in. In order to use a new window manager, you must install the appropriate package. You have the following choices:

- xubuntu-desktop: a lightweight window manager, perfect for lower-end systems
- kubuntu-desktop: a feature-rich window manager
- ubuntu-desktop: the standard window manager, used by default

To install one of these packages, you should first load a terminal window, using the Applications > Accessories > Terminal link in the main menu, and then use the following command.

```
sudo apt-get install xubuntu-desktop
```

Managing Your Edubuntu Clients

Although you will not be installing anything on your clients, it is important to realize that there are still some maintenance tasks specifically directed toward the clients.

Updating the Client NFS Root

You may have an up-to-date server, but this does not necessarily mean that the system the clients run on is up to date. Remember that essentially you have two versions of Ubuntu installed on the Edubuntu server. One is the server and another is a very slimmed down version that simply provides clients with enough capability to be able to boot and log in.

First, open a terminal window using the Applications > Accessories > Terminal link in the main menu. You need to copy your list of package sources from the server to the client. To do this, type the following line into the terminal window, press Enter, and type your password when prompted.

```
sudo cp /etc/apt/sources.list /opt/ltsp/i386/etc/apt/
```

Your root directory must be altered so that you are inside the NFS client root. That way, when you enter commands, they will be run on the client system and not on the main server. To do this, issue the commands shown here. The first makes sure that all programs running inside the chroot will work as expected.

```
sudo chroot /opt/ltsp/i386
mount -t proc proc /proc
```

Although you copied the list of package sources from the server to the client, you'll need to update the actual list of packages available to be installed or upgraded. To do this, you must issue the following command, which will download the latest list of packages from the Internet.

```
apt-get update
```

Once this has completed, it is time to start the upgrade. To do this, enter one final command:

```
apt-get upgrade
```

This will show you a list of all packages that need to be upgraded and will prompt you to continue. If you are happy with the selection, press y to confirm and to begin the installation process. When the installation is completed, you'll need to reboot the client machines for the changes to take effect.

Important: Don't forget to unmount the proc in the chroot by typing sudo umount /proc and pressing Enter, and then leave the chroot by pressing Ctrl-D.

Upgrading the Client's Kernel Version

Once in a blue moon, or if a security update is available, it is necessary to upgrade the kernel version of the client machine. This process should be treated with caution and should really be performed only if you are experiencing problems with your client's hardware. To upgrade the kernel version in the client NFS root, you must explicitly tell it to install the new kernel. Much like in the upgrading of the client root software described in the previous section, you must first load a terminal and enter the client chroot, using this command:

```
sudo chroot /opt/ltsp/i386
mount -t proc proc /proc
```

Once here, update the latest version of the packages using the following command:

```
apt-get update
```

If you know there is a newer kernel available and you know the package name, the next step is easy. If you don't know whether there is a new kernel and would like to check, follow these steps.

You first need to find out what kernel image you currently have installed. Issuing the following command will yield an output similar to that seen below. Remember that you *must* be in the chroot to run these commands; otherwise you'll just be looking at the kernel versions of the main server and not the client's chroot.

```
root@ubunt:~$ dpkg -l | grep linux-image
ii  linux-image-2.6.24-12-generic              2.6.24-12.22
  Linux kernel image for version 2.6.24 on x86
ii  linux-image-generic                        2.6.24.12
  Generic Linux kernel image
root@ubunt:~$
```

From here we can see that the latest version of the Linux kernel image is 2.6.24-12.22. Running the following command shows what the latest version of the kernel is currently in the repositories. Again, remember that you should be in the chroot when issuing this command.

```
root@ubunt:~$ apt-cache show linux-image-2.6.24-12-generic \
| grep Version
Version: 2.6.24-12.22
root@ubunt:~$
```

Notice how the package name from the previous output of code, linux-image-2.6.24-12-generic, is now used again in the second command to find the latest version of the currently installed kernel. In this example, the two kernel versions are the same. However, if they differed, using the following command would update the kernel version in the chroot environment.

```
apt-get install linux-image-2.6.24-12-generic
```

Once the kernel has been upgraded, you must then run the LTSP script for updating the chroot with the correct information that allows the new kernel to be used in preference to the old one. To do this, first unmount proc, as shown before, and then exit the chroot by pressing Ctrl-D. Then run the following command:

```
ltsp-update-kernels
```

After the script has finished, you should reboot your clients' machines to have them start using the new kernel.

TIP   In the previous examples, while administrating the LTSP chroot, notice that the sudo command was *not* needed. This is because when using the sudo chroot command, we automatically take on the persona of the root user inside this environment. So be careful!

Controlling and Managing the Users' Desktops

Thin Client Manager began life as Student Control Panel in Dapper 6.06 and was written by Oliver Grawert. It was then revamped and feature-enhanced in 6.10, and again in 7.04 by Pete Savage and Oliver Grawert. Thin Client Manager now offers many of the features you would find in a commercial network management package. Designed specifically to administrate and manage the LTSP thin client environment, it provides the following features.

- Stop a process on the client's machine.
- Log users out of their sessions.
- Send users a message.
- Run an application on the client's machine.
- Blank or lock users' screens.
- Lock down clients using Pessulus.
- Add users to groups for ease of filtering.
- Use a plug-in framework to perform simple tasks.

Using Thin Client Manager

Upon loading Thin Client Manager for the first time, you will be presented with a screen similar to the one shown in Figure 9-16. The screen is basically split into two sections. The first is the user list, on the left-hand side, which shows a constantly updating list of all users who are logged onto the LTSP server. The second section, on the right, contains the Process View and Screen Viewer tabs. This section is tab operated so that you can switch between viewing the currently selected processes/running applications and, in the future, a selection of four screenshots of currently running clients.

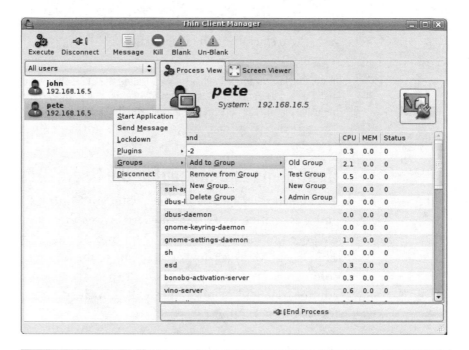

Figure 9-16 Thin Client Manager

Managing Processes

You can end a user's running applications by first choosing a user, selecting a process from the right-hand side, and then clicking on the End Process button. You will then be asked to confirm your actions. After you do, an internal message is sent to the client's session asking for the program to terminate.

Logging Users Out of Their Sessions

If desired, you can log a user out of his or her session by first selecting the user and then clicking on the Disconnect button. (You can also select multiple users.) You will then be asked to confirm your actions. After you do, an internal message is sent to end the user's session. This will log the user out of the current session.

Sending Messages

You can send short messages to users, for example, "You have 5 minutes left for this lesson." To do this, first select a user (or multiple users) and then click the Message button. You will then be presented with a box to type in your message. After you click OK, the message will be sent to the selected user.

Starting Programs

It is also possible to start an application or process in a client's session from Thin Client Manager. To do this, simply select the user (or multiple users), and click the Execute button. You will then be presented with a dialog box to enter a command to be run in the user's session. After you click OK, an internal message will be sent to the user's session asking for the chosen command to be run.

Locking or Blanking Screens

Sometimes it may become necessary to temporarily prevent users from accessing the computer. To do this, select the user (or multiple users) and click the Blank button. This will then activate a locked screensaver on the client's machine, forcing the user to stop and wait until you have unlocked the machine. Unlocking is done the same way, but using the Un-Blank button instead.

The Lockdown Editor

By selecting only a single user and right-clicking on that user, you can use the context menu to lock down a specific user. Selecting Lockdown will open Pessulus, the GNOME lockdown editor. Ticking and unticking options in Pessulus will enable and disable certain functions for the user. Ticking the padlock next to an option will make it unchangeable by the user. This is called a mandatory setting. Pessulus has been altered for integration with Thin Client Manager so that mandatory keys are now per user, instead of per system. For further help with Pessulus, please refer to the Pessulus documentation, www.gnome.org/learn/admin-guide/latest/lockdown.html.

Managing Users with Groups

The latest version of Thin Client Manager comes with a users group and filtering system. This is all accessed by the context menu. By right-clicking in the user list, you will be presented with a menu that has an option called Groups. From this menu, you can create new groups, delete old groups, and assign users to groups.

To assign users to a group, simply select the users required from the user list and then right-click to bring up the context menu. From here you can move through the menu, Groups > Add to Group > *Group Name*. The process is identical for removing users from groups.

Once your groups are all assigned, you can use the filter combo box above the user list to show only members of a particular group. The groups and members are persistent across Thin Client Manager sessions and are automatically saved once they have been altered. If you wish to access the file that stores the groups and members, it is located at /etc/tcm/users.conf.

Plug-ins

The plug-in framework allows you to expand the way Thin Client Manager works. Select a set of users in the left-hand panel and right-click to bring up the context menu. From the Plugins option, you'll see a list of all the plug-ins installed in Thin Client Manager. On a fresh installation, this will consist of a single plug-in, which is used purely as an example. You can also look at the example plug-in file located in /usr/lib/python2.4/site-packages/studentcontrolpanel/plugins/cheap_plugin. Put simply, a plug-in consists of a class and a registration function. The plug-in is provided with a list of users, which you can use to write a routine to perform operations based on that list.

Troubleshooting LTSP

Sometimes when administrating your LTSP system, you may come across problems that you can't solve immediately. This section has been written to try to give some helpful hints about how to diagnose and fix common LTSP problems. The LTSP Web site, www.ltsp.org, has a large wiki and knowledge base to help you find answers to your LTSP problems.

The Computer Is Not Obtaining an IP Address

If your client machines are not receiving IP addresses, it is likely that there is a problem with the DHCP server. In order to check this, you must load a terminal window and run the following command:

```
pidof dhcpd3 2&>1 >/dev/null && echo OK
```

If this shows the result is okay, the problem lies elsewhere. If the result shows that the DHCP server is not running, it is time to check the DHCP logs for errors. To do this, you must restart the DHCP server and then view the logs. Restart the server by using the following command:

```
sudo /etc/init.d/dhcpd3-server restart
```

If at this stage you see a FAIL message on starting the DHCP server, you know that there must be a problem with the dhcpd configuration. Checking the logs in the way shown should lead you to the problem. You can easily see the last errors that the dhcpd server had by running the following command:

```
tail /var/log/daemon.log
```

A variety of problems can be shown by using this method, and after you have a better idea of what the problem is, you may be able to solve it yourself. You can also contact the Edubuntu team for help by using the information provided at the end of this chapter.

NFS Server Is Not Responding

If your clients exhibit an error, similar to `nfs warning: server not responding`, it is possible that the kernel is using too large a block size for the NFS packets. In essence the kernel uses a 32K block size, which must be broken down into 1,500 byte datagrams. Since this results in a large number of small datagrams being sent, the client can time out before receiving all the data. Fortunately, the fix is simple enough.

You must load the file /var/lib/tftpboot/ltsp/pxelinux.cfg/default so that it can be edited. To do this you can use any of the methods previously described in this chapter. Once the file is open, there is a line beginning with *APPEND*; to the end of this line, you must add one of the following:

```
NFSOPTS="-o nolock,ro,wsize=2048,rsize=2048"
```

or:

```
NFSOPTS="-o nolock,ro,proto=tcp"
```

After this, your clients should be able to boot normally. If you are using Etherboot or require more information on this, you can find help on the LTSP wiki, under the Troubleshooting section.

VMware Client Crashes While Booting

Some people use VMware, a virtualization suite, to test various aspects of their setup before they roll it out. However, you may find that VMware clients are unable to boot properly. This is a problem with the graphics driver and can be solved simply by taking the actions described in the previous section, but instead of adding the NFSOPTS line, simply remove the word splash from the APPEND line. This will remove the loading screen from Edubuntu and should make your VMware clients bootable again.

Some Intel Boot Agents Will Not Boot at All

Some Intel Boot Agents have a bug that makes them unable to boot at all if your LTSP server (TFTP server) is different from your DHCP server. The reason for this is that the Intel Boot Agent assumes wrongly that the TFTP information resides on the DHCP server, which of course it doesn't. One way to work around this is to make a mirror of the /var/lib/tftpboot/ directory on the DHCP server and install a TFTP server on that machine to serve that directory. Remember that if you update the NFS chroot, you must then update this new mirror. It is also possible there is a firmware update for your NIC.

Finding Help and Giving Back to the Community
Finding Help

There are many forms of help available to establishments using Edubuntu. As different people prefer to get help in different ways, Edubuntu tries to assist in as many ways as possible.

Web Site   The Edubuntu Web sites have a plethora of information available to the user, from troubleshooting to expansion to upcoming features to bug fixes. The following is a list of the major Web sites for Edubuntu and their uses.

- www.edubuntu.org: The main portal Web site for Edubuntu. This site contains information on installing Edubuntu as well as links for downloading CD images and obtaining CDs via the ShipIt system.

- http://wiki.edubuntu.org/Edubuntu: The main wiki landing page for Edubuntu. A wiki is an online collaborative documentation that allows people from all over the world to work together to provide documentation and support for others. In the wiki you will find more detailed information on setting up Edubuntu for more specialist cases, as well as much of the planning documentation that the Edubuntu team uses.

- http://wiki.edubuntu.org/Edubuntu/Launchpad/Teams: The wiki landing page for Edubuntu Launchpad teams. Launchpad is a system used by many Linux distributions and open source projects to keep track of teams, specifications for new features, bugs, and translation material. If you are thinking about contributing to Edubuntu, you will find this site a great resource of information.

- http://lists.ubuntu.com: A portal for seeing the archives or signing up to mailing lists. The lists are sorted in alphabetical order for easy navigation.

Mailing List   The mailing list for Edubuntu consists of several different smaller mailing lists. You are free to join as many of them as you wish. Traffic on some is lighter than others. Once you have signed up your e-mail address on a mailing list, you are given a special e-mail address to send e-mails to. When you send an e-mail to this address, it is forwarded to every other member of the list. In Edubuntu, the following lists are currently in use.

▪ edubuntu-users: A list where other users of Edubuntu communicate about how they are using it and ask questions about any problems they may be having.

▪ edubuntu-devel: A list geared more toward the developer community of Edubuntu. This often contains a lot of information that general users of Edubuntu will not be interested in.

Internet Relay Chat   A lot of communication in the Ubuntu community is done via IRC. IRC is a kind of conference environment where people communicate via real-time text-based messaging. IRC also has the provision to handle private messaging between two individuals. The Edubuntu channel can be found using the following information:

Server: irc.freenode.net
Port: 8001
Channel: #edubuntu

Using a program like X-Chat, anyone can join the channel and ask questions of the Edubuntu team. There are people in the channel from all over the world, so there should be someone around to answer your questions at pretty much any time.

Forums   Edubuntu also has a section in the www.ubuntuforums.org Web site. Forums are like mailing lists, except that no e-mails are sent or received. Everything is accessed via the Web site, for which you have to register to be able to post replies and topics.

Giving Back to the Community

Edubuntu always welcomes help in every area. It doesn't matter if your skills are in artwork, documentation, testing, coding, or feedback—there is always something you can contribute. Please introduce yourself to the Edubuntu team and start helping the community grow.

Summary

Edubuntu is already used in many educational and noneducational establishments worldwide. From its humble beginnings, the project has grown into a fantastic team of people, and a professional and worthwhile product. In addition to LTSP thin client support, Edubuntu includes many educational packages that are of use to children of many ages and abilities.

CHAPTER 10

Ubuntu-Related Projects

- **Officially Supported Derivatives**
- **Recognized Derivatives**
- **Other Distributions**
- **Launchpad**
- **Bazaar**
- **Summary**

UBUNTU IS NOT MERELY A COMPLETE operating system; it is also the center of a growing ecosystem of distributions. Some, referred to as the partner projects, work closely with and within Ubuntu. Others prefer to work outside the project and are considered full derivatives. Often, these projects are created in order to highlight a specific selection of software or use case, such as the nUbuntu project, which focuses on security and networking tools. Others, like the gNewSense project supported by the Free Software Foundation, exist for philosophical or social reasons.

Others are created for reasons connected to the international nature of Linux and open source software. While most Ubuntu development happens in English, there are large developer and user communities in other languages and countries. Thus, a derived distribution might spring up to satisfy that need. There are derived distributions targeted at Christians, Muslims, people with slow computers, and people who prefer to have an Ubuntu system optimized for any of several alternative user interfaces or for use in several different schools and government bureaucracies around the world. Should you use any of these over Ubuntu? We can't answer that question for you. Some of these projects are fully within and, as a result, not mutually exclusive from Ubuntu. Others might be more appropriate depending on your preferences or circumstances. You can mix, match, and sample these distributions until you find one that works great for you. As we mentioned in Chapter 1, Ubuntu sees these derivatives as a sign of a healthy and vibrant community. One of the goals of the project is to make it easier for this type of distribution to appear. We can all expect to see more of them in the future.

Officially Supported Derivatives

Officially supported derivatives, formerly called Partner projects, are those projects that work in close relation with Ubuntu. They share a common repository of packages and release in sync with Ubuntu. These derivatives are officially supported by Canonical in both development and security.

Kubuntu

Kubuntu is the first and oldest of all the partner projects. First released alongside Ubuntu 5.04 (Hoary Hedgehog), Kubuntu, which means "toward humanity" in Bemba, builds on the strengths of the K Desktop Environment (KDE) rather than GNOME as Ubuntu does. The project is led by Jonathan Riddell, who now works for Canonical, Ltd.

As with Ubuntu, Kubuntu is a complete desktop, but one built around KDE and Qt. Rather than Ubuntu's brown theme, Kubuntu opts for a more traditional blue and makes only a few other visual changes. Rather than the two panels and three menus of Ubuntu with GNOME, Kubuntu uses two menus and a single lower panel, closer in style to that of Microsoft Windows.

Kubuntu also comes with OpenOffice.org, the same office suite included in Ubuntu. Along with this office suite, Kubuntu also includes Krita, a photo manipulation tool, the K3b CD Kreator tool, and the media player Amarok, all parts of KDE. Kubuntu is explored in much more depth in Chapter 8 and so is not given a full treatment here.

TIP   **Kubuntu**
Kubuntu can be found at www.kubuntu.org.

Edubuntu

As the name implies, Edubuntu is a version of Ubuntu for use in schools and other educational environments. Edubuntu uses the thin client technology of the Linux Terminal Server Project (LTSP) as well as a number of programs aimed at the educational market, such as GCompris and the KDE Education suite. Oliver Grawert, a Canonical, Ltd. employee, leads the Edubuntu development. Like Ubuntu, Edubuntu uses the GNOME desktop environment. One of Edubuntu's unique features is the inclusion of the LTSP in an easy-to-use, out-of-the-box installer. LTSP uses a different method of deploying clients over a network than is used in traditional computer deployments. Instead of full-powered computers, LTSP uses thin clients, less capable, cheaper computers that connect to a larger server and have it do all the processing work.

Edubuntu has grown rapidly over the last two years. As a result, we've included a full chapter on the subject at the expense of a longer section here. Worth noting perhaps is the fact that rather than simply a different distribution, Edubuntu is now distributed as an add-on to a standard Ubuntu install. To learn much more about this and about the project, take a look at the in-depth overview in Chapter 9.

TIP   **Edubuntu**
Edubuntu can be found at www.edubuntu.org.

Ubuntu Server Edition

Ubuntu Server Edition was created with the aim of making Ubuntu easy to install and use on servers. The Server Edition was officially launched with Ubuntu 5.04 and initially focused on making certain that the highest quality server applications were available, including MySQL, Apache, and others.

The most recent work has been the creation of Ubuntu JeOS, or Just-enough-Operating-System, designed for virtual environments, and a specialized version of Ubuntu for Amazon's EC2.

TIP   **Ubuntu Server Edition**
Ubuntu Server Edition can be found at
www.ubuntu.com/products/whatisubuntu/serveredition

Recognized Derivatives

Beyond the officially supported derivatives, recognized derivatives use all the same repositories as Ubuntu and release on the same schedule, but they are not officially supported by Canonical in development or security.

Xubuntu

Xubuntu is a version of Ubuntu built on top of the Xfce window management system. In Xubuntu, Xfce and its associated applications play a role analogous to KDE in the context of Kubuntu. Xfce is small and lightweight compared to the much fancier GNOME and KDE. It uses less memory and fewer CPU cycles than either of the alternatives in a normal configuration.

While this means that Xubuntu is often seen as having fewer features or being less user-friendly than Ubuntu or Kubuntu, it also means that it runs faster, is more responsive, and tends to run very quickly on older or less powerful computers, where the weight of either GNOME or KDE may make the system prohibitively slow. As a result, Xubuntu has been used frequently by computer recyclers, by the owners of old computers, and by those who just want to squeeze out better performance from their hardware using a more efficient interface.

Like Kubuntu, Xubuntu is community driven and began outside the project in the universe repository of Ubuntu. In releases 5.04 (Hoary Hedgehog) and 5.10 (Breezy Badger), Xfce 4 was supported by a special Xfce Team in Ubuntu. Due to the great work done on Xfce, Xubuntu was brought into the fold and became Ubuntu's third partner project and a part of the main Ubuntu repository, for release 6.10 (Edgy Eft).

TIP   **Xubuntu**
Xubuntu can be found at www.xubuntu.org.

Mythbuntu

MythTV is one of the most popular pieces of home theater software, but it has a bit of a reputation as a beast to set up. Mythbuntu is designed to make that setup easy. Like Xubuntu, Mythbuntu uses Xfce as a desktop environment, has a custom-made Mythbuntu Control Center, and has a LiveCD for easy testing.

Ubuntu Studio

Ubuntu Studio is a derivative of Ubuntu that is designed and optimized for multimedia production. The system includes a wide variety of applications useful to those engaging in audio and video recording, mixing, editing, synthesis, and production as well as graphics production and manipulation. It contains a modified kernel that allows the system to reduce latency for audio in ways that dramatically improve performance in professional audio recording and manipulation, but the kernel may be inappropriate in other environments. Its first release was based on Ubuntu 7.04.

TIP   **Ubuntu Studio**
Ubuntu Studio can be found at ubuntustudio.org.

Other Distributions

Some distributions usually work outside of the Ubuntu community and usually have their own package repositories. They may not release at the same time as Ubuntu. In the past, several derived distributions have been built upon other distributions such as Debian. The list of derivative distributions has grown rapidly, and as distributions come and go, the list is constantly in flux. While in the first edition of this book, our list was nearly comprehensive, the size of the derivative distribution community has grown so much that compiling a complete list for this book is no longer possible. Instead, we provide a bit of the flavor of the diversity of derived distributions with some examples of the oldest and most visible derived distributions to give you an idea of the scope of the community.

Guadalinex

Guadalinex is the GNU/Linux distribution promoted by the regional government of Andalusia, the most populated autonomous community in Spain with almost 8 million inhabitants. It is currently one of the biggest free software implementations worldwide, with more than 200,000 desktops—and increasing. The project is a consequence of the unanimous support of the Andalusian Parliament on the Information Society and Innovation policies approved in 2002 and 2003, urging all the regional institutions to promote and use free software and open licenses. This makes the Guadalinex initiative unique in the world.

Guadalinex was initially released in 2003, and the first two versions were based on Debian. In 2005 the Guadalinex project decided to develop the third version deriving from Ubuntu. Guadalinex version 3 was released in January 2006 based on Ubuntu 5.10 (Breezy Badger), making it the first major Ubuntu derivative. The project is part of a government plan to implement free software as the default option in the public schools. At the beginning of 2006, this project involved 500 schools and approximately 200,000 desktops equipped with Guadalinex and free software only. These numbers increase every year as new courses start every September and new computers are purchased (about 40,000 in 2006). This initiative alone puts Guadalinex in the top position as the biggest free software implementation worldwide. Additionally, the software is used in public Internet access centers, senior centers, libraries, and women's associations, as well as citizens' homes. Guadalinex is merely one example of many Ubuntu derivatives created by or in cooperation with governments for use in schools and bureaucracies. It is now only one among many massive deployments of Ubuntu in these settings.

TIP **Guadalinex**
Guadalinex can be found at www.guadalinex.org.

gNewSense

While Ubuntu has a strong commitment to free and open source software and software freedom, it makes several compromises for binary-only firmware and drivers whose exclusion renders hardware inoperable. These drivers and firmware are placed in the restricted repository. The multiverse and commercial repositories, while not officially supported, reside in the Ubuntu archive and contain software that does not live up to Ubuntu's standards of software freedom. While Canonical, Ltd. was seriously considering the creation of what eventually became the Gobuntu project, the gNewSense project, spearheaded by Irish Ubuntu community members, was launched. Both continue their work in parallel: on Gobuntu, because the name references and indirectly advertises for Ubuntu, even though Ubuntu uses some proprietary software drivers, and more importantly, because Gobuntu is highly dependent on and integrated with Ubuntu's proprietary Launchpad infrastructure, which is implemented, controlled, and kept largely secret by Canonical, Ltd.; and on gNewSense, for pretty much the same reasons.

gNewSense is a pun on the word *nuisance*—Richard Stallman, the father of the free software movement and the GNU project, is often jokingly referred to as "chief gnuisance"—but also tries to evoke images of "new sense" that comes from a commitment to software freedom. Like Gobuntu, the project aims to stay as close to Ubuntu as possible, forking only where necessary to maintain a high level of software freedom. As a result, the project is primarily reductive.

TIP   **gNewSense**
gNewSense can be found at www.gnewsense.org.

U-lite

U-lite, formerly Ubuntulite, is an Ubuntu derivative targeted at low-power computers. Its slogan, "Ubuntu Power for Slow Machines," is an apt tagline for a project that targets computers as slow as 75Mhz Pentiums with no more than 32MB RAM. The project aims to provide a solution for computers that most operating system developers, including Ubuntu, have written off as impossibly antiquated. Most of the bells and whistles from Ubuntu have been stripped out in the process, but the system provides a compelling option for computers that would be useless with almost any modern operating system.

TIP   **U-lite**
U-lite can be found at u-lite.org

Nexenta OS

Nexenta OS is the first Ubuntu operating system that is not based on the Linux kernel. Instead, it is built on Sun Microsystems's OpenSolaris kernel, which was previously proprietary but is now being distributed as free software. It is the first distribution that combines the GNU system—all imported from Ubuntu—with OpenSolaris.

TIP   **Nexenta OS**
Nexenta OS can be found at www.nexenta.org/os.

Launchpad

As we mentioned in Chapter 1, most of Canonical, Ltd.'s technical employees do not work on Ubuntu. Rather, they work on infrastructure. The majority of this infrastructure is a large collection of services that work together to provide the framework through which Ubuntu is built. This superstructure of related applications is collectively referred to as Launchpad. While it has several non–Web-based systems, it is almost wholly accessible over the Web.

While Launchpad is primarily used to develop Ubuntu, the infrastructure was designed to be useful for any free software project and is becoming more popular. It aims to provide these projects with the code-, bug-, and translation-tracking software necessary to more easily and more powerfully collaborate with others and to develop free and open source software. Each of these functions (code, bug, and translation tracking) is highly integrated, making it much more ambitious, and potentially much more powerful, than traditional Web-based solutions with similar goals. Early on, the Launchpad Web page described the project as follows:

> A collection of services for projects in the Open Source universe. You can register your project, and then collaborate with the Open Source community on translations, bug tracking, and code.

That description continues to be valid even as the project has expanded with support and specification modules. In addition to code, bug, and translation tracking, Launchpad provides the ability to deal with code, not just on a per-package or per-project level, but on the distribution level as well. If a bug has been reported against a piece of software in Ubuntu, it is visible to both the upstream and downstream projects. The project can track how its software evolves over time and see, at a glance, whether bugs apply or not. Developers can track translations in a similar way.

A source of controversy in the free and open source software world is the fact that the source code to Launchpad is not distributed. While Launchpad is designed to help free software, it is not free itself. This has led to fear by some about the risk of enclosure or dependence that comes from using a tool that developers cannot change, update, or copy. Also, while all code and history can be fully copied, some information (such as bug information and metadata) stays within the Launchpad system. Some developers have felt insecure about providing this data to Canonical, Ltd. in such a way that they cannot copy or replicate it. Mark Shuttleworth has replied to these fears by saying that the goals of Launchpad required that he build a community before the code that allows forking is distributed but that, with time, the code to all of Launchpad will be distributed. While several pieces of Launchpad have been made open, the vast majority currently remains proprietary.

The best way to understand Launchpad is to see it in action. This section walks through the individual pieces of Launchpad in more depth. Much of the Ubuntu infrastructure is highly integrated into Launchpad. If you have created an account for contributing to the wiki or ordering CDs at http://shipit.ubuntu.com, you already have a Launchpad account.

TIP   **Launchpad**
Launchpad can be found at www.launchpad.net.

Soyuz

Soyuz is the distribution and archive management software integrated into Launchpad. It handles all of the automatic building of software in Ubuntu on each of the architectures and the integration of successfully built software into the archive. Soyuz means "union" in Russian and is the name of the spacecraft that Mark Shuttleworth traveled in during his voyage to space.

Soyuz works almost entirely behind the scenes. It was first activated in early February 2006, but had no initial effect on the way software was uploaded or downloaded in Ubuntu. What Soyuz does is to integrate the process by which software is built and inserted into different parts of the Ubuntu archive. The building of software cannot be tracked using the Launchpad Web infrastructure.

TIP   **Recent Builds**
The status of recent builds in Ubuntu can be found at https://launchpad.net/distros/ubuntu/ +builds.

Rosetta

Rosetta is a Web-based translation system integrated into Launchpad. It was the first piece of Launchpad to be publicly released. It was named after the Rosetta Stone, the famous piece of dark gray granite with the same text in three scripts that led to the deciphering of Egyptian hieroglyphics.

Rosetta is a Web-based version of a "PO" file editor. In other words, it provides a simple mechanism by which translators can view a list of untranslated phrases or strings and then translate each of them into their language. At the moment, the system works only with translations *from* English. Rosetta's non–Web-based predecessors include Kbabel and Gtranslate, both of which can be downloaded and installed on Ubuntu. By putting this functionality on the Web and integrating it into the archive management scripts, Rosetta lowers the barrier of entry for translation and lowers the chance that a translation will not make it into the distribution.

Rosetta includes each of the translatable strings contained in every application in Ubuntu. When new software is uploaded into Ubuntu, Rosetta will check to see if any strings have changed or been added. Changes to a string that has previously been translated will result in the translation being marked as fuzzy until a translator can check the translation and the new string, make any necessary changes, and then mark the translation as no longer fuzzy. By tracking new strings, Rosetta can easily prompt translators with new strings to translate as they appear as well as provide statistics on the percentage of strings within a particular application or within all of Ubuntu that have been translated into a particular language.

As users translate strings, they build up positive "karma" within the system—an innovation that has now been deployed to many other parts of Launchpad. Users can also work together in localization teams (called l10n teams because the word *localization* has ten letters between its first and last letters). Rosetta provides a great way for Ubuntu users to get involved in the distribution. Anybody who knows English and another language can begin contributing. Because the system is integrated into Launchpad, users do not need to submit their translations to have them included in Ubuntu—the project already has them. Several days later, new translations are pushed out to Ubuntu users who use Ubuntu in those languages.

TIP   **Rosetta**
Rosetta can be found at www.launchpad.net/rosetta.

Malone

Malone is a Web-based bug system like the Mozilla project Bugzilla, which might be familiar to some users. It provides a location where users can file bugs they find in their Ubuntu software by using easily accessible pieces of software such as Bug Buddy and the command-line `reportbug` or by reporting over the Web. Malone's name is a reference to the gangster movie musical *Bugsy Malone*.

Malone's first role is to provide a location where users can submit bugs. Malone is not just a way to collect complaints, though. Rather, its job is to track and record a bug through its full life cycle, from report to close. Bugs can be assigned to a particular developer or reassigned. If the bug is, in fact, the result of another application, the bug can be reassigned to another package. Bugs can be rated according to severity, or tagged and categorized in any number of useful manners. Information, files, and patches that fix a bug can be uploaded into Malone. When the bug has been resolved, it can be closed. The Malone bug report provides a single venue in which to collect information from the bug submitter, the bug fixer, the upstream maintainer if necessary, and any other involved party.

All of this, of course, is exactly what you would expect from any usable modern bug tracker. Where Malone aims to distinguish itself from its competitors is through its integration in Launchpad. First and foremost, this means that users of Malone can track the status of a bug as it relates to a particular patch or a particular piece of code. Because Ubuntu supports *every* release for 18 months and some releases, such as Ubuntu 6.06 LTS, for much longer, it's important that Ubuntu be able to track which bugs show up in which releases. As derivative works of Ubuntu are created in Launchpad, Malone also allows these derivatives to use Malone to see whether bugs submitted against Ubuntu or other distributions apply to their code and, if so, to quickly grab a fix.

As with Rosetta, Launchpad karma can be built up by fixing, reporting, and interacting with bugs over time. Bug triage that involves closing irreproducible bugs and merging duplicate bugs is one way that users can build up their karma. Of course, simply running developer versions and submitting new bugs is another great way to build good karma.

TIP   **Malone**

Malone can be found at www.launchpad.net/malone.

Blueprint

Blueprint is Ubuntu's custom specification and feature-tracking system. Blueprint provides a way that users can create specification pages, linked into the existing Ubuntu wiki, for features they would like to see in Ubuntu. Other interested parties can use Blueprint to subscribe to specifications or proposals they are interested in to collaborate on the development of the specification and to track progress. Over time, users working in the wiki and in Blueprint help new ideas through a process that starts with "braindump"—a very rough collection of ideas and brainstorming—and ends with an implemented feature. In Ubuntu, this process involves (1) review by the community and trusted members and (2) approval by decision makers and the Ubuntu Technical Board or by appropriate team leaders and councils. Blueprint provides technology to support this process and ensure that nothing important is dropped on the floor.

In particular, Blueprint helps leaders and decision makers on Ubuntu prioritize features and specifications and ensure that work is progressing on necessary features toward on-time completion for releases. As a result, Blueprint is used as both the primary specification tracker and the major release management tool for Ubuntu.

While Blueprint is extremely useful for technical specifications, it is also used heavily for developing and tracking community-related proposals as well as for brainstorming stages into implementation. Blueprint also has features designed around sprints and conferences to help organize sessions and coordinate groups to bring forward specifications. As a final bit of trivia, it's interesting to note that Blueprint was also written largely by Ubuntu founder and financier Mark Shuttleworth himself!

TIP   **Blueprint**
Blueprint can be found at www.launchpad.net/blueprint.

Answers

Answers is a technical support tracker built within Launchpad for use by Ubuntu and other free software projects hosted in the system. It allows community members to file support requests and other community members to help resolve those requests. Unlike most other systems, questions can be asked and answered in a variety of languages. Answers tries to complement other forms of community support in Ubuntu by providing a familiar ticketing system that also catalogs answered questions, allowing users to easily find answers to questions that others have asked before. Users can file support requests and communicate with volunteer community support contacts to provide more information, to discuss issues, and to note that their issues are resolved. In addition to storing the answers in a way that makes them searchable, Answers helps contextualize support requests by integrating them with other Launchpad features to show the connections and context of relevant bugs, translations, people, teams, and the variety of versions in the variety of releases tracked by Launchpad. Of course, karma can be built by interacting with Answers and, in particular, by answering questions.

TIP   **Answers**
Answers can be found at https://answers.launchpad.net.

Other Functionality

In addition to Malone, Rosetta, Blueprint, and Answers (the visible flagship products within Launchpad) and Soyuz (the hidden but diligent workhorse that allows Ubuntu to work), Launchpad has several other important uses. We've already alluded to the fact that Launchpad handles all the authentication for all the Ubuntu Web sites. If you want to edit or create a Web page in the Ubuntu wiki or even order a CD, you must first create an account in Launchpad. In addition to holding a username and password, a Launchpad account can contain rich information about each individual, including a GNU Privacy Guard encryption key, wiki pages, contact information, and more. More important, Launchpad also contains representations of every team and group within Ubuntu and handles permission within the entire Ubuntu world. For example, the only people who are allowed to upload core packages to Ubuntu are people who are part of the Ubuntu Core Developers Team in Launchpad.

NOTE The system is also playing an increasingly important role in coordinating sprints and tracking events in a calendar. With time, Launchpad's functionality is only likely to grow and its help in supporting the new type of development with it.

Bazaar

Bazaar is a distributed revision control system. What does that really mean? A revision control system is a program that tracks how the source code of a program changes. It tracks what the specific change was, such as the addition of a new piece of code, as well as who made the change. It also allows a developer to roll back to a previous version or create a branch to try a new idea.

The second key piece about Bazaar is that it is distributed. Traditional revision control systems have a single place where the code is stored. Only certain people can access this place and change the code there. A distributed revision control system is different in that there is no single place for code storage. Each branch a developer is working on is equal, and they all take code from each other. This system is much like a number of equal merchants at a bazaar, hence the name.

Bazaar started out as a fork of the Arch distributed revision control system. (A fork means that the developers disagree on where to take the program, and they break into different groups to work toward each group's different goals.) However, Bazaar 2 was completely rewritten, as it was found that the then-current code did not work in the long term.

TIP **Bazaar**
Bazaar can be found at www.bazaar-ng.org.

Summary

In addition to building a great OS that many people use, the Ubuntu project has developed an OS that those building other operating systems use as a basis to build from. This has come in the form of both internal partner projects and external derivative distributions. Together, these span languages, continents, and markets. Also, Ubuntu is tightly linked to Canonical, Ltd.'s other projects, Launchpad and Bazaar. While Bazaar provides a compelling version control system, Launchpad provides a one-stop show for bugs, translations, and much more.

CHAPTER 11

Introducing the Ubuntu Forums

THIS CHAPTER INTRODUCES THE Ubuntu Forums by describing what they are, why they exist, and some of the history and fun quirks that make them a place where people come for the tech support and end up staying for the community. Whether you have used Internet forums in the past or not, this chapter will give you a good introduction to an official Ubuntu presence on the Web, a place that is helpful, welcoming, and an enjoyable community in which to participate.

What Are the Ubuntu Forums?

An Internet forum is a Web site where people may sign up for an account and then communicate with one another in discussions of varying types in a casual and free-flowing manner. Most forums are divided into smaller areas, each dedicated to a particular topic or set of related topics. For those who have participated in online activities for a long time, Internet forums are an easy-to-find and easy-to-use equivalent of local dial-up bulletin board systems (BBSs) from the 1980s and early 1990s, as well as a prettier looking version of Usenet news groups.

The Ubuntu Forums were created as a place for people to come and help one another learn how to install, use, and customize Ubuntu. The goal was to create a place on the Internet that was easy to access for those who are not especially adept at or experienced with technology. The site is divided into a number of different topical areas to make finding information easy and to make asking questions and finding answers simple.

In addition, the forums exist in a very informal, sometimes whimsical atmosphere, where the information and tech advice are both solid and useful; the community is kind, gentle, and welcoming; and the spirit is often playful.

A Brief History of the Ubuntu Forums

The Ubuntu Forums were created in October 2004 by Ryan Troy, aka ubuntu-geek (we talk more about forum usernames later in the chapter). The forums were started as a personal project, an unofficial resource provided by one man who was having fun and trying to help people at the same time. Quickly the forums became known as a wonderful place to find other Ubuntu users who are knowledgeable, helpful, and friendly. The forums caught the eye of Canonical very early on, and in November 2004, in recognition of the solid foundation and great atmosphere that had already been established, the forums became the Official Ubuntu Forums. The forums hosting continued to be paid for by Ryan and the occasional donations of forum community members until March 2006, when Canonical graciously offered to host the forums on its own servers. In June 2007, the forums' domain name, license, and assets were all transferred to Canonical, which now maintains sole ownership.

Over the years, the forums have changed their look and feel several times, but one thing has always remained: the feeling of community. The Ubuntu Forums began as a small group of playful geeks (meant in the best of ways) who gathered to have some fun and help one another with a new and interesting Linux distribution in a lighthearted and welcoming atmosphere. As of this writing, the forums have well over 750,000 members, with an average of between eight and fifteen thousand online at any given time, and yet the friendliness and helpful community feeling remains.

How May I Participate?

To browse the forums, read questions and answers, and get a feel for the community, simply point your browser to ubuntuforums.org. You don't need an account to benefit from the information that already exists on the site. You can read and even search the forums to see if others have asked questions about the things you are interested in learning.

However, to really begin to participate in the community, you will want to sign up for an account. Do so by browsing to the main page at ubuntuforums. org and clicking the Register link, as shown in Figure 11-1.

You will be asked to read and agree to the forum rules shown in Figure 11-2. The complete Ubuntu Forums Code of Conduct is summarized later in this chapter.

After doing so, choose and provide a username and password, along with an e-mail address. You may choose a username that is serious, whimsical, informative, or secretive, almost anything you want as long as it is clean and

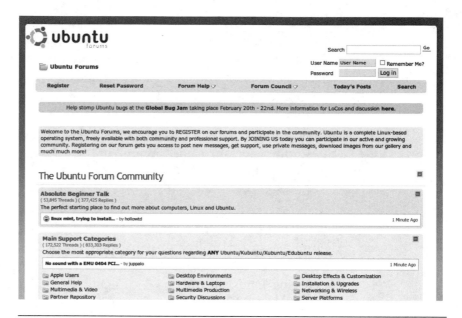

Figure 11-1 UbuntuForums.org Web site front page

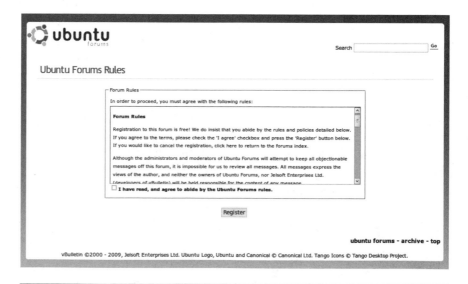

Figure 11-2 UbuntuForums.org rules agreement

work/school appropriate. There is also some optional information that may be included in your registration, such as the username of another forums community member who referred you, and your time zone. When you have entered all the information, click the Complete Registration box, as seen in Figure 11-3. You will receive an e-mail at the address you entered and will need to follow the instructions it contains to complete your registration.

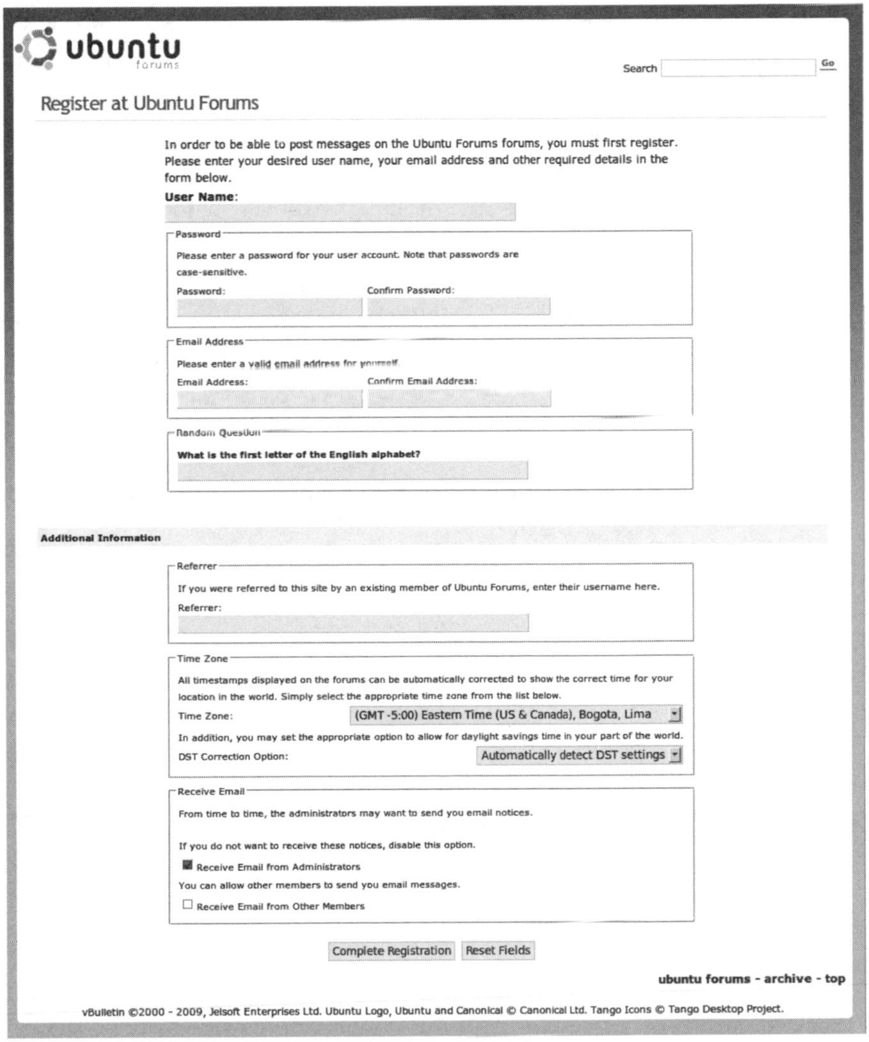

Figure 11-3 UbuntuForums.org account signup page

Now that you have an account, you probably want to ask a question. To do so, pick a category from the list on the front page. For example, if you have a specific issue with multimedia program configuration or your video card not working correctly, you might want to post in the section under Main Support called Multimedia & Video. Click to open that section and click the small box at the top of the list of topics containing the words New Thread, as shown in Figure 11-4.

Topics are called *threads*, and individual comments and contributions within a thread are called *posts*. You will be "posting a new thread" in a specific *subforum*. You will need to give your new thread a proper title and clearly explain your question.

One of our forum staff members, who uses the username aysiu on the forums, wrote a wonderful set of instructions on how to get the best help in Internet forums. You can read his entire guide at http://ubuntucat. wordpress.com/2007/08/06/getting-the-best-help-on-linux-forums/. Following is a basic outline of his helpful advice.

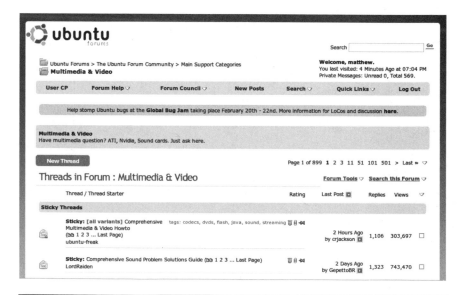

Figure 11-4 UbuntuForums.org posting a new thread example

When posting a new thread with a request for assistance, it is a good idea to follow these steps for the greatest effectiveness:

1. Show that you tried to do some research on your problem. Mention the results of searching the forums or via Google, what you have tried, and the results of your attempts thus far.

2. Come up with a thread title that accurately describes your problem. A title like "help, it doesn't work" is less likely to attract attention and receive quick assistance than one titled "Installing nVidia video driver on laptop with GeForce 9300M GS."

3. State the important facts, but don't ramble. All of the forum community members are volunteers. Not a single one is paid to read or answer questions. You want to keep your post short and to the point, with enough detail to be helpful for understanding the problem but not so long that people get bored or overwhelmed.

4. Focus on the problem you are trying to fix, and stick to one issue per thread. If you have multiple problems, please feel invited to post multiple threads asking questions. If you do this, each issue is more likely to be seen and answered.

5. Be polite to those who help you, and ignore anyone who is rude. Better yet, use the "report post" function to inform the staff of problems by clicking an icon at the bottom left corner of any post that is in violation of the Forum Code of Conduct (discussed later in this chapter). If you aren't sure which icon, hover over each of them with your mouse pointer, and a tool tip will pop up for each one to tell you what it does.

6. When your problem is solved, please say so. If the solution was posted by someone in the thread you started, please acknowledge their help. If you found the answer elsewhere, please post it in the thread where you ask your question. This will help other members in the future who may be struggling with the same problem.

Once you have a feel for the community and for how things work, please know that you are invited to help out as well. One of the pleasures of the Ubuntu Forums is that anyone who knows something is welcome and invited to assist another member. In fact, many of today's most helpful members of the community started out knowing nothing and asking questions. This community is filled with people who are grateful, most of whom are helping others solely because they themselves were once helped and a desire arose to give something back.

With time, many members distinguish themselves as incredibly helpful, friendly, and polite. Many of them are invited to be a part of the forums staff, or members of forum teams with specific goals. A great example of a forum team is the Unanswered Posts Team, which searches for threads and questions that have never received a reply, in the hopes of finding a way to help answer the more difficult questions.

Questions, Locations, Conversations, and Activities

Most community members first visit the forums to find help with adjusting to a new operating system, with understanding how things work and the underlying principles involved, or to ask specific questions regarding hardware or software configurations or problems.

Those first questions are often quite simple, and that is okay. The Ubuntu Forums welcome beginners and beginner-level questions. There is even a special location in the forums called Absolute Beginners Talk that is dedicated to inviting beginners to ask any questions they may have, in whatever way they are able to ask them. This is also a location where the more experienced users work to give their answers in the least technical language possible and to give the most detail in their answers, trying not to assume any prior knowledge while giving the steps necessary to complete a task.

As time goes on and community members learn more of the foundational information they need, they become more confident and tend to gravitate to areas of specific interest, both to learn and often to assist other users with fun and useful items that have been discovered. This is when the Main Support categories start to receive more and more use.

It is also around this time in a member's entry into the community that she may discover a new trick that she hasn't read about anywhere on the forums, and many enjoy sharing those in Tutorials & Tips. Members often discover that those who "hang out" regularly in the forums are fun and friendly people with whom they would like to interact in a less formal style. The Community Cafe, which is kind of like the water cooler at work, exists for just that purpose. People drop in to discuss things that are unrelated to Ubuntu, Linux, or tech support, and the topics are often silly and playful.

There is a lot more to explore in the forums. There are sections on gaming, art and design, education and science, running a server, security, multimedia production, and a whole lot more. There are even localized forums for groups based on physical location, called LoCo Teams, most of whom hold regular meetings in the real world as well as conduct some of their business in our forums.

Key People in the Forums

The Ubuntu Forums are led by a small group of people called the Forum Council. The council is currently made up of seven community members, listed here by their usernames on the forums:

- ubuntu-geek (Council Chairman)
- KiwiNZ
- jdong
- Technoviking
- matthew
- bodhi.zazen
- bapoumba

These five are ultimately responsible for the oversight and operation of the forums. Primarily, ubuntu-geek deals with server and software maintenance and also chairs the council. In addition, he and all the Forum Council members are corporately responsible for maintaining the community atmosphere and dealing with some of the technical aspects of the forums from within the forum software. If a user has a problem, these are the people who will ultimately deal with the issue.

There is an additional group of users who are vital to the smooth running and community atmosphere of the forums. These are the other forum staff. A current list of all staff is available by clicking the "view forum leaders" link on the front page of the Web site. This list includes the extremely important and wonderful community moderators and the leaders of specific teams and LoCo groups.

Fun Stuff

A discussion of the Ubuntu Forums would be incomplete without a mention of some of the more frivolous and whimsical aspects of this community. These exist to remind us that life is about more than technology and that we are doing more than answering tech support questions. Ultimately, we are dealing with people, people who have names and faces and personalities and feelings. We want to give good and accurate information in the forums, and we want to be completely safe for browsing at work or school, but we do not strive for a stark, professional-only sort of atmosphere.

To begin, community members are given the opportunity to express their personality through their forum account. To access the various settings and personalization options, click UserCP and select User Control Panel from the front page of the forums.

From here you may create or edit a signature, a short bit of text that will be added to each of your posts in the forums. Some users put useful information there, others whimsical quotes. You can edit your avatar, which is a small graphic image that you use to identify or represent you to other forum members. You can also add an additional profile picture to be displayed to any user who chooses to view your profile on the forums. There are lots of options for customization, with the opportunity to be as public or private about your real-life identity as you desire.

You will also notice that each user has a few things related to him or her that have some connection to coffee. User titles like "Dark Roasted Ubuntu" and "Ubuntu Extra Shot" are just a fun way to reward community members as they post in the tech support areas. Every time you post in those areas, you earn a bean. As your bean count grows, your coffee-based user title changes, as does your user rank image—the set of coffee-based icons that appears near your username. You will see things like green beans, roasted beans, coffee cups of various styles and fill levels, and more. All of this is done for fun and is not intended to imply that users with high bean counts are any more or less capable than users with low bean counts. Rather, it is an amusing way to say thank you to those who have the time and willingness to hang around and help the community.

There are lots of other surprises in the forums as well. Occasionally forum staff will call a random "tribute" week, inviting users to change their avatars to honor someone or something dear to the heart of the community. There are avatar dress-up times, such as before Halloween, and the staff has been known to change the entire forum look for April Fool's Day.

The Foundation of the Ubuntu Forums

The foundation of the Ubuntu Forums is the Forums Code of Conduct. It is based on the Ubuntu Code of Conduct but is specifically written to cover forum usage, behavior, and expectations. Please refer to the link on the front page of the Ubuntu Forums, under Forum Help, for the most recent version, as this document is occasionally updated.

The basics of the Forum Code of Conduct are simple and are summed up in the first rule: "Be respectful of all users at all times. This means please use etiquette and politeness. Treat people with kindness and gentleness. If you do this, the rest of the Code of Conduct won't need more than a cursory mention."

Summary

This chapter introduced you to the Ubuntu Forums. It began with a little history and then moved on to specifics of usage and the nature of the forums.

Welcome to the Command Line

ONE OF THE MOST powerful parts of any Ubuntu system is the command line. It can also be one of the most daunting to dive into. It seems there is often little help, and that the commands are not easy to find or figure out. If you are willing to learn, the power of the command line will speed up your work and will be a great education that will serve you for years by increasing your ability to do exactly what you want to do with your computer with greater efficiency.

While the command line is a nice addition to a desktop user's life, it is completely invaluable if you run a server. The Ubuntu server installs without any graphical user interface, so the tools explained in this chapter and other books will be absolutely critical to success. And hey, remember to have fun!

Starting Up the Terminal

The terminal can be found under Accessories > Terminal. When it first launches, you will see something similar to what Figure A-1 shows.

You will see a blinking cursor immediately preceded by some letters, and perhaps numbers and symbols, ending with a $. The first word in that string of characters is your username, followed by the @ symbol. After the @, the hostname of your computer is listed, followed by a colon and the name of the directory you are currently in (you always start in your home directory, which is represented by a ~ symbol).

There are many dozens of commands. This appendix presents just a few useful ones in a narrative style to get you started, then lists some more with just a basic description and broken down by category.

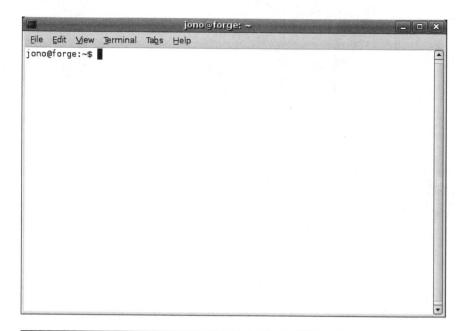

Figure A-1 The terminal window

Getting Started

First have a look at the files in your home folder by running the following command:

```
username@computer:~$ ls
```

The `ls` command lists the files in your current folder. The default command just displays a collection of items that are in your current directory, or location in the filesystem. To make `ls` more useful, you can type it with options:

```
username@computer:~$ ls -al
```

The `-al` parts are options that can be passed to the command. In this example, two options, a (list all files) and l (use a long display format to display file permissions, dates, sizes, and more), are used with `ls` to display all of the files (including hidden files) and their details.

TIP   **To Dash or Not to Dash?**

In many command-line tools, options are added after a dash (-). Some tools, however, don't need the dash. It isn't particularly consistent, so you must pay attention as you learn new commands.

Now move to a different directory:

```
username@computer:~$ cd Desktop
```

The cd command changes the directory to the place you specify after the command (in this case, the desktop directory). A nice shortcut that you can use when typing files and folders is to type the first few letters and then press the Tab key to fill in the remainder of the file/folder name. As an example, in the previous command, you could type cd Des and press the Tab key to fill in the rest of Desktop.

When inside a directory, you may want to have a quick look at the contents of a text file. To do this, use the cat command:

```
username@computer:~$ cat myfile.txt
```

This command prints the contents of the file on the screen (a more correct way to say this in computer geek jargon would be "outputs to the screen").

Building Pipelines

The power of the command line really comes into its own when you start combining commands by using pipelines. A pipeline uses the pipe symbol (|) to string together a number of commands to perform a specific task. As an example, if you use the cat command to display the contents of a file to the screen, but the file scrolls past you, create a pipeline and use the less command so you can browse the file:

```
username@computer:~$ cat foo.txt | less
```

To see how this works, break the command into parts, each separated by the pipe. The output of the part on the left (cat'ing the file) is fed into the less command on the right, which allows you to browse the file with the arrow keys.

Pipelines can be useful for finding specific information on the system. As an example, if you want to find out how many particular processes are running, you could run a command like this:

```
username@computer:~$ ps ax | grep getty | wc -l
```

Here you count how many getty processes are running (getty is the software that runs a console session). The ps ax command on the left lists the processes on the system, and then the grep command searches through the process list and returns only the lines that contain the text "getty." Finally, these lines are fed into wc, which is a small tool that counts the number of words or lines. The -l option specifies that the number of lines should be counted. Cool, huh?

Running Commands as the Superuser

When you log in to your computer, the account you use is a normal user account. This account is restricted from performing various system administration tasks. The security model behind Ubuntu has you run as a normal user all the time and dip into the system administrator account only when you need to. This prevents accidental changes or malicious installation of unwanted programs and similar things.

To jump to this superuser account when using the terminal, put the sudo command before the command you want to run. As an example, if you want to restart the networking system from the command line, run:

```
username@computer:~$ sudo /etc/init.d/networking restart
```

The command to the right of sudo is the command that should be run as the administrator, but sudo lets you run the command as the current user. When you run the above command, you are asked for the administrator password. This is the same password as the one you established for the first user you added when you installed Ubuntu on the computer. If you are using that user's account, just enter your normal password.

When you have authenticated yourself to sudo, you will not be asked for the password again for another 15 minutes.

Finding Help

Each command on your computer includes a manual page—or man page—that contains a list of the options available. Man pages are traditionally rather terse and intended only for referencing the different ways the command should be used. For a friendlier introduction to using commands, we recommend a Google search.

To view a man page (such as the man page for `ls`), run:

```
username@computer:~$ man ls
```

The man page command itself has a number of options (run `man man` to see them), and one of the most useful is `-k`. This option allows you to search the man pages for a particular word. This is useful when you don't remember the command. As an example, you could find all commands related to processes by running:

```
username@computer:~$ man -k processes
```

The remainder of this appendix gives a brief introduction to some of the more common and useful commands you will encounter and want to learn, organized in categories based on how they are used. We will end with a short list of some other resources for further research.

Moving Around the Filesystem

Commands for navigating in the filesystem include the following.

- **pwd:** The `pwd` command allows you to know the directory in which you're located (`pwd` stands for "print working directory"). For example, `pwd` in the desktop directory will show ~/Desktop. Note that the GNOME terminal also displays this information in the title bar of its window, as shown in Figure A-1.

- **cd:** The `cd` command allows you to change directories. When you open a terminal, you will be in your home directory. To move around the filesystem, use `cd`.
  - Use `cd ~/Desktop` to navigate to your desktop directory.
  - Use `cd /` to navigate into the root directory.

- Use cd to navigate to your home directory.

- Use cd .. to navigate up one directory level.

- Use cd - to navigate to the previous directory (or back).

- If you want to go directly to a specific, known directory location at once, use cd /directory/otherdirectory. For example, cd /var/www will take you directly to the /www subdirectory of /var.

Manipulating Files and Folders

You can manipulate files and folders with the following commands.

- **cp:** The cp command makes a copy of a file for you. For example, cp *file* foo makes an exact copy of the file whose name you entered and names the copy foo, but the first file will still exist with its original name.

- **mv:** The mv command moves a file to a different location or renames a file. Examples are as follows: mv *file* foo renames the original file to foo. mv foo ~/Desktop moves the file foo to your desktop directory but does not rename it. You must specify a new filename to rename a file. After you use mv, the original file no longer exists, but after you use cp, as above, that file stays and a new copy is made.

- To save on typing, you can substitute ~ in place of the home directory, so /home/jono/pictures is the same as ~/pictures.

NOTE   If you are using mv with sudo, which is often necessary outside of your home directory, you will not be able to use the ~ shortcut. Instead, you will have to use the full pathnames to your files.

- **rm:** Use this command to remove or delete a file in your directory, as in rm file.txt. It does not work on directories that contain files.

- **ls:** The ls command shows you the files in your current directory. Used with certain options, it lets you see file sizes, when files where created, and file permissions. For example, ls ~ shows you the files that are in your home directory.

- **mkdir:** The `mkdir` command allows you to create directories. For example, `mkdir music` creates a music directory.

- **chmod:** The `chmod` command changes the permissions on the files listed. Permissions are based on a fairly simple model. You can set permissions for user, group, and world, and you can set whether each can read, write, and/or execute the file. For example, if a file had permission to allow everybody to read but only the user could write, the permissions would read `rwxr-r-`. To add or remove a permission, you append a + or a - in front of the specific permission. For example, to add the capability for the group to edit in the previous example, you could type `chmod g+x file`.

- **chown:** The `chown` command allows the user to change the user and group ownerships of a file. For example, `chown jim` *file* changes the ownership of the file to Jim.

System Information Commands

System information commands include the following.

- **df:** The `df` command displays filesystem disk space usage for all partitions. The command `df-h` is probably the most useful. It uses megabytes (M) and gigabytes (G) instead of blocks to report. (`-h` means "human-readable.")

- **free:** The `free` command displays the amount of free and used memory in the system. For example, `free -m` gives the information using megabytes, which is probably most useful for current computers.

- **top:** The `top` command displays information on your Linux system, running processes, and system resources, including the CPU, RAM, swap usage, and total number of tasks being run. To exit `top`, press Q.

- **uname -a:** The `uname` command with the `-a` option prints all system information, including machine name, kernel name, version, and a few other details. This command is most useful for checking which kernel you're using.

- **lsb_release -a:** The `lsb_release` command with the `-a` option prints version information for the Linux release you're running. For example:

```
user@computer:~$ lsb_release -a

No LSB modules are available.
Distributor ID: Ubuntu
Description:    Ubuntu 9.04
Release:        9.04
Codename:       jaunty
```

- **ifconfig:** This reports on your system's network interfaces.

- **iwconfig:** The `iwconfig` command shows you any wireless network adapters and the wireless-specific information from them, such as speed and network connected.

- **ps:** The `ps` command allows you to view all the processes running on the machine.

The following commands list the hardware on your computer, either of a specific type or with a specific method. They are most useful for debugging when a piece of hardware does not function correctly.

- **lspci:** The `lspci` command lists all PCI buses and devices connected to them. This commonly includes network cards and sound cards.

- **lsusb:** The `lsusb` command lists all USB buses and any connected USB devices, such as printers and thumb drives.

- **lshal:** The `lshal` command lists all devices the hardware abstraction layer (HAL) knows about, which should be most hardware on your system.

- **lshw:** The `lshw` command lists hardware on your system, including maker, type, and where it is connected.

Searching and Editing Text Files

Search and edit text files by using the following commands.

- **grep:** The `grep` command allows you to search inside a number of files for a particular search pattern and then print matching lines. For example, `grep blah` *file* will search for the text "blah" in the file and then print any matching lines.

- **sed:** The `sed` (or Stream EDitor) command allows search and replace of a particular string in a file. For example, if you want to find the string "cat" and replace it with "dog" in a file named pets, type `sed s/cat/dog/g pets`.

Both `grep` and `sed` are extremely powerful programs. There are many excellent tutorials available on using them, but here are a couple of good Web sites to get you started:

- https://help.ubuntu.com/community/grep
- http://manpages.ubuntu.com/manpages/intrepid/en/man1/sed.1.html

Three other commands are useful for dealing with text.

- **cat:** The `cat` command, short for concatenate, is useful for viewing and adding to text files. The simple command `cat FILENAME` displays the contents of the file. Using `cat FILENAME file` adds the contents of the first file to the second.
- **nano:** Nano is a simple text editor for the command line. To open a file, use `nano filename`. Commands listed at the bottom of the screen are accessed via pressing Ctrl followed by the letter.
- **less:** The `less` command is used for viewing text files as well as standard output. A common usage is to pipe another command through `less` to be able to see all the output, such as `ls | less`.

Dealing with Users and Groups

You can use the following commands to administer users and groups.

- **adduser:** The `adduser` command creates a new user. To create a new user, simply type `sudo adduser $loginname`. This creates the user's home directory and default group. It prompts for a user password and then further details about the user.
- **passwd:** The `passwd` command changes the user's password. If run by a regular user, it will change his or her password. If run using `sudo`, it can change any user's password. For example, `sudo passwd joe` changes Joe's password.

- **who:** The who command tells you who is currently logged into the machine.

- **addgroup:** The addgroup command adds a new group. To create a new group, type sudo addgroup $*groupname*.

- **deluser:** The deluser command removes a user from the system. To remove the user's files and home directory, you need to add the -remove-home option.

- **delgroup:** The delgroup command removes a group from the system. You cannot remove a group that is the primary group of any users.

Getting Help on the Command Line

This section provides you with some tips for getting help on the command line. The commands –help and man are the two most important tools at the command line.

Virtually all commands understand the -h (or –help) option, which produces a short usage description of the command and its options, then exits back to the command prompt. Try man -h or man –help to see this in action.

Every command and nearly every application in Linux has a man (manual) file, so finding such a file is as simple as typing man *command* to bring up a longer manual entry for the specified command. For example, man mv brings up the mv (move) manual.

Some helpful tips for using the man command include the following.

- **Arrow keys:** Move up and down the man file by using the arrow keys.

- **q:** Quit back to the command prompt by typing q.

- **man man:** man man brings up the manual entry for the man command, which is a good place to start!

- **man intro:** man intro is especially useful. It displays the Introduction to User Commands, which is a well-written, fairly brief introduction to the Linux command line.

There are also info pages, which are generally more in-depth than man pages. Try `info info` for the introduction to info pages.

Searching for Man Files

If you aren't sure which command or application you need to use, you can try searching the man files.

- **man -k foo:** This searches the man files for *foo*. Try `man -k nautilus` to see how this works.

NOTE `man -k foo` is the same as the `apropos` command.

- **man -f foo:** This searches only the titles of your system's man files. Try `man -f gnome`, for example.

NOTE `man -f foo` is the same as the `whatis` command.

Using Wildcards

Sometimes you need to look at or use multiple files at the same time. For instance, you might want to delete all .rar files or move all .odt files to another directory. Thankfully, you can use a series of wildcards to accomplish such tasks.

- `*` matches any number of characters. For example, `*.rar` matches any file with the ending .rar.
- `?` matches any single character. For example, `?.rar` matches a.rar but not ab.rar.
- **[*characters*]** matches any of the characters within the brackets. For example, `[ab].rar` matches a.rar and b.rar but not c.rar.
- `*` **[!*characters*]** matches any characters that are not listed. For example, `[!ab].rar` matches c.rar but not a.rar or b.rar.

Executing Multiple Commands

Often you may want to execute several commands together, either by running one after another or by passing output from one to another.

Running Sequentially

If you need to execute multiple commands in sequence but don't need to pass output between them, there are two options based on whether or not you want the subsequent commands to run only if the previous commands succeed or not. If you want the commands to run one after the other regardless of whether or not preceding commands succeed, place a ; between the commands. For example, if you want to get information about your hardware, you could run lspci ; lsusb, which would output information on your PCI buses and USB devices in sequence.

However, if you need to conditionally run the commands based on whether the previous command has succeeded, insert && between commands. An example of this is building a program from source, which is traditionally done with ./configure, make, and make install. The commands make and make install require that the previous commands have completed successfully, so you would use ./configure && make && make install.

Passing Output

If you need to pass the output of one command so that it goes to the input of the next, after the character used between the commands, you need something called a *pipe*, which looks like a vertical bar or pipe (|).

To use the pipe, insert the | between each command. For example, using the | in the command ls | less allows you to view the contents of the ls more easily.

Moving to More Advanced Uses of the Command Line

There are a great number of good books out there for working the command line. In addition, because most of the command line has not changed in many years, a large body of information is available on the

Internet. If you need help with something, often simply searching for the command will turn up what you need.

As you can imagine, there are hundreds and hundreds of different commands available on the system, and we don't have the space to cover them here. A number of superb Web sites and books can help you find out about the many different commands.

To get you started, here are some recommendations.

- *A Practical Guide to Linux® Commands, Editors, and Shell Programming* by Mark G. Sobell (Prentice Hall, 2005) is a good book for any user of the shell in Linux to have on his or her bookshelf.

- **LinuxCommand.org**, found at http://linuxcommand.org/, is an excellent Web site designed to help people new to using the command line.

- **The Linux Documentation Project**, found at www.tldp.org/, is an excellent and free resource for many things Linux.

APPENDIX B

Ubuntu Equivalents to Windows Programs

FOR THOSE OF YOU who are moving to Ubuntu from Windows, often simply knowing which application to use is half the battle. This appendix shows common Windows applications and their Ubuntu counterparts. Your Windows-using friends shouldn't be completely shut out, so there are some applications for them to use also.

On the Ubuntu Desktop

Listed here are common Windows applications that already have an equivalent installed on the Ubuntu desktop. Some common alternatives are also listed.

Word Processing

- **Windows:** Microsoft Word
- **Ubuntu:** OpenOffice.org Writer
- **Alternative:** Abiword

Spreadsheet

- **Windows:** Microsoft Excel
- **Ubuntu:** OpenOffice.org Calc
- **Alternative:** Gnumeric

Presentation

- **Windows:** Microsoft PowerPoint
- **Ubuntu:** OpenOffice.org Impress

Database

- **Windows:** Microsoft Access
- **Ubuntu:** OpenOffice.org Base
- **Alternative:** Glom

Web Browser

- **Windows:** Internet Explorer or Mozilla Firefox
- **Ubuntu:** Mozilla Firefox
- **Alternative:** Epiphany

NOTE   Mozilla Firefox runs on Windows as well as Linux, allowing you to have the same browsing experience.

E-mail

- **Windows:** Microsoft Outlook Express, Microsoft Outlook, or Mozilla Thunderbird
- **Ubuntu:** Evolution
- **Alternative:** Mozilla Thunderbird

Media Players

- **Windows:** Windows Media Player, iTunes, Winamp
- **Ubuntu:** Rhythmbox, Totem Movie Player
- **Alternatives:** Banshee, Muine, Beep Media Player

NOTE   Due to patent restrictions, Ubuntu cannot install the codecs for some media codecs. Please see Chapter 3 for information on how to do this.

Photo Editor

- **Windows:** Adobe Photoshop or GIMP
- **Ubuntu:** GIMP

Instant Messaging

- **Windows:** AIM, Yahoo, ICQ, or Pidgin
- **Ubuntu:** Pidgin

NOTE   Pidgin can connect to AIM, Yahoo, ICQ, and Google Talk networks.

Voice Over IP

- **Windows:** Skype or GizmoProject
- **Ubuntu:** Ekiga Softphone or Skype

NOTE   Skype uses a proprietary protocol that only Skype can understand. Ekiga uses an open protocol, called SIP, so if you are just starting out with Voice Over IP, use Ekiga to avoid being tied to one program. Ekiga can also talk H.323, so you can connect with Windows NetMeeting clients as well.

Additional Applications

The Ubuntu desktop does not cater to everybody, so there are some classes of applications that, by default, are not installed. Some of the common ones are listed in this section.

Office and Finance

Personal Accounting

- **Windows:** Quicken, Microsoft Money
- **Ubuntu alternatives:** Grisbi, Gnucash

Accounting

- **Windows:** Intuit Quickbooks
- **Ubuntu alternative:** TurboCASH

Desktop Publishing

- **Windows:** Microsoft Publisher
- **Ubuntu alternative:** Scribus

Project Management

- **Windows:** Microsoft Project
- **Ubuntu alternative:** Planner

Drawing and Modeling

Vector Drawing

- **Windows:** Adobe Illustrator, Inkscape
- **Ubuntu alternative:** Inkscape

3D Modeler

- **Windows:** Alias Maya, Blender
- **Ubuntu alternative:** Blender

Diagram Editing

- **Windows:** Microsoft Visio
- **Ubuntu alternative:** Dia

Games and Edutainment

Planetarium

- **Windows:** Starry Night, Voyager III
- **Ubuntu alternative:** Stellarium

Space Simulator

- **Windows:** Orbiter
- **Ubuntu alternative:** Celestia

Flight Simulator

- **Windows:** Microsoft Flight Simulator, FlightGear
- **Ubuntu alternative:** FlightGear

Typing Tutor

- **Windows:** Mavis Beacon Teaches Typing
- **Ubuntu alternatives:** Tux Typing, KTouch

Index

The definitive, authorized Ubuntu server guide: The server companion to the world's best-selling Ubuntu book!

- The complete guide to using the powerful Ubuntu server capabilities that Canonical has been aggressively upgrading and promoting
- Modern, easy-to-use best practices for deploying, managing, and securing any type of Ubuntu server
- Two CD-ROMs contain the latest version of Ubuntu Server Edition 9.04 and the Long Term Support (LTS) Ubuntu Server Edition 8.04.2.

The Official Ubuntu Server Book covers everything mere mortals need to know to install, configure, and administer efficient low-cost Ubuntu servers in any environment. Ideal for both new and experienced Ubuntu and Linux administrators, this book covers a wide spectrum of core admin tasks, including automated Kickstart and FAI installation techniques; package management; security; backup; monitoring; and even virtualization. Readers will also find detailed, step-by-step recipes for installing and configuring each leading type of server, including web, database, DNS, DHCP, file, mail, print, and many other types. Beginning administrators and power users can rely on this book from the moment they decide to install and configure their first Ubuntu servers. Advanced sysadmins and netadmins can save time with elegant, streamlined techniques that fully leverage the major improvements to Ubuntu and Linux administration that have been implemented in recent years.

PRENTICE
HALL

PRENTICE HALL

REGISTER

THIS PRODUCT

informit.com/register

Register the Addison-Wesley, Exam Cram, Prentice Hall, Que, and Sams products you own to unlock great benefits.

To begin the registration process, simply go to **informit.com/register** to sign in or create an account. You will then be prompted to enter the 10- or 13-digit ISBN that appears on the back cover of your product.

Registering your products can unlock the following benefits:

- Access to supplemental content, including bonus chapters, source code, or project files.
- A coupon to be used on your next purchase.

Registration benefits vary by product. Benefits will be listed on your Account page under Registered Products.

About InformIT — THE TRUSTED TECHNOLOGY LEARNING SOURCE

INFORMIT IS HOME TO THE LEADING TECHNOLOGY PUBLISHING IMPRINTS Addison-Wesley Professional, Cisco Press, Exam Cram, IBM Press, Prentice Hall Professional, Que, and Sams. Here you will gain access to quality and trusted content and resources from the authors, creators, innovators, and leaders of technology. Whether you're looking for a book on a new technology, a helpful article, timely newsletters, or access to the Safari Books Online digital library, InformIT has a solution for you.

informIT.com

THE TRUSTED TECHNOLOGY LEARNING SOURCE

Addison-Wesley | Cisco Press | Exam Cram
IBM Press | Que | Prentice Hall | Sams

SAFARI BOOKS ONLINE

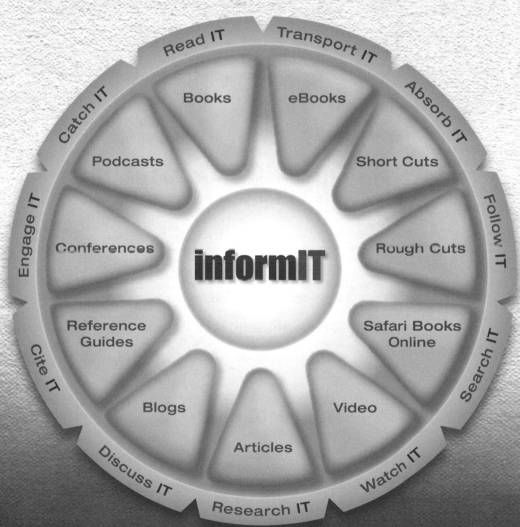

Try Safari Books Online FREE

Get online access to 5,000+ Books and Videos

FREE TRIAL—GET STARTED TODAY!
www.informit.com/safaritrial

Find trusted answers, fast

Only Safari lets you search across thousands of best-selling books from the top technology publishers, including Addison-Wesley Professional, Cisco Press, O'Reilly, Prentice Hall, Que, and Sams.

Master the latest tools and techniques

In addition to gaining access to an incredible inventory of technical books, Safari's extensive collection of video tutorials lets you learn from the leading video training experts.

WAIT, THERE'S MORE!

Keep your competitive edge

With Rough Cuts, get access to the developing manuscript and be among the first to learn the newest technologies.

Stay current with emerging technologies

Short Cuts and Quick Reference Sheets are short, concise, focused content created to get you up-to-speed quickly on new and cutting-edge technologies.

DVD Warranty

Prentice Hall warrants the enclosed DVD to be free of defects in materials and faulty workmanship under normal use for a period of ninety days after purchase (when purchased new). If a defect is discovered in the DVD during this warranty period, a replacement DVD can be obtained at no charge by sending the defective DVD, postage prepaid, with proof of purchase to:

Disc Exchange
Prentice Hall
Pearson Technology Group
75 Arlington Street, Suite 300
Boston, MA 02116
Email: AWPro@aw.com

Prentice Hall makes no warranty or representation, either expressed or implied, with respect to this software, its quality, performance, merchantability, or fitness for a particular purpose. In no event will Prentice Hall, its distributors, or dealers be liable for direct, indirect, special, incidental, or consequential damages arising out of the use or inability to use the software. The exclusion of implied warranties is not permitted in some states. Therefore, the above exclusion may not apply to you. This warranty provides you with specific legal rights. There may be other rights that you may have that vary from state to state.

More information and updates are available at:
informit.com/ph

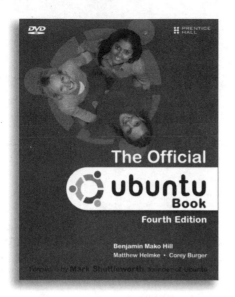

FREE Online Edition

Your purchase of *The Official Ubuntu Book, Fourth Edition* includes access to a free online edition for 45 days through the Safari Books Online subscription service. Nearly every Prentice Hall book is available online through Safari Books Online, along with more than 5,000 other technical books and videos from publishers such as Addison-Wesley Professional, Cisco Press, Exam Cram, IBM Press, O'Reilly, Que, and Sams.

SAFARI BOOKS ONLINE allows you to search for a specific answer, cut and paste code, download chapters, and stay current with emerging technologies.

Activate your FREE Online Edition at www.informit.com/safarifree

> **STEP 1:** Enter the coupon code: RJUDREH.

> **STEP 2:** New Safari users, complete the brief registration form.
> Safari subscribers, just log in.

If you have difficulty registering on Safari or accessing the online edition, please e-mail customer-service@safaribooksonline.com